Praise for *Value Above Cost*

"*Value Above Cost* reminds us that superior financial performance must be at the heart of every decision and every action we take as business professionals. And in addition to bringing fresh insight and accompanying techniques, the Customer Value Added™ metric provides a formula with which to measure results and the tools to deliver on that responsibility."

—**Mark Yolton,** Senior Vice President, SAP

"Marketers can always spend money to hide a flawed business strategy. When money is tougher to come by, we need to be much smarter about how we spend it. *Value Above Cost* shows us how to be smarter. It underscores the potential contribution marketers can deliver if they diligently pay attention to this ratio."

—**Chris Gaebler,** Vice President, Corporate Marketing,
Sony Electronics

"CVA® is such a simple yet ingenious concept. Every businessperson from marketing to operations to finance should put this concept into everyday practice. All organizations need to get back to the basics of measuring, monitoring, and increasing customer value. After all, customer value is the net value created for society. Don's book gives a great framework on how to achieve that nirvana."

—**Alfred Lin**, Chairman and COO/CFO, Zappos.com

"In challenging economic times, it is essential to have a clear path for extracting the maximum value from your investments in product design and development. This book offers the tools to plan and evaluate your marketing program."

—**Ed Reilly**, Chief Executive Officer, American
Management Association

"Finally, a straightforward and practical way to show the value of marketing efforts in terms of revenue and profits. Don Sexton clearly explains why marketing works and how to determine whether or not your marketing efforts are effective."

—**Bernd Schmitt**, Robert D. Calkins Professor of International Business,
Faculty Director, Center on Global Brand Leadership;
author, *Big Think Strategy*

"The book is really a substantial step in bringing marketing and finance together. Corporations have been grappling with the problem of overlapping effects of these decisions, and Don's book provides a simple paradigm that can be measured and implemented in most industries in most countries."

—**Kamal Sen**, Regional Director, Business Research
and Corporate Planning, Hindustan Lever Ltd.

"CVA® is an important topic in today's world of budgetary control. It makes a no-nonsense case for marketing and finance working closely together in assessing appropriate and necessary spend through the perspective of customers. The future of business is directly tied to the concepts which Don has crafted through his outstanding work."

—**Mark C. Kershisnik**, Executive Director, Eli Lilly and Company

"Securing long-term preference by managing customer perceived value should have as much strategic focus as managing costs. There are great insights in *Value Above Cost*: to strategically manage both sides of the equation to ensure customer loyalty and drive superior financial performance."

—**Steven Haro**, Brand Manager, Boeing Commercial Airplanes

"Don Sexton renders a simple yet profound truth visible when he defines marketing as 'managing perceived value.' Customer Value Added (CVA®) is breakthrough thinking about the way customers understand value and how organizations can deliver and measure value. His 40 years of award-winning teaching, writing, and research in the field of marketing at Columbia University are now concise and actionable insights for the mere price of a book."

—**Kevin Clark**, President and Founder, Content Evolution
LLC Worldwide; Program Director emeritus,
IBM Brand & Values Experience

"If marketing is about creating value, some marketers struggle with staying focused on the objective. Others struggle with proving they've achieved it. Dr. Sexton's book is a must-read for both."

—**Steve Smith**, CMO, Enterprise Rent-A-Car

"CVA® will be a powerful addition to the business lexicon, helping to bridge the gap between the CMO's budget request and the CFO's perceived value of marketing spend. *Value Above Cost* should be required reading for both."

—**Shailendra Ghorpade**, Group Managing Director,
Europe, Middle East, and India, MetLife

"Effective brand management requires a solid understanding of the value being delivered by the brand and how the business strategies link together in delivering the value of the brand. The concepts that Don Sexton has summarized in *Value Above Cost* provides practical tools and many examples on how to understand the value components. With these tools, marketers and business managers should be able to improve the performance of their businesses while delivering the best value to their customers."

—**Dean Adams**, Principal Brand Strategist, LEVEL

"Marketing commitments can be viewed as an expense or as an investment. Don Sexton's *Value Above Cost* establishes the framework for differentiating between investment with payback that should be optimized and an expense that should be minimized."

—**Tom Finneran**, EVP, Agency Management Services,
American Association of Advertising Agencies

"In describing how Customer Value Added™ can be used by organizations to improve their financial performance, Professor Sexton has bridged the gap between theory and application…between marketing and finance. Using his techniques, CEOs and marketing executives can evaluate alternatives and make decisions to maximize market share and profitability."

—**Daniel C. Petri**, Group President—International (retired),
Verizon Communications

"Don Sexton writes like he lectures: clearly, succinctly, relevantly, and always sprinkled with a good sense of humor."

—**James R. Gregory**, CEO, CoreBrand

"Don Sexton has managed to weld key ideas from marketing, economics, finance, and statistics to explain clearly how marketing drives the financial performance of a company. Furthermore, he has given us forward control through his Customer Value Added™ metric that allows us to predict a company's future performance."

—**JC Larreche**, INSEAD Alfred H. Heineken Professor of Marketing;
author of *The Momentum Effect*

"In synthesizing basic economic, financial, and brand marketing concepts under the banner of 'Customer Value Added™,' Don Sexton has designed a powerful tool that creates a foundation for a company-wide shared view of how to think about and how to measure the financial impact of its brand marketing efforts. In this time of heightened scrutiny of expenditures and strict accountability, we should all keep *Value Above Cost* close at all times."

—**Frank Cooper III**, Chief Marketing Officer, Sparkling Beverages,
Pepsi-Cola North American Beverages

"Price, marginal cost, gross profit, product attribute cost/benefit analysis, advertising effectiveness, and marketing ROI all have value in the senior manager's toolkit, but CVA® is the one metric I have found that brings these together, creating a common reference for operations, marketing, sales, and finance. This is a powerful tool every manager needs to understand and use."

—**Mark Osterhaus**, Vice President and Assistant General Manager,
Harrah's Council Bluffs

"A book that blends the disciplines of finance, economics, marketing, and branding in a logical and thought-provoking way is one that provides real 'Customer Value Added™.'"

—**John Dodds**, Global Branding and Marketing
Communications Director, Air Products

"A probing discussion and rewarding read. Don's premise on the valuation of brands contains the analytics, relevant business examples, and commentary of what to do and how to do it. Take advantage of his insights."

—**Gary Elliott**, Vice President, Brand Marketing, Hewlett-Packard

"Don Sexton's book clearly lays out best practices for gaining maximum value for your marketing investment. This is a must-read in these tough economic times when every marketing dollar is being seriously questioned. This book will help you to charter unchartered waters!"

—**Ed Faruolo**, Principal, VitaLincs, LLC

"Too many business people take a conventional view of pricing as a simple cost plus exercise. This doesn't take into consideration the value of a brand, nor consumers' willingness to buy a brand versus a mere product—as a sum of its raw material plus margin. In *Value Above Cost*, Don Sexton gives us ideas as well as methods to more accurately understand the value of our brands to consumers and to maximize profit and grow brand equity. I will recommend his book to anyone who has influence over 'brand pricing' as a way to better manage brands and their businesses."

—**Marshall Dawson**, cofounder, Deviate Marketing; former
Global Brand Director, Bombay Sapphire Gin

"Customer Value Added™ combines a discipline with an insightful approach to assessing and capturing the intrinsic value of business opportunities."

—**Scott Fuson**, Vice President, Specialty Chemicals and
Global Executive Director Life Sciences, Dow Corning

"Marketing no longer has a seat at the boardroom table in many companies because they can't discuss CVA® and link it to the financial performance of their company. Read on."

—**Grahame Dowling**, Professor of Marketing, Australian School
of Business, The University of New South Wales

"CVA® serves to normalize data for multinationals like Lenovo that seek to attract both up-market and emerging market audiences. This is no easy feat, but Don Sexton's book demonstrates that it can be done. As marketers increasingly are held accountable for return on their in-market investments, this kind of sensible construct can only help provide them with the ammunition they so desperately need!"

—**Glen Gilbert**, VP, Brand Management & Marketing Strategy, Lenovo

Value Above Cost

Value Above Cost

Driving Superior Financial Performance with CVA®, the Most Important Metric You've Never Used

Donald E. Sexton, Ph.D.

Vice President, Publisher: Tim Moore
Associate Publisher and Director of Marketing: Amy Neidlinger
Acquisitions Editor: Tim Moore
Editorial Assistant: Pamela Boland
Operations Manager: Gina Kanouse
Digital Marketing Manager: Julie Phifer
Publicity Manager: Laura Czaja
Assistant Marketing Manager: Megan Colvin
Cover Designer: Alan Clements
Managing Editor: Kristy Hart
Project Editor: Chelsey Marti
Copy Editor: Harrison Ridge Services
Proofreader: Leslie Joseph
Senior Indexer: Cheryl Lenser
Compositor: Nonie Ratcliff
Manufacturing Buyer: Dan Uhrig

© 2009 by Pearson Education, Inc.
Publishing as FT Press
Upper Saddle River, New Jersey 07458

FT Press offers excellent discounts on this book when ordered in quantity for bulk purchases or special sales. For more information, please contact U.S. Corporate and Government Sales, 1-800-382-3419, corpsales@pearsontechgroup.com. For sales outside the U.S., please contact International Sales at international@pearson.com.

Company and product names mentioned herein are the trademarks or registered trademarks of their respective owners.

Printed in the United States of America

First Printing April 2009

ISBN-10: 0-13-604332-1
ISBN-13: 978-0-13-604332-4

Pearson Education LTD.
Pearson Education Australia PTY, Limited.
Pearson Education Singapore, Pte. Ltd.
Pearson Education North Asia, Ltd.
Pearson Education Canada, Ltd.
Pearson Educación de Mexico, S.A. de C.V.
Pearson Education—Japan
Pearson Education Malaysia, Pte. Ltd.

Library of Congress Cataloging-in-Publication Data

Sexton, Donald E., 1943-
 Value above cost : driving superior financial performance with CVA/E, the most important metric you've never used / Donald E. Sexton.
  p. cm.
 Includes index.
 ISBN 0-13-604332-1 (hbk. : alk. paper) 1. Marketing—Management. 2. Economic value added. I. Title.
 HF5415.13.S458 2009
 658.8—dc22
                2008040502

To all the members of my wonderful family:
Laura, Mitra, Daniel, Jonathan, Ian, Matt, and Nan,
who are always in my thoughts.

Contents

             Scorecard 275
             General Practice 276
             Use of Specific Marketing ROI Measures 279
             Searching for a Marketing Accountability
             Scorecard............................. 284
             Conclusions 291

Chapter 11: Organizing to Manage CVA® 293
             How Individuals and Organizations Behave ... 295
             Task Clarity............................ 297
             Effort.................................. 299
             Rewards 300
             Capabilities............................ 301
             Environment............................ 307
             Results................................. 309
             Conclusions............................. 310

             Endnotes 311
             Index 329

Foreword

Customer Value Added is the most critical concept for the business community to understand, embrace, and practice. The greater the value added, the greater the opportunity to drive profitability and, therefore, increase shareholder value—which is the primary objective of the CEO.

As business people, our primary responsibilities are to drive shareholder value by selling sufficient quantities of preferred and profitable products and services to consumers and customers. The key word in that sentence for marketers is *preferred*. Preference by consumers and customers may be *real* or it may be *perceived*—but it is a preference nonetheless.

Our job as marketers is to create *preference* via distinctive and differentiated communications. Not only must marketers create preference, but we must also try and grow it over time to ensure that the product or service can contribute positive cash flow to the business enterprise over the longer term. Preference equals perceived value. The more preference that marketers can drive, the more perceived value can be delivered to customers—thereby driving increasing levels of cash flow and shareholder value.

Professor Sexton can certainly explain these business dynamics far better than I—and he does—in this eloquent masterpiece of business marketing and economics. What is magnificent in Professor Sexton's work is that he provides the fundamentals of how this business model effectively operates. By paying attention to these core fundamentals, marketers will improve their odds for delivering upon the CEO's ultimate objective—driving shareholder value.

Many successful marketers have paid attention to the fundamentals—and have succeeded as a result. Let's take a look at a few recent examples:

- Apple's iPod was brilliant—not in its technology—but in its marketing. Apple didn't invent MP3 players or flash technology or recorded music. But what it did so well was it marketed the perceived benefits of portable and customized music. Apple's technology was easily replicated—but not its leadership position. Consumers *perceived* that Apple was the preferred device for *personal, customized music management.* Customer value added could not have been higher as it reflected substantial marketplace *preference.*

- Procter & Gamble's Pampers brand is reinventing how parents choose diapers. Pampers created enormous equity and customer value by changing the conversation with consumers. While parents care about keeping their babies dry, Pampers went one step further and expanded the focus on *total baby care.* By doing so, Pampers tapped into the reservoir of parental goodwill, which was rapidly transferred to Pampers in terms of trust and *preference.* That meant marketplace leadership and growing profits. Was Pampers necessarily a better diaper? Probably not, but in the minds of parents it certainly was.

Does a lot of this sound familiar? Well it should—because this is the essence of building a successful brand. There is no greater responsibility for a marketer than to preserve, if not build, brand value. Building strong brands creates the core customer loyalty and long-term demand that gives marketers great latitude for creating price premiums among a sea of commodity-like products. What kind of price premium can marketers charge? Quite simply, it's the *perceived value* that consumers ascribe to the product and service. The greater the perceived value, the greater opportunity to build margins via price, thereby increasing positive cash flows and brand profitability.

Professor Sexton's book wonderfully and easily navigates the marketplace strategies and theories that serve as beacons for successful brand management. As you leap into the contours of this outstanding brand management perspective, know that there are many pitfalls lurking that can undercut a marketer's ability to deliver the goods. Good marketers must follow core brand management practices that can often escape even the most savvy of marketers, for example:

- **Strong marketing accountability practices.** Insufficient metrics and measurements can derail any good brand building management. In fact, it's an old axiom, "You can't manage what you can't measure." Marketers must continue to work to link marketing, finance, and a solid analytics to create targeted metrics that provide quick and compelling feedback on the impact of brand management programs.

- **Effective integrated marketing communications.** As marketers have an expanding array of media to pursue their customer and consumer targets, they need to have a good foothold as to how they select the most effective media and decide on the levels of financial resources to devote to the use of various marketing approaches.

- **Outstanding marketing and media talent.** The field of marketing has received increasing criticism for failing to keep the marketing management pipeline full of holistic business thinkers that can blend great creativity with dynamic leadership potential and superb business savvy. Those needs are critical, not only at the brand management level, but also in terms of the support resources at advertising and media agencies.

It's certainly not easy being a marketer. But Professor Sexton makes it a lot easier by providing guidance on how to think about managing the significant challenges marketers face each and every day. And, now, it's time for you to move from my take on Professor Sexton's work and to create your own perspective. Enjoy the good reading. You probably won't come across this wonderful path again.

Many thanks Professor Sexton—not many could have said it as well as you.

Bob Liodice
President & CEO
ANA—The Association of National Advertisers

Acknowledgments

Many thanks to many people: Peter Farquhar, Jim Gregory, and Don Lehmann, professional colleagues and friends, whose ideas are always fresh, always stimulating. Bob Liodice, CEO of the Association of National Advertisers, for his breadth of vision, thoughtful marketing insights, and long-time encouragement. Barbara Bacci Mirque for her much-appreciated support. All the executives who generously shared their experience and insights in their sidebars: Dean Adams, Susan Avarde, Serdar Avsar, Michael Bentivegna, Jeff Berman, Robert Bordley, Kevin Clark, Eduardo Conrado, Marshall Dawson, Jamie DePeau, John Dodds, Gary Elliott, Carlos Falchi, Ed Faruolo, Tom Finneran, Lauren Flaherty, Amy Fuller, Scott Fuson, Chris Gaebler, Shailendra Ghorpade, Andrew Giangola, Steven Haro, Tony Hsieh, Peter Neiman, Mark Osterhaus, Evan Oster, Dan Petri, Ed Riley, Cheryl Sawyer, Becky Saeger, Kamal Sen, Steve Smith, and Jon Spector, all singularly effective managers whose paths I have had the good fortune to cross. Rajinder Balaraman and Venu Gorti for our vigorous discussions. Ashleigh Brilliant, whom I met in Santa Barbara many years ago and whose wit provides perspective on everything. Tim Moore, Gina Kanouse, and Anne Goebel of Pearson for the many ways they have helped. Thanks to all.

About the Author

Donald E. Sexton is Professor of Marketing and Decisions, Risk, and Operations, and Director of the Jerome A. Chazen Institute of International Business, Columbia University. Don received his B.A. in mathematics and economics from Wesleyan University and his Ph.D. and M.B.A. in business economics and mathematical methods and statistics from the University of Chicago. He has been teaching at Columbia for more than 40 years in the areas of marketing, international business, and quantitative methods, and is a recipient of the Business School's Distinguished Teaching Award. Don is a visiting professor at the China Europe International Business School in Shanghai and has also taught at the University of California-Berkeley, INSEAD, the Indian School of Business, the Australian Graduate School of Management, Skolkovo (The Moscow School of Management), the University of Tehran, the US Business School in Prague, and the Hong Kong University of Science and Technology. He has more than 100 publications and has published articles in numerous journals such as the *Harvard Business Review*, *Journal of Marketing*, *Journal of Marketing Research*, *Journal of Advertising Research*, and *Management Science*. He is frequently quoted in media such as the *New York Times*, *BusinessWeek*, *Ad Age*, *Brandweek*, and Beijing's *China Economic Daily*. Don is the Program Director of the Conference Board's Marketing Effectiveness Conference and Marketing Research Councils and is a frequent speaker at Association of National Advertisers events. His research concerns marketing return on investment and marketing and branding strategy. His best-selling book on marketing management, *Marketing 101* (Wiley), has been translated into several languages including Chinese, Turkish, Polish, and Indonesian. His book on building and managing brands, *Branding 101* (Wiley), was published in 2008. Don is the principal of The Arrow Group, Ltd.®, which has provided consulting and training services to companies such as GE, IBM, Pfizer, Unilever, Citigroup, DuPont, and Verizon. You can reach Don at donsexton@mindspring.com or log onto www.cva.us.com.

1

Marketing and Financial Performance

Today's competitive environment creates enormous pressures on all managers to be more effective (Exhibit 1.1). Managers at every level from Chief Executive Officer, Chief Marketing Officer, and Chief Financial Officer to the assistant to the Assistant Brand Manager feel these pressures.[1]

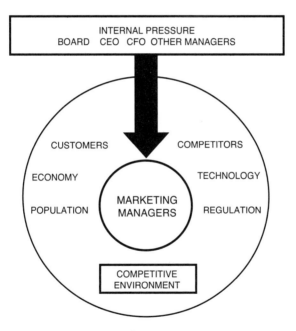

Exhibit 1.1   Pressures on marketing

Marketing managers feel not only the external pressures of the competitive environment but also internal pressures from fellow managers who ask reasonable questions within their organizations, such as:

- What is the return on our marketing efforts?
- What would our sales or profits be if we cut back on the marketing budget?
- Why should we increase efforts in marketing?

In their surveys of marketing managers, the Association of National Advertisers (ANA) has found that relatively few managers are satisfied with their ability to estimate the return on their marketing efforts, and relatively few believe that they can forecast the impact of a 10 percent cut in the marketing budget (Exhibit 1.2).[2]

Exhibit 1.2   Marketing manager's views on their ability to evaluate marketing

How would you evaluate your ability to determine marketing ROI?

	Very Satisfied or Satisfied
2005 (ANA)	13%
2006 (ANA)	23%
2007 (ANA)	11%
2008 (ANA)	13%

"I can forecast the impact of a 10% cut in the marketing budget."

2005 (ANA)	16%
2006 (ANA)	28%
2007 (ANA)	18%
2008 (ANA)	10%

It is, therefore, not at all surprising that about 60 percent of finance managers surveyed by *Financial Executive Magazine* have doubts about marketing forecasts (Exhibit 1.3).[3] In fact, given the discouraging opinions of marketing managers regarding their own forecasts, it is surprising that about 35 percent of the finance executives were found to be willing to believe the marketing numbers!

Exhibit 1.3   Financial managers' views on marketing's ability to evaluate marketing return

	No
Given that marketing forecasts are often input to financial guidance, do you believe these forecasts are audit-ready?	60%
Do you believe that marketing has adequate understanding of financial controls?	63.1%

Financial Executive Magazine and Marketing Management Analytics, 2008.

*Few managers are satisfied with their ability
to estimate the return on their marketing efforts.*

These findings are remarkably consistent—not only over studies conducted by a wide range of organizations including the ANA, the Conference Board, the American Productivity and Quality Center, the CMO Council, and various consultancies—but also over time. In fact, in all these various studies, the percentage of managers very satisfied or satisfied with their ability to evaluate marketing ROI is generally between 10 percent and 20 percent, with no upward trend. At the same time, 80 percent of senior marketing managers surveyed in late 2008 believed that the demands of board members and C-level executives for proof of the effectiveness of marketing and branding initiatives were *increasing*.[4]

Today's intensely competitive environment makes it increasingly difficult to determine marketing accountability. Marketing returns are affected by numerous, powerful marketplace forces such as knowledgeable customers, aggressive competitors, shifting macro trends, and technological changes—evolutionary changes that produce new industry leaders and revolutionary changes that produce new industries.

This book provides marketing managers and other managers, including finance managers, with tools to answer questions about the impact of marketing efforts on an organization's financial performance. The heart of the book is the concept of Customer Value Added (CVA®). CVA® is the difference between the value an organization provides customers and the cost of providing that value—Value Above Cost (Exhibit 1.4).

CVA® = Perceived Value Per Unit – Variable Cost Per Unit

- Total net value per unit created as
  perceived by customer

- Associated with contribution,
  profit, and cash flow

- Net value shared by the producer, resellers,
  and customer

Exhibit 1.4   Customer Value Added

CVA® is the net value to society created by an organization. The higher the CVA®, the more economically successful the organization. The lower the CVA®, the less successful the organization. It is that simple.

CVA® is the net value to society created by an organization.

This chapter explains how you can use CVA® to improve marketing decision-making.

Unum: Marketing and Shareholder Value

Scroll half way down the Fortune 500 list and you'll find a company called Unum. Rooted in a 150-year heritage, it was known primarily to Human Resource and Benefits professionals as the leading disability insurance company in the country. It was also known for having stumbled early this decade due to litigation issues and some strategic missteps. In fact, the stock price had fallen from a high of $33 in May, 2001, to just $6 in March, 2003.

Because Unum products are sold through brokers and offered through the workplace, the company's previous promotional campaigns had been trade-focused. But in the summer of 2007, to help give more visibility to Unum's brand—and to reposition the company from a disability insurance company to a leading employee benefits company, Unum launched a multi-million dollar advertising and branding campaign. The work centered on the company's new tagline "better benefits at work" and included a new logo, visual identity system, sales literature, television advertising, trade print, consumer print and a sponsorship of ESPN's Injury Report.

The new work energized the sales force and gave them something new to talk about with brokers and companies. In the past year, Unum's corporate reputation has improved dramatically with brokers, employers of all sizes, and most importantly, with Wall Street and the ratings agencies. In fact, today the stock price is back up to almost $24 a share.

—Peter Neiman, Vice President, Advertising and Branding, Unum

Reprinted with permission of Peter Neiman

Determining Marketing Accountability

Interest in how marketing affects financial performance has a long history. Nearly 40 years ago, the author's first published journal articles concerned marketing accountability (Exhibit 1.5). Over the years, many qualified researchers have spent considerable time and effort attempting to estimate the return from marketing activities. Yet the answers have remained elusive, and today marketing accountability remains one of the most important issues facing marketers.[5]

35 + years!

"Estimation of Marketing Policy Effects on Sales," *Journal of Marketing Research*, August 1970.
"Overspending on Advertising," *Journal of Advertising Research*, December 1971.

"Pricing, Perceived Value, and Communications," *The Advertiser*, April 2006.
"Hidden Wealth in B2B Brands," with James R. Gregory, *Harvard Business Review*, March 2007.

Exhibit 1.5   Personal involvement in marketing accountability research

Marketing managers seem to believe that the evaluation of the return on the marketing investment is important. In 2006, members of the CMO Council placed issues involving marketing ROI as three of their top five concerns.[6] A 2007 Conference Board survey found nearly 80 percent of the respondents considered marketing ROI and marketing metrics among their most important challenges.[7]

Given the amount of interest and efforts over many years, one would expect some success. Yet, a 2008 study by the Conference Board found that only 19 percent of the organizations surveyed felt that they had made good progress in measuring marketing ROI, and more than 50 percent had not started or had just started their efforts to measure marketing ROI.[8] A 2007 Marketing NPV study found fewer than 10 percent of respondents felt their ability to measure marketing ROI to be "as good as it needs to be."[9] While a 2008 study by the Lenskold Group found that 26 percent of the firms surveyed calculated some profitability measure for at least some marketing investments, that is still far from a majority.[10]

This lack of progress is reflected in the budgeting process. Nearly two-thirds of marketing budgets are set based on history—last year's budget, according to the ANA surveys and corroborated by other studies.[11]

In Chapter 11, "Organizing to Manage CVA®," the reasons for this lack of progress are examined in detail.[12] In brief, numerous studies suggest that the main factors slowing progress in determining marketing accountability are:

1. **Lack of clarity as to what marketing return is.** Many managers report that there is no definition of marketing ROI within their organization.[13]

2. **Lack of time devoted to marketing return.** Time spent on marketing return is one of the most useful predictors of progress, but many organizations have not even started to develop systems to examine marketing return.

3. **Lack of motivation for people to work on marketing return.** Relatively few compensation or recognition systems seem to encourage work on marketing return.

4. **Lack of skills and resources.** Many organizations feel they do not have the appropriate data or the appropriate analytical skills to evaluate marketing return.

5. **Lack of cooperation between marketing and finance.** Marketing and finance silos still seem to be the reality in many organizations.

6. **Inertia.** Many managers seem comfortable with what they are currently doing and neither feel the pressure to change nor have the time to change their approaches.

This book focuses on how to think about the return on marketing activities. It shows how a company's marketing and branding efforts play a major role in determining the financial performance of any organization, including revenue, profits, cash flow, and shareholder value and how those efforts can be monitored and evaluated for maximum impact.

Will this book solve all the problems in determining marketing accountability? No, of course not. But it provides methodologies and approaches that are broadly rooted in many disciplines—marketing, economics, finance, and accounting—and which are supported by multiple studies. The book explains how to evaluate marketing efforts with a straightforward concept—CVA®—that has a direct relationship to contribution. Its use has been proven in practice by the author's corporate clients.

©Ashleigh Brilliant, 2008. Used with permission.

The Value of a Business

The value of a business depends on its future, not its past.

Managers, investors, and others concerned about the well-being of an organization need to look at where it is going, not where it has been. A company's future financial performance depends on its long-term abilities to manage both the value it provides customers and its costs. Expected future financial performance, in turn, determines shareholder value. The company value meltdowns in the Fall of 2008, such as that of AIG, were due to lack of confidence in the future financial performance of those organizations.[14]

There is a huge body of thought and writing devoted to the determinants of the value of a corporation.[15] Many factors have been suggested, including managerial talent, resources, innovation ability, and core competencies. While all of these factors surely affect the financial performance of an organization, none of them provide a direct link to financial performance. Managerial talent and resources are very broad categories. Innovation may be managed but is difficult, by its nature, to predict. Core competencies are specific but look inward (at the organization) rather than outward (toward the customers and competitors). Intangible assets, such as brands, have appeared to pose especially difficult valuation problems for many companies.[16]

In lieu of factors that are linked directly to financial performance, many managers attempt to predict performance by relying on various financial ratios such as return on sales and turnover.[17] The problem with many of those measures is that they look backward rather than forward .[18] A manager should always prefer leading indicators to lagging indicators because forward control is preferable to backward control. One wants to steer by looking through the windshield, not through the rear-view mirror.

CVA® is both outward looking—toward customers and competitors—and forward looking, in that it indicates the future performance of an organization.

3M: Relation of Loyalty to Growth and Profit

3M has more than 50,000 products, 36 divisions spanning almost all major markets and subsidiary companies in 65 countries. With that complexity, building powerful brands is a difficult task. A key element of powerful brands is delivering relevance and differentiation. Maintaining relevance and differentiation over a long period of time can be difficult without a solid new product engine. Fortunately, one of 3M's greatest strengths is it's strong culture of innovation and new product development.

To accelerate growth and build lasting customer relationships, 3M has processes for measuring end user loyalty to its brands. In studies over time, 3M has seen loyalty increase as it focuses it efforts on improving the specific drivers of end user loyalty. The businesses that have achieved above average loyalty, compared to the Corporate average, enjoy faster growth and higher margins.

An example is the Dental business at 3M. The 3M Dental business won the Baldridge award in 1997 which included tough customer measures. The business measured end user satisfaction and loyalty. The measures were connected to the drivers of loyalty and programs put in place to correct any gaps that were detected. The 3M businesses that have successfully aligned programs against the gaps have achieved above average growth.

Measures and processes are necessary but not sufficient to achieve the superior performance. Business leadership and programs that align the resources against the priorities are required. Leadership that inspires employees is necessary. No strong brand can be built without employees who know what to do, have the resources to do what is needed and are supported by their management. The Dental business has consistently delivered its brand promise over many years with several changes in management.

—Dean Adams, Director, Corporate Brand Management, 3M
Reprinted with permission of 3M Company

Customer Value and Costs

In the long-run, an organization's financial success depends on how well they manage two things: value to customers and costs. Both determine margin and demand, and both need to be managed in concert.

Over the years, some management gurus have suggested that being the customer value leader or the cost leader produces winning strategies.[19] That is not the case. Focusing solely on customer value or cost can lead to implementation of lopsided strategies.

Having the highest customer value does not guarantee success, just as having the lowest costs does not guarantee success. High customer value can lead to high costs. Low costs can lead to low customer value. Customer value and costs must be in *balance*.

What determines financial success is how well an organization maximizes the difference between the value to customers and the costs of providing that value. That difference is known as Customer Value Added (CVA®), the focus of this book.

CVA® has two important components: perceived value and cost. Perceived value is discussed at length in Chapter 4, "Perceived Value," and costs are explored in Chapter 5, "Costs."

Perceived Value

In CVA®, customer value is defined as the value *perceived* by the customer.

Perceived value is the maximum that the customer will pay for your product or service.

Perceived customer value is not price—it is the ceiling on price. It can be both measured and managed.

Perceived customer value may well be different from actual value. In fact, most of the time perceived value is less than the actual value a customer receives because a customer rarely knows all the value a product or service provides.

Perceived value alone has been found to be an important leading indicator of financial performance in a variety of studies conducted by different researchers with different sets of data (Exhibit 1.6). In a process the author facilitated for members of the Conference Board's Council on Corporate Brand Management (described in Chapter 10, "Building the Marketing Accountability Scorecard"), perceived value was selected as the most important single measure of brand health by a nearly 2:1 margin over the next most frequently mentioned measure.

> *"The relationship between brand equity and stock return was...strong."*
> —Jacobson and Aaker, EquiTrend data
>
> *"Brand differentiation and relevance are leading indicators of brand success."*
> —Agres, BrandAsset Valuator data
>
> *"There is no doubt that relative perceived quality and profitability are strongly related."*
> —Buzzell & Gale, PIMS data
>
> *"...brand equity is found to have nearly as strong an influence as ROI [on stock return]."*
> —Jacobson and Aaker, Techtel data
>
> *"...Corporate brand image actually has some degree of influence on a significant 75 percent of the key factors that explain stock price."*
> —Gregory, Fortune 500 data

Exhibit 1.6   Research findings regarding perceived value and financial performance[20]

A New Definition of Marketing

Many people routinely define marketing as the "4 P's": product, pricing, place, and promotion. The author *never* uses the 4 P's definition of marketing. Except perhaps for product, the 4 P's definition of marketing concentrates on the tactical aspects of marketing such as pricing, distribution, and advertising and promotion. While tactics are certainly important, the marketing strategy, including in particular target marketing and positioning, must be appropriate in order for the tactics to have effect.

Marketing is managing perceived value.

The author's definition of marketing is *managing perceived value*. Managing perceived value incorporates both the strategic and tactical areas of marketing. Frances Farrow, executive member of the board of Virgin Atlantic, described how their marketing focuses on managing value to the customer "…the customer viewpoint remains the heart of our companies' origins…[We evaluate opportunities by asking:] Are we meeting a gap where there is a need? Does it offer consumers a better deal? Can we offer both substance and a unique Virgin flair across many consumer touchpoints?"[21]

To attain high value perceived by target customers, it is necessary to think strategically and design or position the product or service for a target group. It is also necessary to think tactically, for example, by communicating the product or service position effectively to the target customers.

Products with on-target design that no one knows about do not sell. Products that are communicated widely but that have poor design may sell once, but not again. There is a saying in advertising, "Great advertising makes poor products fail even faster"—since people are persuaded to try them and find they do not like them.

Perceived value per unit can be increased with managerial attention, and it can also be decreased through managerial inattention. However, for any level of costs, the higher the perceived value, the stronger the company's position in the market, both now and in the future.

While CVA® depends on both perceived customer value and costs, much of this book concerns perceived value because managing the value perceived by the customer should be the primary purpose of all marketing and branding efforts.

CVA®

CVA® is the difference between perceived value per unit and the variable cost per unit for a product or service (Exhibit 1.7). CVA® is the net value—as perceived by customers—that an organization provides society.

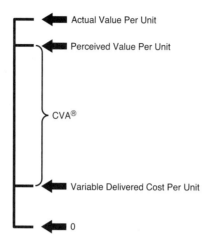

Reprinted with permission from "How Marketing Affects Shareholder Value," The Arrow Group, Ltd.®, New York, NY, 2008.

Exhibit 1.7   Customer Value Added

If CVA® is high, an organization is perceived as providing value to society and will be rewarded with strong financial results. However, if CVA® is low, the financial results will be weak. At the extreme, if CVA® is negative, in a free market the organization will likely go out of business because the inputs it is using cost more than the value of the products or services it is producing. In open markets, such organizations fail.

Keep in mind, as mentioned earlier, that perceived value per unit is typically below actual value, as shown in Exhibit 1.7, because customers usually do not know all the benefits that they receive from a product or service.

Cost Orientation

Unfortunately, all too often managers become preoccupied with costs to the detriment of value to customers. With a cost orientation, managers pay minimal attention to customer value (Exhibit 1.8).

According to Boyd Beasley, the senior director of customer support at Electronic Arts, the successful producer of video games, "In years past, we [EA] were very much a cost center operation and our vision was to come in on budget...We are turning the ship to be significantly more customer centric" by providing more services to customers and bringing them into the product development process earlier.[22]

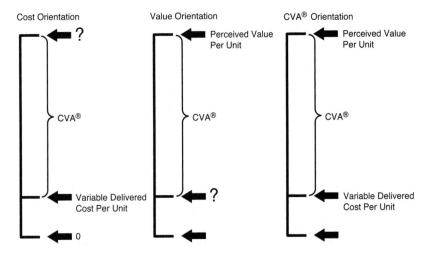

Reprinted with permission from "How Marketing Affects Shareholder Value," The Arrow Group, Ltd.®, New York, NY, 2008.

Exhibit 1.8   Orientations

There are at least two problems with a single-minded cost orientation:

1. Cost reduction programs may lower value to the customer more than they lower costs.
2. Cost preoccupation is often, but not necessarily, associated with low pricing strategies.

Hollowing-Out

If lowering costs leads to an even greater lowering of perceived value, CVA® is being decreased, and the organization is contributing less to society and will, therefore, have a lower level of financial performance. Decreasing CVA® when lowering costs represents the *hollowing out* of a brand.[23]

During a hollowing-out process, because CVA® depends on the perceptions of customers, there may be a time lag between the lowering of costs and the lowering of perceived value. There is inertia in perceptions—customers may be forgiving at the first signs of lowered product or service value.

An example of how easy it is for managers to begin the hollowing out of a brand: Typically the author travels to China two or three times a year with a major US airline. In the past, they provided sandwiches in the middle of the trip—the time in the air is 14 to 15 hours so the sandwiches were welcome. Recently, the airline decided to eliminate the sandwiches, cutting back on their value to customers. Notice the price of a round-trip business class ticket is in the vicinity of $10,000; the cost of providing a sandwich perhaps a dollar or two. By cutting back on costs, they risk losing the entire fare because there are other carriers flying the same route that are not cutting back on the small comforts that make a trip bearable. Truly, the airline is following a policy of "penny wise, pound foolish."

When the author mentioned the loss of sandwiches to a flight attendant, she said, "Yes, they are just getting very chintzy—and I am tired of reporting the negative passenger reactions. The managers don't understand." Perhaps it would be helpful if the cost-cutters were asked to experience a 15-hour flight sometime and learn how the world looks from a passenger's point of view.

Incidentally, whenever the author sees one of this airline's expensive print ads, he immediately thinks, "How many sandwiches is that ad worth?" Glossy advertising does not offset perceived product or service deficiencies—as eventually the top managers of this airline might learn. In fact, glossy advertising makes customers more sensitive to perceived value deficiencies.

One can see hollowing out actions all the time and everywhere. When a local bank promises wonderful service and a customer does not receive that level of service, perceived value falls even faster than any cost savings. When a chemical produces lags in their delivery, perceived value may decrease more than any shipping costs saved.

The time lag between when a cost is cut and when customer value falls can tempt a senior manager to cut costs because they can appear to be successful with a cost-cutting program as long as customers have not yet noticed the decline in customer value. Their successor will discover later that the cost decreases have eroded the customer value and brand reputation of the organization, compromising the brand's power to generate revenue, profits, and cash flow, sometimes irretrievably.[24]

All cost reduction programs should be calibrated against the impact on customer value as perceived by the customer—value engineering from the customer's point of view. Unfortunately, many organizations are cost-oriented because they do not know the perceived value associated with their product or service and, therefore, are unable to discover the impact of cost changes on value as perceived by their customers.

An infamous example of failing to consider CVA® is the Schlitz beer story. In the 1970's, Schlitz was the number two brewer in the US. Concerned with their stock price, top management cut costs by using less expensive hops and reducing the time to age the beer. In the short run, profits increased and so did the stock price, but then customers started to realize that the Schlitz taste had deteriorated and they stopped buying the beer. Schlitz was never able to climb back to their number two position. It was a classic case of deliberately decreasing CVA® for short-term gain and consequently hollowing out a once strong brand.[25]

Price-Cutting

Organizations focused on costs often seem to focus on price-cutting strategies. As a result, they risk training their customers to be concerned about price to the exclusion of value and often incite price wars. The airline, telecommunications, and automotive industries include competitors that seem to have adopted this approach.[26]

There is usually only one winner of a price war: the customer. Of the companies involved in the price war, the lowest-cost producer may do the best; but their financial results may or may not be attractive. As demonstrated in Chapter 5, as prices are lowered, unit volume must increase substantially simply to maintain contribution.

Meanwhile, in such an industry, many customers become price-shoppers instead of value-shoppers. That simply intensifies the pressure to lower prices and accelerates the vicious spiral of price cuts. Price wars not only erode profits, but also train customers to expect the same prices and to assume that all products and services perform the same—even if that is not true.

Appropriate Costs

A preoccupation chiefly with costs can keep one from achieving an optimal strategy for all the reasons above. But the situation is even worse. As discussed in Chapter 5, many organizations do not even know their appropriate costs and, instead, use some form of average full-costing, which compounds the errors associated with a cost orientation.

Value Orientation

Some time ago the author listened to an economist, a colleague, discuss his research concerning luxury products. At one point, he said, "You will not believe this, but in the luxury product industry, prices do not follow costs." In that one sentence, he captured the key difference between economics and marketing—one of point of view, not theory.

Economics and marketing are both consistent in concept. However, an implicit assumption in economics is the movement of markets toward equilibrium as prices decline and profit margins across industries approach some equivalent levels. That equilibrium, in fact, would be achieved in open markets with free flows of information, resources, and products and services.

However, marketers try to interrupt the forces driving markets to equilibrium through innovation, continual redesign, and communications—a focus on customer value. While economists might declare that prices should follow costs if a market reaches equilibrium, marketers would say that their job is to keep a market from reaching that equilibrium by continually adding value and communicating those value increases to the customer.

All marketers try to keep prices from following costs. The marketing task is to break away from the pack of commodity products and services and distinguish their product or service for their target customers. The CVA® for differentiated products or services will generally be high, while the CVA® for commodity products and services will generally be low (Exhibit 1.9).

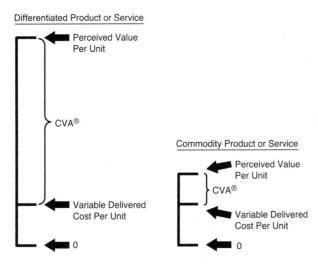

Reprinted with permission from "Pricing, Perceived Value, and Communications," Donald E. Sexton, New York, NY, 2008.

Exhibit 1.9   Differentiated products and services versus commodity products and services

However, a value orientation that translates as value at any cost should not be the objective. Many books on customer satisfaction and customer loyalty often employ the phrase, "Delight your customers." Yes, one wants to delight customers, but one needs to make a profit while doing so. One should not try to increase continually perceived value without regard to the increases in costs associated with those value changes. At some point the costs of delighting customers may become greater than the value that they are willing to pay for.

There was an industrial supply distributor that held a much higher percentage of parts in their catalog in inventory than did their competitors. Their customers were delighted with the higher chance of finding the parts they needed at this distributor. They were less delighted when the distributor went out of business due to its high inventory costs.

Costs and perceived customer value must be monitored, measured, and managed together.

CVA® Orientation

A CVA® orientation is about *balancing* perceived customer value and costs. Because CVA® is the difference between perceived value per unit and cost per unit, it rewards those organizations that can measure, monitor, and manage *both* customer value and costs.

How many people in the typical organization measure, monitor, and manage costs? Usually a lot of people. How many people in the typical organization measure, monitor, and manage customer value? All too frequently, very few.

> *How many people in the typical organization measure, monitor, and manage customer value?*

There are some organizations that are proficient at evaluating customer value, and managers from many of those organizations have provided sidebars for this book. Often, however, when the author addresses audiences on the topic of marketing accountability and asks how many people know the perceived value for their products or services, very few raise their hands. A follow-up question concerns how many of the attendees know about some of the techniques for measuring perceived value—and again very few raise their hands. The CVA® orientation forces managers to look at customer value and costs and then rewards them for their efforts with strategies that are more effective in achieving desired financial goals. Gordon Bethune dramatically raised the performance of Continental Airlines by examining the implications of all decisions on both customer value and cost. For example, before the Bethune takeover, pilots were given bonuses for using less fuel—which they accomplished by going more slowly resulting in missed connections for Continental passengers. The pilot incentives constituted a classic example of single-minded thinking, lowering costs without regard to the impact on CVA®—an attitude that Bethune completely changed with dramatic results.[27]

American Association of Advertising Agencies: The Role of Marketing

Marketing is a dynamic and foundational component of all commerce. Marketing resides at the intersection of the seller's economic interests and the buyer's behavioral values. When done well, marketing can and will inform, inspire, and motivate consumers into action.

Over the course of the past thirty years, there are countless examples of marketing strategies and advertising tactics that have dramatically changed the fortunes of companies, product categories, and individual brands:

- Graphics and design elements define many categories and brands—think Chanel (perfume category), Method (cleaning products), or Absolut (vodka).

- Pricing strategy has become a communications vehicle that establishes an audience profile and value framework that can range from prestige and luxury (Hermès, Rolls-Royce, Gucci, Haagen-Dazs) to everyday affordable (Wal-Mart, Costco, Ikea, Southwest Airlines).

- Business model innovations are almost always predicated on insightful marketing (eBay, Nintendo, TiVo, Google)

- Advertising initiatives have introduced revolutionary products (Swiffer, Palm's PDA), changed pop culture (Apple's iPod), altered societal norms (Viagra—Bob Dole, Friends Don't Let Friends Drive Drunk—Nat'l Highway Traffic Safety), rejuvenated tired categories (Got Milk—California Milk Processors Board), and won presidential elections (George H.W. Bush's Willie Horton release from prison ad in 1988).

- Iconic Ad campaigns now define a significant number of Fortune 500 company brands. To name just a few: Just Do It (Nike), Priceless (MasterCard), You're in Good Hands (Allstate), or When it Absolutely, Positively has to be there overnight (FedEx).

Marketing is the seller's investment in their brand, which defines the distinctive public face of a product or service. For sellers the question is not if they should market their brands. The operative questions are how, where, when and how much should be invested in order to optimize a brand through marketing.

Don Sexton's seminal work in the areas of marketing accountability, pricing, metrics scorecards and now "Customer Value Added" has advanced the dialogue that sellers need to consider in order to optimize their commercial interests.

—Tom Finneran, EVP, American Association of Advertising Agencies

Reprinted with permission of Tom Finneran

Strategic Themes

The power of the CVA® concept can be seen in a comprehensive industry study conducted by William Hall. He studied 64 companies in eight industries, four business-to-business industries and four consumer industries.[28] The industries Hall studied included steel, tire and rubber, heavy-duty trucks, construction and materials handling equipment, automotive, major home appliances, beer, and cigarettes. All were characterized by single-digit annual growth and intense competition.

In each industry, Hall identified two companies that were leaders in regard to annual revenue growth rate and return on equity, not only in their respective industries, but among all US companies. In his seminal article, he described the strategies of these winning companies with what the author calls the *Strategic Themes Matrix* (see Exhibit 1.10).

In Hall's formulation of the matrix, the horizontal axis is "relative delivered cost." *Relative delivered costs* are all costs involved in placing the product or service in the hands of the customer: operations costs, but also costs such as distribution costs and marketing costs. The vertical axis of Hall's matrix is "relative product/service differentiation" and refers to product or service performance relative to competitors.

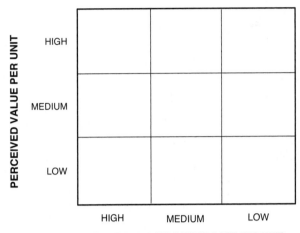

Source: Adapted from William K. Hall, "Survival Strategies in a Hostile Environment,"
Harvard Business Review, September 1980, pp. 74-85.

Exhibit 1.10   Strategic Themes Matrix

In the reformulation of Hall's matrix for this book, the definitions of the horizontal and vertical axes have been refined.

The horizontal axis is defined here as "variable delivered cost per unit"—all the incremental costs involved in bringing a unit of the product or service to the customer. That definition is fairly close to that of Hall.

The vertical axis is defined here as "perceived value per unit." Recall that the perceived value per unit is the maximum that a customer is willing to pay for a unit of a product or service. That definition varies from Hall's definition with the addition of the word *perceived*. Even if a product or service is differentiated from its competitor's product or service, that differentiation must be *perceived* by the customer to have an impact on their purchases.

The most powerful strategic position on the Strategic Themes Matrix is the upper right position—lowest cost per unit and highest perceived value per unit. However, among the 16 leading companies that Hall identified, only 2 companies occupied that position at the time of his study: Caterpillar in earthmoving equipment and Philip Morris in cigarettes. Today, companies in the upper right position arguably include companies such as Southwest Airlines and Trader

Joe's.[29] There are two other winning positions on the matrix—the highest perceived value per unit combined with the medium (or acceptable) cost per unit and the medium (or acceptable) perceived value per unit combined with the lowest cost per unit. In Hall's study, in heavy-duty trucks those positions were occupied, respectively, by Paccar and Ford.

A company would not want to be in the four cells on the lower left-hand side of the matrix—low or medium perceived value coupled with high or medium costs, which Michael Porter of Harvard Business School has memorably termed *stuck in the middle*. Stuck-in-the-middle companies lose their performance-minded customers to their higher perceived value competitors and their economy-minded customers to their lower cost competitors.

The upper left position is filled by elite companies with high value products such as Hermès, Chanel, or Carlos Falchi.[30] The lower right position is filled by companies producing cheap but shoddy products or services. A company can succeed in either of those two positions, but they require very special types of managerial thinking. Elite companies typically focus on market niches, while shoddy product companies do not expect much repeat business.

The Strategic Themes Matrix clearly shows the two main factors driving business success: perceived customer value and cost. These same themes have been identified and discussed by numerous highly regarded management thinkers such as Michael Porter, Peter Drucker, Al Reiss, and Frederick Reicheld. When such diverse thinkers agree, that is a signal that the idea is significant.

The importance of perceived customer value and cost in determining financial performance has also been validated by several diverse empirical studies over many years. (See Exhibit 1.6.) Different researchers such as Jim Gregory of CoreBrand, Stuart Agres of Young and Rubicam, and Robert Buzzell and Brad Gale of the PIMS Project, and professors including David Aaker, Robert Jacobson, Dominique Hanssens, and Natalie Mizik have all arrived at similar conclusions using different data bases—*perceived value is clearly linked to measures of financial return*.[31]

When an idea is supported *both* by well-known management gurus and by highly respected researchers, the idea is not only significant, but one that works and has been proved in practice.

Carlos Falchi: The Real Meaning of Luxury

LUXURY—EXPENSIVE…DOES NOT SYSTEMATICALLY MEAN QUALITY.

INEXPENSIVE DOES NOT AUTOMATICALLY MEAN CHEAP.

A PRODUCT CARRIED BY A CELEBRITY DOES NOT MAKE IT LUXURY.

Real luxury and value are beyond celebrities photographed wearing them and all the brand advertising.

The value and luxury that a customer receives when making her purchase is in the caring, thoughtfulness, time spent, and top quality materials assembled to achieve a product of distinction. A product that I can offer with pride.

When I see a customer who is still carrying one of my handbags after 30 years and wearing it with the same pleasure she had the day she bought it, I am deeply touched she has had so many years of pleasure from something made with care. Thirty years of wear and still worn with pride. That is satisfying.

Quality is a lasting value.

Some countries show their appreciation of this principle by making people who excel in their trade a "National treasure." Be it the best rice grower, best scientist, best artist, best photographer or best tailor. The title is given for constant Zen dedication in achieving the best.

When all these ingredients come together everyone is satisfied.

Thank you,

Carlos Falchi

—Carlos Falchi, Designer, Design and Development Lab, LLC
Reprinted with permission

Design and Communication

To succeed, an organization needs to provide customer value at acceptable costs and communicate that value to target customers. Design and communications must both be focused on the customer. As Tony Davidson, president of the D&AD Global Awards, pointed out, "In the end, it's not just about whether something [an advertisement] is a good idea. It's about whether it's a good idea and relevant."[32]

Customer value comes from *innovations in design*—the new products and services or improvements in products, services, and processes that a company generates over time. At the heart of communications is *branding*—the reputation of the company in the minds of its target customers. Without innovation, branding withers. But without branding, the company is not rewarded for its innovations.

For example, many years ago Xerox developed many innovations in computing—but never truly received credit for their achievements in terms of their brand. On the other hand, Levi's has been a very powerful brand, but failures to keep pace with innovations in styling eroded the brand's value.[33]

In the long run, *both* innovation and branding are required for success, as shown in the sidebar, a 30-year tale of two companies: Harley-Davidson and Norton Villiers Triumph.[34]

Winners and Losers: The US Motorcycle Industry

The 1970s

In the 1970s, the motorcycle market in the United States was under fierce attack from the Japanese motorcycle manufacturers. At one time, Harley-Davidson held nearly 100 percent of the US motorcycle market, but by 1981, the Japanese companies had secured 94 percent of that market (Table 1.1).

Table 1.1　United States Motorcycle Shares

Year		Honda	Yamaha	Kawasaki	Suzuki	Harley Davidson	BMW	NVT
1974	TOTAL	43.0%	20.0%	13.0%	11.0%	6.0%	.9%	1.4%
1981	TOTAL	38.0	25.0	17.0	14.0	5.0	.4	.2
	<750 CC	41.0	27.0	18.0	14.0	0	.2	N/A
	>750 CC	31.0	21.0	16.0	14.0	17.0	.8	N/A
1991	TOTAL	26.0	9.5	14.5	17.0	31.0	2.0	0
2001	TOTAL	26.6	20.0	11.2	11.1	24.0	1.8	0
2005	TOTAL	28.6	17.4	9.6	12.5	25.6	1.3	.8

Source: "Top Motorcycle Makers." Dealer News, Market Share Reporter, Thomson Gale, various years.

The Japanese motorcycle manufacturers used a classic international strategy to defeat Harley: They obtained a beachhead in the market with innovative products—small motorcycles—then built their brand and introduced larger and larger bikes.

Compared to Harley, the Japanese manufacturers Honda, Kawasaki, Yamaha, and Suzuki were more efficient producers, built more reliable motorcycles, and spent more on customer advertising. When AMF merged with Harley, they increased output three-fold. The speed of the expansion had its consequences. More than half the Harley's produced were missing parts, and the others leaked oil. Bikers said you needed to buy two Harley's, one to provided spare parts to keep the other on the road.

The 1980s

Harley-Davidson and Norton Villiers Triumph (NVT) both lost share to the Japanese companies during the 1970s. In the 1980s, NVT eventually went out of business, but Harley-Davidson used innovation and branding to not only survive, but also regain its position as a force in the motorcycle industry.

At the beginning of the 1980s, both Harley-Davidson and NVT, arguably, were stuck in the middle in the Strategic Themes Matrix.

In the middle of the top row was BMW, which was widely regarded as a high-performance, reliable motorcycle and, seemingly, content to stay in that position. In the right-most column were the four Japanese producers, led by Honda, all driving toward the upper-right hand high value/low cost position.

Meanwhile, the situation was getting worse for both Harley and NVT. Their bikes had poor reputations for reliability, and they were behind in product design. Both Harley-Davidson and NVT had to take action if they were to survive. In 1981, 13 Harley managers purchased the company from AMF and proceeded to decrease their costs by cutting their workforce by 40 percent, decreasing salaries by 9 percent, and then freezing hiring and salaries. They adopted cost-lowering methods such as just-in-time inventory, which they learned from visits to the production lines of their Japanese competitors. They also improved their quality control.

These changes in operations required time. Their chief designer, William "Willie G." Davidson, provided that time. He designed new Harley bikes such as the Super Glide that did not require substantial time for retooling. Davidson's designs permitted Harley to increase their perceived value per unit in the short-run, while they waited for their longer-term efforts to pay off. In 1984, for example, they introduced a new engine, the Evolution, which was very well-received.

The Harley brand was in danger of being hollowed out by the prior actions of AMF. While Harley had improved their product, their brand had to be revived by communicating the product improvements to their customers.

Once they had restored the performance of their product, Harley used print ads to communicate with their target customers, including a memorable print ad showing a group of tough-looking bikers with the headline, "Would you sell an unreliable motorcycle to these guys?"

Another key part of the revival of their brand was the Harley Owners Group (HOG). Started by Harley in 1983, today it is the largest motorcycle club in the world—and an excellent example of how to build relationships with your customers.

Increasing CVA® by simultaneously increasing perceived customer value per unit and decreasing cost per unit worked for Harley. In 1991, they had more than a 30 percent share of the total US market for motorcycles and nearly 50 percent of the cruiser (large) motorcycle market.

Meanwhile, during the 1980s, NVT was struggling and continuing their retreat strategy of the 1970s, dropping models from their line. They had labor problems. Their motorcycles continued to have product defects. Their policy with regard to warranty claims could be described as *grudging*. Spare parts were difficult to find. They lost orders destined for police departments in the UK.

Their brand was spiraling down the failure route, and their cash flow problems made it difficult for them to innovate. In efforts to lower costs, they cut models from their line until, finally, they could no longer cover their overhead. In 1983, NVT closed their Meriden factory and the company was liquidated.

The 1990s and Beyond

Honda eventually reached the upper right-hand corner—the high value/low cost position on the Strategic Themes Matrix—and remains a formidable competitor to Harley-Davidson. Harley occupies a position on the high perceived value top row. They continuously reinvigorate their brand with a stream of new engines, new transmissions, and new bikes (10 new models launched in 2005-6). They have also focused their efforts on lucrative new segments among older bikers. In 1987, the median age of a Harley buyer was 35; in 2006, it was 47. More than 20 percent of their sales are outside the US, in markets such as China and Japan, where Harley has the leading share in heavyweight motorcycles.

Going forward, Harley still faces challenging decisions concerned with younger riders. The competitive environment does not get quieter.

Lessons

In the 1970s, both Harley-Davidson and Norton Villiers Triumph were multi-domestic companies, succeeding in their home markets and selected export markets. They did not seek competitors, but the competitors—the Japanese motorcycle companies—came to them. Both Harley and NVT were slow to react, and both lost share in the US market in the 1970s. However Harley-Davidson was able to use innovation and branding to recover. NVT was unable to innovate and reverse their brand failure route.

Harley-Davidson's recovery is even more dramatic if one recalls the backdrop. In the 1970s and 1980s, many managers of US companies were complaining about the "unfair" practices of Japanese companies. One Harley executive commented, "First, we thought it was the Japanese pricing, then we thought it was the Japanese culture…. Finally, we realized the problem was us, not them."

Although NVT disappeared, Triumph motorcycles live on. A new, privately-owned company—Triumph Motorcycles Limited—was started in the mid-1980s. Six brand new Triumph motorcycles were launched in 1990, followed by more innovations and more models. One might say that innovation and branding Triumph once again.[35]

CVA® and Economic Development

This book is about how CVA® can be used by organizations to improve their financial performance. CVA® also has implications for how economies are managed to increase Gross Domestic Product (GDP).

There continues to be substantial discussion regarding the economic futures of China and India. To the extent managers in either country are successful with their marketing and branding efforts to develop specialty products and services, the GDP of their country will increase far beyond what might be expected were they producing commodity-like products or services.[36]

In the most recent *Business Week* listing of the 100 most valuable brands in the world as estimated by Interbrand, there are 52 brands from the United States; 10 from Germany; 8 from France; 7 from Japan; 5 from Switzerland, 2 from Sweden, 2 from South Korea; 1 each from Finland and Spain; but none from China and none from India.[37] Lenovo is thought by some to be the strongest Chinese global brand; with strong global potential, but, in 2007, their global brand awareness was estimated by Interbrand to be 59 percent—far below that of Sony (98 percent) and Samsung (96 percent).[38]

Both China and India have demonstrated substantial economic growth. However, their growth rates are especially astounding given that they have not included substantial branding success in world markets, although Indian companies seem to be more successful than Chinese companies in certain product categories (Table 1.2)

Table 1.2   Country preferences for selected products

Product	Preferred Country	
	China	India
Pet Food	22%	78%
Prescription Drugs	26%	74%
Toys	27%	73%
Makeup	30%	70%
Skincare Products	26%	74%

Source "China's Recall Woes Bad for Wal-Mart," *Brandweek*, September 10, 2007.

A study by a colleague shows that the efficiency of capital in China and India is similar to that of the US in heavy industries, but well below that of the US in consumer packaged industries.[39] Most likely this comparison reflects the relative strengths of US marketing and branding efforts—especially in consumer packaged goods.

Many Chinese and Indian companies have exceptionally low costs. For example, Pearl River in China, the world's leading producer of pianos, is known for very low costs. The challenge of companies that rely on low costs is to increase CVA® by building perceived value in the minds of their target customers.

Because of their low cost positions, price has often been a major weapon of many Chinese and Indian companies for acquiring customers. For example, from 2000 to 2003, local Chinese cell phone manufacturers such as Bird, Amoi, and Panda moved from a 0 percent market share to nearly 50 percent by cutting prices against Nokia, Motorola, and other international brands. Tata has produced an extraordinarily low-priced automobile. Unfortunately, low price strategies often foment price wars. Preoccupation with low prices can be a major distraction to building customer perceived value.

While they are in position to build their brands, Chinese and Indian companies especially need to be wary of the temptation to enter foreign markets by offering low prices. While such an approach may provide a quick market entry, there are long-term consequences—both to their own brands and to their country's brands.[40] If a company starts at a low price point, then it can take much longer to build a brand that connotes value to customers. Today Samsung and Hyundai are valuable brands; but when each entered the United States, they exploited low prices. It took many years of brand-building for Samsung to raise their customer perceived values to their deserved position and Hyundai, one of the top three on J.D. Powers and Associates' automobile overall product quality list, continues their efforts to raise their perceived value to their actual value.[41]

Akio Morita, the founder of Sony, used to tell this story: One of the first very successful products of Sony was the transistor radio. Supposedly a department store in New York City told Mr. Morita that they wanted to order thousands for the holiday sales season. His reply was, "No."

Akio Morita knew that at that point in time the reputation of the "Japan Brand" was low. If something broke, at that time people in the United States often said that, "It must have been made in Japan." Morita knew that if he tried to produce the thousands of units the store wanted, the Sony quality control would falter—and the products would not represent the brand he was trying to build. So he said no to the large order the department store wanted, but agreed to furnish them the number of transistor radios he felt he could produce at a quality level of which he could be proud. How important was his decision? It was the foundation for the Sony brand in the US. Actions today determine the brand tomorrow.

If Chinese and Indian companies succeed with their marketing efforts to increase their perceived value, then the GDPs of both China and India will increase substantially—perhaps by 30 percent—even without increases in production capacity! The same observation can be made of most fast-developing economies.

Conclusions

Marketing is managing customer perceived value. In turn, customer perceived value is a key component of CVA®. Perceived value per unit and cost per unit—CVA®—determine the net value an organization provides society according to the perceptions of customers. CVA® has a direct relationship to the contribution earned by an organization, which in turn affects profit, cash flow, shareholder value, and share price.

Managing CVA® provides forward control over the financial performance of an organization as well as the financial performance of an economy.

The next chapter explains exactly how CVA® determines financial performance.

2

How CVA® Affects Financial Performance

CVA®, or Customer Value Added, has a direct and clear relationship to the financial performance of any business. This relationship is based on marketing concepts and economic ideas coupled with accounting and financial methodologies. In this chapter, the relationship between CVA® and financial performance is explored and explained.

CVA® and Financial Performance: Executive Summary

The linkage between CVA® and financial performance is straightforward and involves several steps (Exhibit 2.1).

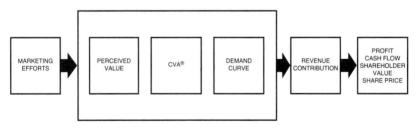

Reprinted with permission from "How Marketing Affects Shareholder Value," The Arrow Group, Ltd.®, New York, NY, 2008.

Exhibit 2.1   The relationship of marketing efforts to contribution

1. Marketing affects perceived value.
2. Perceived value affects CVA®.
3. Perceived value affects demand curve.
4. Demand curve affects revenue.
5. CVA® affects contribution.

1. Marketing efforts manage perceived value, one of the two components of CVA®. For example, how well products and services are designed to meet the needs of the target customers determines the actual value the target customers receive. Advertising and personal selling communicate the actual value and determine the value customers perceive they receive from the product or service.

2. If the increase in perceived value per unit is greater than any associated increase in cost per unit, then CVA® increases. Alternatively, if a decrease in cost per unit is greater than any associated decrease in perceived value per unit, CVA® increases.

3. Any increase in perceived value leads to a shift to the right in the demand curve for the product or service. A shift in demand is accompanied by an increase in price or in units sold—or more likely in both. Price and unit demand increases produce an increase in revenue.[1]

4. Changes in demand are related to changes in revenue.

5. Changes in CVA® are related to changes in contribution since CVA® involves both perceived value and cost.

If any *fixed costs* associated with the increase in CVA® do not exceed the increase in contribution, then profits increase. The profit increase, in turn, can usually be expected to increase cash flow. An increase in cash flow also increases shareholder value and share price.

The rest of the chapter explains these steps in detail.

Verizon: Rebranding Omnitel: A Carefully Planned Transition Pays Off

The more competitive an industry is, the more important company brands and images are—and the more risks a company takes on when it decides it needs to change or modify its brand. This is particularly true in the mobile phone industry in Europe, where the number of mobile telephones outnumbers the population by about 50%.

Vodafone, the world's largest mobile phone carrier, faced a critical branding-transition challenge in 2000 when it acquired a smaller

European carrier and its assets, including Omnitel, the second-largest mobile phone company in Italy. Through this acquisition, Vodafone owned 77% of Omnitel; Verizon Communications, then the largest telephone company in the U.S., owned the remaining 23%.

The Omnitel brand was strong in Italy, where the company had a reputation for innovation and high quality of service. However, Vodafone, based in the United Kingdom, was not well-known in Italy, even though the company has a global brand. Vodafone needed to devise a way of putting Omnitel under the Vodafone umbrella by transferring Omnitel's brand equity to Vodafone in Italy.

Vodafone did its homework: It conducted market surveys to determine the strengths of the Omnitel and Vodafone brands in Italy and to establish a baseline from which to measure progress toward the Vodafone brand. For two years, Vodafone took steps to create in customers' minds an association between the Omnitel and the Vodafone brands. These steps included brand advertising and sponsorships that introduced the new brand alongside the existing brand.

This enabled Vodafone to transition the Omnitel brand to Omnitel-Vodafone, then to Vodafone-Omnitel, and finally to Vodafone—all without any deterioration of the market survey results. At the end of the two-year period, surveys showed that the positive image of the Omnitel brand had been maintained and successfully grafted on to the Vodafone brand in Italy.

—Daniel Petri, Group President—International,
Verizon Communications

Reprinted with permission

Perceived Value and Price

CVA® determines financial performance primarily through its effect on price and demand for a product or service.

The range between perceived value per unit and variable cost per unit, CVA®, is the *range of possible prices* that might be charged for a unit of the product or service (Exhibit 2.2). By definition, a customer would not pay more for a unit of the product or service than whatever they consider to be the perceived value per unit. An organization will not usually price their products below variable cost per unit—at least not for any appreciable volume or time—because then they would be losing money on every unit sold.

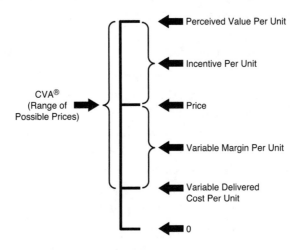

Reprinted with permission from "Pricing, Perceived Value, and Communications," Donald E. Sexton, New York, NY, 2008.

Exhibit 2.2   Customer Value Added and Price

Any price divides the CVA® range into two parts. The distance from the price to the variable delivered cost per unit is the *variable margin per unit* or *incremental profit per unit*. The distance from the perceived value per unit to the price is the *incentive per unit* for the customer to purchase. The higher that incentive, the more the *unit demand*.

The higher the CVA®, the higher an organization's per unit margin and unit demand—the two components of contribution (Exhibit 2.3). A higher CVA® leads to higher contribution—either due to higher margin per unit or more units sold, or more likely both. A higher CVA® usually means *both* a price premium and a volume premium.

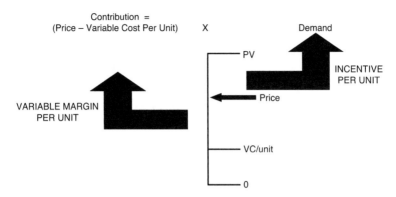

Reprinted with permission from "Pricing, Perceived Value, and Communications," Donald E. Sexton, New York, NY, 2008.

Exhibit 2.3   How CVA® affects contribution

A low price strategy yields high volume with a low margin—what is known as a *penetration pricing strategy*. A high price strategy yields low volume with a high margin—what is known as a *skimming pricing strategy*.

CVA® represents the *total net value per unit* for the product or service, as perceived by customers. The pricing question is how much of this value the organization will capture (variable margin per unit) and how much will the organization give to the customer (incentive per unit)?

Hindustan Lever Ltd.: Pricing and Brand Equity

The source of long term profitability for a consumer goods business has to be linked with brand equity through the lever of strategic long-term pricing. Even though this is intuitively well known in business, operationally, day to day pricing decisions are not based on this knowledge. If pricing power could be measured and placed within a competitive framework that made sense to both marketing and finance, a dialogue can emerge to make better business decisions.

Studying brands and their key competitors across markets within
the "perceived value" framework provides a comprehensive man-
ner in which to assess likely competitive pricing responses and
their outcomes.

In 2007 the senior management of Unilever's Asian and African
businesses was evaluating unprecedented price increases in the
wake of severe cost inflation. Crude oil prices were spiraling
beyond what had been anticipated and this was having a knock-on
effect on vegetable oil prices, a key ingredient required to manufacturing soaps. Management believed competitors would also
raise prices to manage this cost pressure. No one could predict
how these price changes would influence market dynamics and
relative market shares. Based on this uncertainty the business
decided that pricing based on "perceived value" or a long term
consumer based evaluation of pricing power was a superior
approach compared to being driven by internal metrics of cost
neutralization.

Kamal Sen the head of Business Research and Corporate Planning
led a "perceived value" measurement exercise which revealed that
Unilever's brands enjoyed high perceived value compared to competition although with different degrees of pricing power. The
exercise illustrated that consumers were willing to pay higher
prices for our brands if we could improve the delivery of specific
benefits they were seeking. The business accordingly took strategic
price increases coupled with improvements in product mixes and
communication of the benefits that consumers were seeking.

Another valuable learning emerged from this exercise by estimating
the pricing power of key competitors. Unilever faced competition
from a local discount manufacturer who had grown market shares.
The perceived value analysis revealed that this competitor had poor
perceived value and poor incremental pricing power. Consumers
were buying the brand more because of rising awareness rather
than for a strong benefit led reasons. If this manufacturer were to
follow the price increases planned by other major brands then the
study predicted it stood to lose significant market share. The study's
prediction of the likelihood of this event ensured that Unilever had
the right plans in place.

> As the competitor brand started raising prices and losing some market share, Unilever raised prices in a planned manner keeping cost increases and perceived value in perspective.
>
> —Dr. Kamal Sen, Regional Director, Business Research and Corporate Planning, Hindustan Lever Ltd.
>
> Reprinted with permission of Business Analytics and Strategic Planning, Unilever

Demand Curves

A demand curve shows the relationship between price and units sold (Exhibit 2.4). Typically, at high prices few units are sold and at low prices many units are sold. For most situations, demand curves may be expected to have negative slopes.[2]

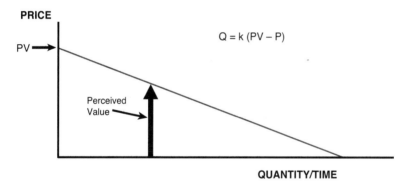

Reprinted with permission from "Managing Pricing ROI," The Arrow Group, Ltd.®, New York, NY, 2008.

Exhibit 2.4   The demand curve

Perceived value is the height of the demand curve for a specific group of customers, a market segment. A *market segment* can be defined as a group of customers who share the same perceived value for a specific product or a service. As price for a unit of that product or service is decreased, it falls below the value perceived for the product or service, leading customers in that segment to make a purchase.

> *A market segment is a group of customers who share the same perceived value for a specific product or a service.*

How a demand curve works can be understood with what is known as a *Dutch Auction*. Suppose a can of beer is auctioned to an audience. Initially, the price is set high, say $50, and the audience asked, "Who will buy?" Then the price is lowered systematically. Usually no one will buy the can until the price falls below a reasonable level, such as $5. Why? Because the person's perceived value for the can of beer is around $5; and, only when the price is at or below $5, he or she will purchase it. As one continues to lower the price, more and more people will agree to purchase the can of beer as the price reaches their perceived value. For those who do not like beer, one can provide a negative price—a gift or coupon, known as a *promotion*—to provide them with an incentive to purchase. If one cumulates the purchases for each price (someone willing to buy at $4 should also buy at $3), then one can trace out a demand curve.

© Ashleigh Brilliant, 2008. Used with permission.

There are many ways to estimate demand curves ranging from utilizing subjective estimates to employing econometric methods. These approaches are surveyed in Chapter 4, "Perceived Value."

The demand curve's y-intercept—where the demand curve intersects the vertical axis (PV in Exhibit 2.4)—is the maximum level of perceived value per unit for the customers in the market represented by the given demand curve. The y-intercept can be used as a proxy measure for the perceived value corresponding to the product or service for that market and provides the linkage between perceived value and revenue.

Perceived Value and Revenue

Revenue is the product of demand in units and price:

$$Revenue = Demand\ in\ Units\ x\ Price$$

With a demand curve, revenue is the area in the rectangle determined by a given price and the corresponding quantity in units sold (Exhibit 2.5).

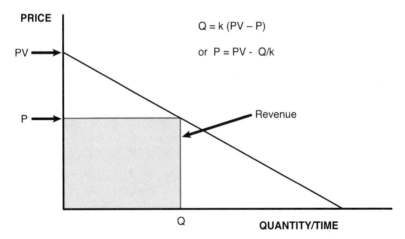

Reprinted with permission from "Managing Pricing ROI," The Arrow Group, Ltd.®, New York, NY, 2008.

Exhibit 2.5   Revenue

The higher the perceived value associated with a product or service, the higher the revenue, other things equal.

Given a demand curve, a manager can select the price that maximizes revenue for those conditions. When the demand curve is assumed to be linear, then the profit-maximizing price depends only on the y-intercept—the perceived value measure given by the formula:

Revenue-Maximizing Price = a/2

Where: a = Max Perceived Value per Unit (y-intercept or PV in Exhibit 2.5)

(See the chapter appendix for the derivation.)

Even if a demand curve is not linear, usually it can be estimated with a piece-wise linear function—several linear functions (lines) that approximate the demand curve (see Exhibit 2.6). The profit-maximizing price formula still can be used—although now it will give an approximate revenue-maximizing price. The approximate revenue-maximizing price will depend on the y-intercept for the appropriate line segment.

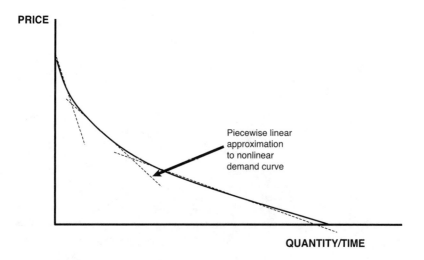

Exhibit 2.6   Approximating a nonlinear demand curve

Contribution

Contribution or *variable margin* is the product of demand in units and price minus the variable cost per unit (equal to the variable margin per unit):

Contribution = Demand in Units x (Price - Variable Cost per Unit)
= Demand in Units x Variable Margin per Unit

In the demand curve diagram, contribution is the area in the rectangle bounded by the price and variable cost per unit and by the corresponding quantity in units sold (Exhibit 2.7).

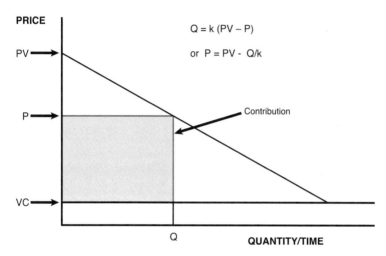

Reprinted with permission from "Managing Pricing ROI," The Arrow Group, Ltd.®, New York, NY, 2008.

Exhibit 2.7   Contribution

Contribution represents the incremental profit from the product or service. The higher the level of CVA®, the higher the contribution a manager can expect to achieve.

A manager can select that price that maximizes contribution or variable margin. For a linear demand curve, the formula is:

Contribution-Maximizing Price = (a + c)/2
    Where: a = Max Perceived Value per Unit (y-intercept or PV in Exhibit 2.4)
        c = Variable Cost per Unit

(See the chapter appendix for derivation.)

Note for linear demand curves that the contribution-maximizing price depends only on the perceived value measure (the y-intercept) and the variable cost per unit. It will also always be higher than the revenue-maximizing price (unless the variable cost per unit is negative, representing a subsidy.)

Fixed costs do *not* play a role in determining the price that optimizes contribution. Regardless of the amount of fixed costs, the price that maximizes contribution would be the same.

Fixed costs *do* determine profit and whether an organization remains in business. If contribution is not sufficient to cover fixed costs over time, then, if not subsidized, the product or service would no longer be produced.

Revenue and Contribution: An Example

Suppose that unit demand for a product is given by:

$$Q = 100 - 4P$$
$$\text{or}$$
$$P = 25 - Q/4$$

And that variable cost per unit is $3.

The demand curve is shown in Exhibit 2.8 and the units sold, revenue, and contribution for different prices are shown in Exhibit 2.9.

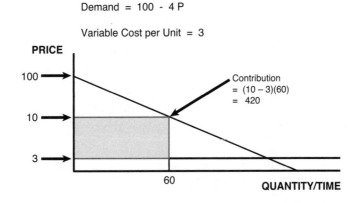

Exhibit 2.8   The demand curve in the revenue and contribution example

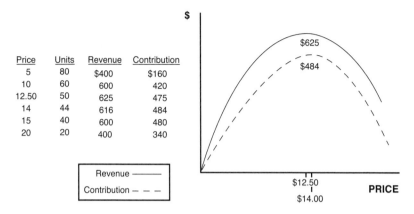

Price	Units	Revenue	Contribution
5	80	$400	$160
10	60	600	420
12.50	50	625	475
14	44	616	484
15	40	600	480
20	20	400	340

Revenue ———
Contribution – – –

Exhibit 2.9   Alternative prices for the revenue and contribution example

The revenue-maximizing price is given by:

Revenue-Maximizing Price = $25/2 = $12.50

The contribution-maximizing price is given by:

Contribution-Maximizing Price = ($25 + $3) / 2 = $14

Notice how sensitive contribution is to price. If the price is too low, then per unit margin is too low—so contribution falls off quickly. If the price is too high, then the incentive to the customer is too low—and again contribution falls off quickly. There is a *sweet spot* for pricing. Managers are punished with low financial performance if they do not price within that sweet spot.

Shifting the Demand Curve

By increasing perceived value, marketing activities such as advertising, promotion, and personal selling can shift the demand curve to the right (Exhibit 2.10).[3] Both the y-intercept and the slope of the demand curve may be changed by marketing activities. The author's research has suggested that the demand curve shifting effect of marketing activities likely has diminishing returns.[4] But, for simplicity, assume that the curve is shifted equally along its length and that only the y-intercept changes.

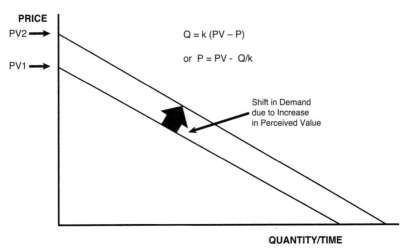

Exhibit 2.10   Shift in demand curve

Marketing efforts change perceived value
and shift the demand curve.

When the demand curve shifts, the maximum revenue increases
(Exhibit 2.11). The price that now maximizes *revenue* differs from
the price prior to the demand shift.

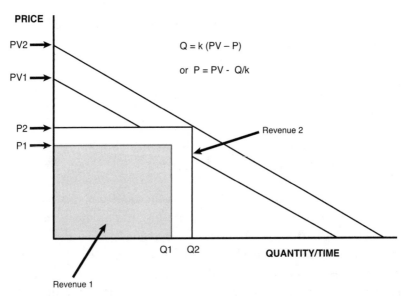

Reprinted with permission from "How Marketing Affects Shareholder Value," The Arrow
Group, Ltd.®, New York, NY, 2008.

Exhibit 2.11   Increase in revenue as the demand curve shifts

When the demand curve shifts, the maximum contribution increases as well (Exhibit 2.12). The price that now maximizes *contribution* differs from the price prior to the demand shift. If the organization is attempting to maximize contribution, generally, the shift in demand curve will lead to both a price premium and a unit volume premium.

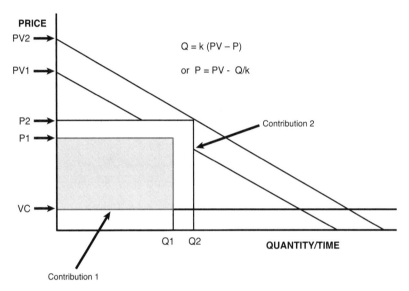

Reprinted with permission from "How Marketing Affects Shareholder Value," The Arrow Group, Ltd.®, New York, NY, 2008.

Exhibit 2.12   Increase in contribution as the demand curve shifts

Table 2.1 shows price and unit sales exhibits for several products, both branded and private label. (Many thanks to the author's colleague, Professor Don Lehmann, for suggesting these examples.) For these brands, the impact of a well-developed brand name resulted in both a price premium and a unit volume premium. These illustrations are meant to be suggestive rather than conclusive. To compare sales of these products, one must also account for likely differences in distribution coverage as well as product and cost differences.

Table 2.1   Examples of Price and Unit Quantity Premiums

CATEGORY	BRAND	PRICE	UNITS°	REVENUE°
GELATIN	JELLO	$3.72	47,393	$176,302
	PRIVATE	2.60	7,572	19,687
BLEACH	CLOROX	$1.20	42,698	$51,238
	PRIVATE	.67	19.090	12,790
CIGARETTES	MARLBORO	$20.37	3,739	$76,163
	PRIVATE	12.54	1,249	15,587
LENS CARE	BAUSCH & LOMB	$5.69	2,635	$14,993
	PRIVATE	2.55	6,833	17,424
MOTOR OIL	PENNZOIL	$1.61	3.379	$5,440
	PRIVATE	1.11	2,764	3,068
PANTY HOSE	NO NONSENSE	$1.54	22,448	$34,570
	PRIVATE	1.28	23,215	29,715
RAZORS	GILLETTE	$1.02	27,885	$28,443
	SENSOR EXCEL	.88	34,197	30,093
	SENSOR PRIVATE	.35	22,980	8.043

° in thousands
Source: *Marketing Fact Book*, IRI, 1997.

Sexton's Laws

If the demand curve for a product or service is assumed to be linear, then some simple but powerful results emerge. (See the chapter appendix for derivations of these laws.)

Sexton's Revenue Law

> *The change in revenue is in proportion
> to the square of the relative change in perceived value.*

While this law (Exhibit 2.13) can be shown with mathematics, it should also be consistent with common sense. An increase in perceived value leads to both an increase in price and an increase in unit demand. Because revenue is the product of price and unit demand, revenue increases with the *square* of the relative change in perceived value.

Perceived Value and Revenue

$$\frac{\text{Revenue 2}}{\text{Revenue 1}} = \frac{(PV_2)^2}{(PV_1)^2}$$

$$= \left\{ \frac{(PV_2)}{(PV_1)} \right\}^2$$

$$= \left\{ \text{ Relative Change in PV} \right\}^2$$

Where: PV is Perceived Value Per Unit

"How Marketing Affects Shareholder Value," The Arrow Group, Ltd.®, New York, NY, 2008. Used with permission.

Exhibit 2.13   Sexton's revenue law

Exhibits 2.14 and 2.15 show how the impact on revenue due to increases or decreases in perceived value can be calculated.

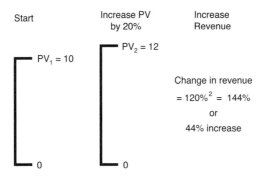

"How Marketing Affects Shareholder Value," The Arrow Group, Ltd.®, New York, NY, 2008. Used with permission.

Exhibit 2.14   How increases in perceived value increase revenue

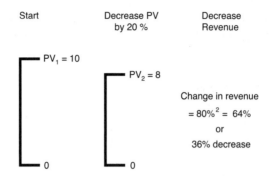

Exhibit 2.15   How decreases in perceived value decrease revenue

Sexton's Contribution Law

The change in contribution is in proportion to the square of the relative change in CVA®.

Sexton's Contribution Law (Exhibit 2.16) is also consistent with common sense. An increase in CVA® leads to an increase in both variable margin per unit and unit demand. Because contribution is the product of variable margin per unit and unit demand, contribution increases with the *square* of the relative change in CVA®.

Exhibits 2.17 and 2.18 show how the impact on contribution due to increases or decreases in CVA® can be calculated.

The derivation of these laws assumes that the demand curve is linear and that marketing activities shift the demand curve to a new curve parallel to the first. These assumptions are perhaps the simplest, but no less powerful for that. Many or most demand curves, if not linear, can be handled with a piece-wise linear approximation as discussed earlier.

CVA® and Contribution

$$\frac{\text{Contribution 2}}{\text{Contribution 1}} = \frac{(PV_2 - VC_2)^2}{(PV_1 - VC_1)^2}$$

$$= \left\{ \frac{(PV_2 - VC_2)}{(PV_1 - VC_1)} \right\}^2$$

$$= \left\{ \frac{CVA^®_2}{CVA^®_1} \right\}^2$$

$$= \{ \text{ Relative Change in CVA}^® \}^2$$

Where: CVA® is Perceived Value Per Unit – Variable Cost Per Unit

"How Marketing Affects Shareholder Value," The Arrow Group, Ltd.®, New York, NY, 2008. Used here with permission.

"How Marketing Affects Shareholder Value," The Arrow Group, Ltd.®, New York, NY, 2008. Used with permission.

Exhibit 2.16   Sexton's contribution law

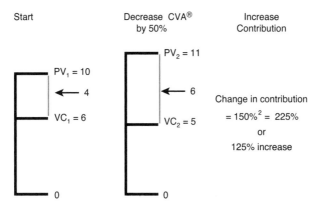

Start   Decrease CVA®   Increase
                 by 50%   Contribution

$PV_2 = 11$

$PV_1 = 10$

← 4

← 6

$VC_1 = 6$

$VC_2 = 5$

Change in contribution
$= 150\%^2 = 225\%$
or
125% increase

0   0

"How Marketing Affects Shareholder Value," The Arrow Group, Ltd.®, New York, NY, 2008. Used with permission.

Exhibit 2.17   How increases in CVA® increase contribution

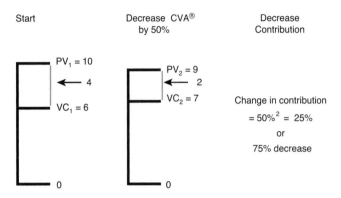

"How Marketing Affects Shareholder Value," The Arrow Group, Ltd.®, New York, NY, 2008.
Used with permission.

Exhibit 2.18   How decreases in CVA® decrease contribution

As long as the price that maximizes revenue and the new price
that maximizes revenue are associated with the linear function and
with the same slope, then the Sexton's Law results still apply (Exhibit
2.19). Only when the two prices are associated with parts of the
demand curve with different slopes do the implications become more
complicated and involve changes in both slopes and intercepts of the
demand curve.

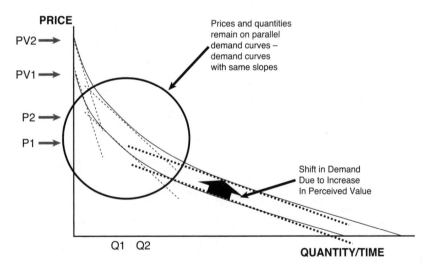

Exhibit 2.19   Shift in nonlinear demand curves

Employing Sexton's Contribution Law

While the relative change in CVA® and its impact on contribution can be computed for any specific case, Exhibit 2.20 provides an overview of the relationship between changes in CVA® and changes in contribution. The columns correspond to CVA® expressed as a percentage of the current perceived value per unit for a product or service. The rows correspond to a proposed change in CVA® expressed as a percentage of the current perceived value per unit for the product or service. Where a column and row intersect is the percentage change in contribution to be expected expressed as a percentage of the contribution currently obtained.

For example, suppose CVA® is currently 40 percent of perceived value (as it is in the examples in Exhibits 2.17 and 2.18). If CVA® as a percentage of perceived value is increased by 20 percent (as in the Exhibit 2.17 example), then contribution will be 225 percent of the current contribution level. If CVA® as a percentage of perceived value is decreased by 20 percent (as in the Exhibit 2.18 example), then contribution will be 25 percent of the current contribution level.

CHANGE IN CVA® AS % OF PERCEIVED VALUE	CVA® AS % OF PERCEIVED VALUE										
	1	10	20	30	40	50	60	70	80	90	100
- 50						0	3	8	14	20	25
- 40					0	4	11	18	25	31	36
- 30				0	6	16	25	33	39	45	49
- 20			0	11	25	36	45	51	56	60	64
- 10		0	25	45	56	64	69	73	76	79	81
0	100	100	100	100	100	100	100	100	100	100	100
+ 10	12100	400	225	177	156	144	136	130	127	123	121
+ 20	44100	900	400	280	225	196	177	165	156	149	144
+ 30	96100	1600	625	400	306	256	225	204	189	177	169
+ 40	168100	2500	900	543	400	324	279	245	225	209	196
+ 50	260100	3600	1225	713	506	400	335	293	264	242	225

Exhibit 2.20   The change in contribution due to change in CVA®

Changes in CVA® have a significant nonlinear impact on contribution because it is the *square* of the relative change in CVA® that determines the change in contribution. When CVA® is increased, that leads to strong financial performance; but when CVA® is decreased—for whatever reason—there is a substantial negative affect on financial performance. Exhibit 2.20 clearly demonstrates the asymmetry of those impacts.

Applying Sexton's Laws: Groupe Le Soleil Case

Groupe Le Soleil* (GLS) is a small Belgian company that processes and packages vegetables and fruit. Their product line includes brussel sprouts, beans, cauliflower, carrots, peas, artichokes, mushrooms, cherries, and pears.

At present, GLS has established itself as a premium producer in Belgium, where its products are known for fresh taste and attractive appearance.

They are considering introducing their mushroom product into France. Based on market surveys and experience, the brand manager estimates demand for their mushrooms in France for various alternative prices to be as follows:

Price (Euros)	Quantity (000)
4.0	10,000
3.0	20,000
1.5	35,000

Per unit variable costs (Euros) are:

Manufacturing	0.8
Transportation	0.1
Distribution	0.5

Given these estimates, the demand curve for mushrooms in France is shown here.

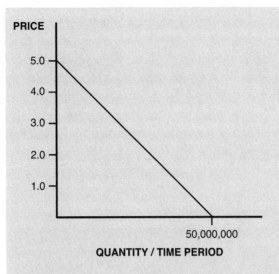

The demand curve (Q in thousands of units) can be estimated to be:

$P = 5 - (1/10,000)Q$

or

$Q = 50,000 - 10,000P$

Revenue and contribution at different prices are:

Price	Quantity (000)	Revenue (000)	Contribution (000)
4.0	10,000	40,000	26,000
3.5	15,000	52,500	31,500
3.0	20,000	60,000	32,000
2.5	25,000	62,500	27,500
2.0	30,000	60,000	18,000
1.5	35,000	52,500	14,000
1.0	40,000	40,000	– 4,000

Given the current situation, the optimal prices are:

Revenue-Maximizing Price = 2.5 euros

Maximum Revenue = 62,500,000 euros

Contribution-Maximizing Price = 3.2 euros

Maximum Contribution = 32,400,000 euros

Suppose that GLS conducts an advertising campaign in France to build their brand position in the minds of French consumers. As a result the maximum perceived value increases 20 percent, from 5 to 6, and the demand curve for GLS mushrooms in France shifts to the right:

$P = 6 - (1/10,000)Q$
    or
$Q = 60,000 - 10,000P$

Now the optimal prices are:

Revenue-Maximizing Price = 3 euros
Maximum revenue = 90,000,000 euros

Contribution-Maximizing Price = 3.7 euros
Maximum Contribution = 52,900,000 euros

The change in maximum revenue is:

$90,000,000 / 62,500,000 = 144\%$

The relative change in perceived value is:

$6 / 5 = 120\%$

According to Sexton's Revenue Law, the change in maximum revenue should be:

$120\%^2 = 144\%$

Similarly, the change in maximum contribution is:

$52,900,000 / 32,400,000 = 163\%$

The relative change in CVA® is:

$(6 - 1.4) / (5 - 1.4) = 4.6 / 3.6 = 128\%$

According to Sexton's Contribution Law, the change in maximum contribution should be:

$128\%^2 = 163\%$

° All names are fictitious and any similarities to real organizations or people are coincidental.

Used with permission from "Groupe LeSoleil," The Arrow Group, Ltd.®, New York, NY, 2008.

Contribution and Profit, Cash Flow, Shareholder Value, and Share Price

CVA® is directly related to contribution. In turn, contribution affects other financial outcomes such as profit, cash flow, and shareholder value (Exhibit 2.21).

Profit is equal to contribution minus relevant fixed costs. There may be changes in fixed costs due to changes in CVA®, and those fixed cost changes need to be included when examining the changes in profit associated with changes in CVA®. It is possible that those corresponding changes in fixed costs can offset any increases in contribution due to increases in CVA®. Contribution can increase, while profit may decrease. However, as discussed in Chapter 5, "Costs," the fixed costs that should be considered in any profit calculations are direct fixed costs—those directly associated with the changes in CVA®.

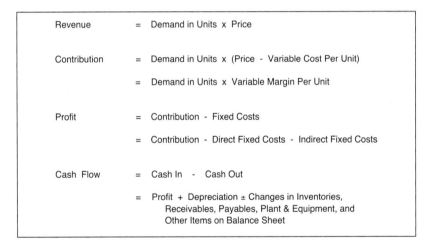

Revenue	=	Demand in Units x Price
Contribution	=	Demand in Units x (Price - Variable Cost Per Unit)
	=	Demand in Units x Variable Margin Per Unit
Profit	=	Contribution - Fixed Costs
	=	Contribution - Direct Fixed Costs - Indirect Fixed Costs
Cash Flow	=	Cash In - Cash Out
	=	Profit + Depreciation ± Changes in Inventories, Receivables, Payables, Plant & Equipment, and Other Items on Balance Sheet

Exhibit 2.21   Finance concepts

Profit is equal to contribution minus relevant fixed costs.

Cash flow is profit adjusted by depreciation and by changes in various items in the balance sheet such as inventories, receivables, payables, and plant and equipment purchases.

The cash in cash flow does not refer to cash as bills or coins. The *cash* in cash flow refers to the relatively liquid assets available to the organization after the end of a day, week, month, quarter, or year.

"Profit is opinion, cash is a fact." Underlying profit figures are opinions regarding many items. For example, *depreciation* is determined by opinion and is a noncash cost that needs to be added to profit to get to cash flow. *Costs* in the income statement are usually costs of goods *sold* or of services *provided*, therefore profit must be adjusted by costs associated with goods-not-sold or services-not-provided to determine a company's cash position. Another major adjustment to profit concerns accounts receivables and accounts payables. Accounts receivable are basically loans—sometimes involuntary—to customers while accounts payable may represent loans—sometimes involuntary—to the company from its suppliers. Both affect a company's cash position.

There is insufficient space in this book to provide a full discussion of cash flow.[5] The main point is that contribution is a major factor in profits and cash flow—and CVA® is a significant determinant of contribution. For most organizations, contribution is the largest component of cash flow. That is the main focus of the following chapters.

Shareholder value is widely regarded as the sum of a company's future cash flows, properly discounted. However, keep in mind that any changes in fixed costs and in balance sheet items such as inventories, receivables, and payables affect cash flow. As a result, improvements in contribution due to CVA® are not the only factors determining shareholder value.

Finally, shareholder value affects share price. Share price reflects the shareholder value per share held in the company.

CVA® and Life Time Customer Value

Life time customer value focuses on the financial impact of marketing efforts on a customer-by-customer basis.[6]

The concept of CVA® can be applied at the customer level as well. As shown in Exhibit 2.22, life time customer value consists of the net contribution per customer—the product of price minus variable cost per unit minus fixed costs specific to each customer, weighted by the cumulative retention rate and the discount factor, and summed over all time periods.[7]

Life Time Customer Value =

$$\sum_{\substack{\text{All time} \\ \text{periods}}} [\ (\text{Price - Variable Cost Per Unit}) (\text{Purchases}) - \text{Fixed Costs}\ ] \\ \times\ (\text{Cumulative Retention Rate}) \times (\text{Discount Rate})$$

Exhibit 2.22   Life time customer value

The *cumulative retention rate* is the probability that an initial customer will continue to purchase the organization's product or service and is the product of the time period retention rate for all time periods (Exhibit 2.23). The retention rate is the probability that a customer will continue to purchase the product or service from one time period to the next.

The discount factor depends on the interest rate assumed and compensates for the time value of money—changing future sums of money into present value.

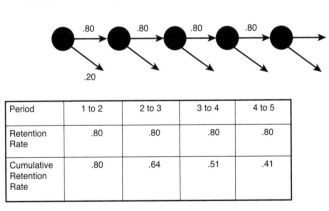

Period	1 to 2	2 to 3	3 to 4	4 to 5
Retention Rate	.80	.80	.80	.80
Cumulative Retention Rate	.80	.64	.51	.41

Reprinted with permission from "Managing Communications ROI," The Arrow Group, Ltd.®, New York, NY, 2008.

Exhibit 2.23   Retention rate and cumulative retention rate

Each customer can be regarded as having an individual demand curve. A marketing activity that increases perceived value per unit shifts the demand curve for each customer to the right—and may also increase variable cost per unit. A contribution-maximizing price can be determined for any customer, given their demand curve.

CVA® predicts the contribution earned
from each individual customer.

The impact of any marketing effort on the life time value of a customer can be seen by summing the changes in contribution per period over all time periods for that customer. The impact of any marketing effort on the contribution to an organization can be seen by summing the changes in contribution over all customers in a target market segment.

There is one major reservation that prevents the sum of the contributions from the individual demand curves from being identical to the contribution predicted by the aggregate analysis examined earlier in the chapter. Increased perceived value increases the retention rate and decreased perceived value decreases the retention rate. In the aggregate model, those adjustments are made through changes in perceived value over time as shown in the perceived value life cycle (see Chapter 4). In the individual model used for life time customer value, the effect of perceived value on retention rate would need to be estimated as well.

If one assumes that the retention rate is constant and that the interest rate is constant over all time periods considered—restrictive assumptions occasionally made in practice—then the aggregate and the individual approaches based on CVA® can be reconciled (Exhibit 2.24).

$$\text{Life Time Customer Value} = \frac{C}{1 - r + i}$$

Where: C = Contribution per time period.

r = Retention rate from time period to time period (assumed constant over time).

i = Interest rate (assumed constant over time).

Exhibit 2.24   Life time customer value—a short cut

CVA® and Life Time Value of Customer: Mobile Telephone*

Suppose that a user of a mobile telephone in a specific small business segment has an individual demand curve for minutes used per month given by:

$$Q = 1120 - 4000P$$
or
$$P = 0.28 - .00025Q$$

Where: P = Price in US $
Q = Minutes Used per Month

Monthly contribution for that customer is, then:

$$C = (P - VC) \times Q$$

Where: C = Contribution per Month
VC = Variable Cost per Minute

If variable cost per minute is assumed to be $.02 (high just for illustration), then the contribution-maximizing price for that customer is:

$$P = \frac{\$.28 + \$.02}{2} = \$.15$$

And the maximum monthly contribution from that customer is:

$$C = (\$.15 - \$.02) \times (520) = \$67.60$$

Suppose there are 100 customers with the identical demand curve. Then the total maximum monthly contribution from that segment is:

$$\text{Total C} = (100) \times (\$67.60) = \$6760$$

Assume that the retention rate is constant and equals .70 and that the interest rate is constant and equals .15. The short-cut formula for life time customer value gives the maximum contribution for this group of customers over time:

$$\text{Total C Over Time} = \frac{\$6760}{(1 - .70 + .15)} = \frac{\$6760}{.45} = \$15,022.22$$

Assume that price maximizes the contribution of a customer in that target segment. Note that in reality, for mobile telecommunications, monthly contribution would depend mainly on the price, since both variable cost per unit and fixed cost per customer are relatively small. The fixed cost for the customer would be the fixed cost of connecting the customer to the system—*not* the average fixed cost calculated by dividing all the telecommunication company's fixed costs by the number of customers.

Suppose that the telecommunication company launches a promotion—for example, a free mobile telephone carrying case—that increases perceived value and shifts the demand curve to the right. In addition, the fixed cost per customer increases due to the cost of providing the customer with the carrying case.

The new demand curve can be represented in this way:

$Q = 1200 - 4000P$

or

$P = .30 - .00025Q$

Given the new perceived value per unit and the assumed variable cost per unit ($.02), the contribution-maximizing price for a customer in this particular segment is now $.16 with sales of 560 minutes. Maximum contribution for the customer is given by:

$C = (\$.16 - \$.02) \times (560) = \$78.40$

The overall impact of the promotion on the telecommunication company's contribution is obtained by summing the new maximum contribution for each customer across all 100 customers:

$\text{Total C} = (100) \times (\$78.40) = \$7840$

If one is willing to make some restrictive assumptions—namely that retention rates and interest rates remain constant over time—the impact of the change in CVA® on life time value of customer is given by the short-cut formula from Exhibit 2.24:

$$\text{Total C Over Time} = \frac{\$7840}{(1 - .70 + .15)} = \frac{\$7840}{.45} = \$17,422.22$$

The change in contribution per customer, total contribution, and total contribution over time due to the promotion represents an increase of nearly 16 percent:

$$\text{Change in Contribution} = \frac{\$78.40}{\$67.60} = \frac{\$7840}{\$6760} = \frac{\$17,422.22}{\$15,022.22} = 1.1598$$

The changes in these various contribution measures are those that are predicted by Sexton's Contribution Law:

$$\left[\frac{CVA_2}{CVA_1}\right]^2 = \left[\frac{(.16 - .02)}{(.15 - .02)}\right]^2 = 1.1598$$

*All names are fictitious and any similarities to real organizations or people are coincidental. Source: "Cellmonterey," The Arrow Group, Ltd.®, New York, NY, 2008. Used with permission.

Conclusions

Perceived value is directly associated with revenue and CVA® is directly associated with contribution. Increases in perceived value and CVA® produce increases in revenue and contribution related to the squares of the changes in perceived value and CVA®.

Managing CVA® provides managers with a forward-looking way to manage the financial performance of their businesses. The next chapter discusses how the concept of CVA® can be applied to develop strategy over time.

Appendix: Derivations

Suppose that:

Price = a - b Quantity

and therefore:

Quantity = $(a/b) - (1/b)$ Price

Sexton's Revenue Law can be derived:

Revenue = Price x Quantity
$$= \text{Price} \times ((a/b) - (1/b)\ \text{Price})$$
$$= (a/b)\ \text{Price} - (1/b)\ \text{Price}^2$$
dRevenue/dPrice = $(a/b) - (2/b)$ Price = 0 when Price = a/2
Maximum Revenue = $a^2/4b$
So $\text{Revenue}_2 / \text{Revenue}_1 = (a_2 / a_1)^2$

Sexton's Contribution Law can be derived:

Contribution = (Price - Variable Cost Per Unit) x (Quantity)
$$= (\text{Price} - c)\ ((a/b) - (1/b)\ \text{Price})$$
$$= ((a + c)/b)\ \text{Price} - (1/b)\ \text{Price}^2 - (a/b)c$$
dContribution/dPrice = $(a + c)/b - (2/b)$ Price = 0 when Price
= $(a + c)/2$
Maximum Contribution = $(a - c)^2 / 4b$
So $\text{Contribution}_2 / \text{Contribution}_1 = [(a_2 - c_2) / (a_1 - c_1)]^2$
$$= [\text{CVA}^{\circledR}_2 / \text{CVA}^{\circledR}_1]^2$$

3

CVA® over Time

The value of an organization depends on how well an organization meets customer needs at levels superior to those of their competitors over time, while controlling costs. For example, Polaroid went bankrupt because a new technology—digital imaging—was superior to instant film (Exhibit 3.1). Even though Polaroid produced digital cameras, their brand was inextricably associated with what was eventually perceived by many customers to be an inferior technology.[1]

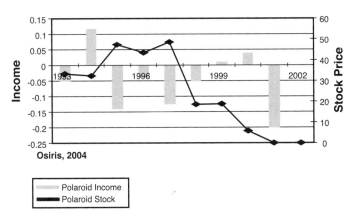

Osiris, 2004

Source: Osiris, 2004

Exhibit 3.1   Polaroid financial performance

Financial performance over time is related to CVA® over time. One can track the value of a business through various life cycles, including the life cycle of CVA®.

Levels of Sales Life Cycles

Sales life cycles show how unit sales of a product or service change over time. There are several levels of sales life cycles.

Life cycles provide insights into the changing competitive environment.

The broadest level of sales life cycle is known as the *market life cycle* (Exhibit 3.2). The market life cycle concerns the need of a customer and consists of all the ways that he or she may satisfy those needs. For example, there may be many ways to lose weight including health clubs, diet, drugs, self-exercise, hypnotism, even surgical procedures. All would be embraced by the market life cycle for losing weight. Similarly, there may be many ways to join metal components in an automobile such as welding, nuts and bolts, rivets, and adhesives. Each would be part of the market life cycle for joining metal parts.

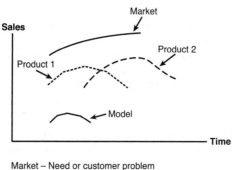

Market – Need or customer problem

Product – Specific way to satisfy need
or solve problem

Model – Specific version of product

Reprinted with permission from "Managing through the Life Cycle," The Arrow Group, Ltd.®, New York, NY, 2008.

Figure 3.2   Levels of life cycles

Each specific way that a customer's need might be satisfied follows a life cycle, known as the *product or service life cycle*. Often product or service life cycles are related to specific technologies. As a new technology appears, often the life cycle for a product or a service related to an older technology disappears or at least drops in prominence. For example, mechanical typewriters gave way to electric typewriters, which gave way to electronic typewriters, which gave way to word processors, which gave way to personal computers.

Most strategic planning focuses on the product or service life cycle, because that often is the most volatile life cycle with introduction, maturity, and decline stages. Within the product or service life cycles are the *model life cycles*. These cycles are specific versions of a product or service. Model life cycles, for example, might refer to different flavors of a soft drink, or different sized laptop computers, or automobiles with different sets of options.

The Competitive Life Cycle

The product or service life cycle (Exhibit 3.3) is more aptly described as the *competitive life cycle* because it is a model that describes competitive conditions over time—how customers are behaving and how competitors are behaving. Consequently, the stages in the competitive life cycle have major implications for the types of strategies an organization might consider.[2]

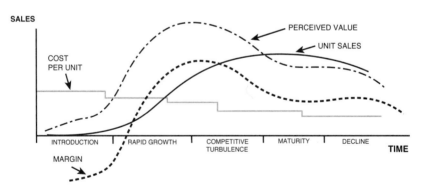

Reprinted with permission from "Managing through the Life Cycle," The Arrow Group, Ltd.®, New York, NY, 2008.

Exhibit 3.3   The competitive life cycle

The competitive life cycle refers to a specific market segment. Over time an organization likely serves customers in many target market segments. While the competitive life cycle shows how financial performance varies over time within a specific market segment, the overall financial performance of an organization depends on its performance in all the markets in which it competes.

The competitive life cycle comes in many shapes and sizes, and it is not uncommon for stages to repeat.[3] The life cycle is not an easy template to use for prediction, although there are numerous new product models that forecast sales well in certain situations.

Here is a brief tour of the common conditions during the various stages of the competitive life cycle:

- **Introduction.** One company pioneers the first version of a product or service. Competing products and services are typically based on old technology.
- **Rapid Growth.** There are a few direct competitors, the pioneer and the fast-followers. There is room for all to grow and be profitable.
- **Competitive Turbulence.** Many direct competitors are in the market. Because most or all functional benefits have been imitated, competition often focuses on price and a shakeout occurs.
- **Maturity.** The market consolidates, and there are only a few direct competitors. It is difficult to add value because most improvements have been introduced.
- **Decline.** New technology emerges or is put in place. Few providers of the old product or service remain, and, except for in niche markets, they compete with price.

There is an enormous difference between the competitive conditions during the Rapid Growth stage and the Competitive Turbulence stage. During Rapid Growth, all competitors may obtain profits. During Competitive Turbulence, there is often an intense price war that destroys profits.

However, most marketing textbooks do not distinguish between Rapid Growth and Competitive Turbulence. In an informal survey of more than 20 marketing textbooks, about 80 percent of them, including several best-selling and famous books, combined the Rapid Growth and Competitive Turbulence stages into one stage that the authors typically called *Growth*.[4] Much of the value of the competitive life cycle rests on the distinctions among the stages, and combining stages with widely different conditions blurs conclusions.

Sales Life Cycle

During the Introduction stage, unit sales usually grow slowly because companies must educate customers and resellers of the value of the new product or service as compared to the existing product or service. During Rapid Growth, sales begin to take off as customers discover the new product or service.

Sales growth slows somewhat during the Competitive Turbulence stage and then levels off during Maturity. During the Decline stage, a product or service with an improved technology displaces the current product or service. Sales decline and may eventually disappear.

Margin Life Cycle

Unit margin is defined as price minus unit cost. Typically the margin curve begins as a negative value in the Introduction stage. It becomes a positive value and often reaches its maximum during the Rapid Growth stage, plunges during Competitive Turbulence stage due to price competition from direct competitors, and then stabilizes for a while during Maturity stage. Margin may even increase during the Maturity stage, but that increase is usually due to cost reductions, not to value enhancements. Margin falls again during the Decline stage due to price competition from new products or services.

The shape of the margin curve may vary due to special circumstances, such as a very attractive product or service. However, in numerous executive seminars conducted by the author, managers confirm that the curves drawn in Exhibit 3.3 are consistent not only with common sense, but also with what they often see as they manage their products and services. These observations have generally been supported by studies by organizations such as the Strategic Planning Institute.[5]

Unit Cost Life Cycle

Typically per unit costs are relatively high at the beginning of the competitive life cycle. Start-up costs for a business may include expenditures for capacity and communications, both selling and advertising. Depending on managerial ability, per unit costs fall over time due to reasons such as new operations technologies, outsourcing, value engineering, and economies of scale. Unit costs do not decrease automatically. The decreases are due to continuous monitoring and continuous efforts. The shape of the unit cost curve is often a step function—capacity is increased, then costs fall as capacity is filled.

© Ashleigh Brilliant, 2008. Used with permission.

Perceived Value Life Cycle

The perceived value per unit curve is crucial to the value of any business. Perceived value is the maximum the customer is willing to pay for the product or service. The focus of marketing is to manage perceived value. While per unit cost reflects the realistic floor on price, perceived value per unit represents the *ceiling* on price.

Marketing efforts manage the perceived value life cycle.

Unless a product or service is associated with a powerful brand, the perceived value per unit curve usually begins low at the start of the Introduction stage. During the Rapid Growth stage, perceived value per unit increases as customers learn about the benefits provided by the product or service. Perceived value per unit often peaks in the Rapid Growth stage. As *me-too* products and services flood the market during the Competitive Turbulence stage, perceived value per unit falls because perceived value depends on comparisons with competing products and services. As competitors copy the product or service, the customer perceives less differentiation, and so perceived value declines, sometimes abruptly.

Perceived value per unit during the Maturity stage is often relatively stable, especially for established brands. Products or services with new technologies appear during the Decline stage, causing perceived value per unit of the original product to fall again.

Downward price pressures on margin typically occur during the Competitive Turbulence and Decline stages as alternative equivalent or superior products and services are introduced to the market. Organizations in Competitive Turbulence that are *shaken out* are organizations that are unable to lower their costs quickly enough to avoid being crushed by the falling perceived value curve.

NASCAR: NASCAR Puts Fans Inside the Helmet

With the only open locker room in sports, NASCAR has always tried to give its customers—the fans—close access to the sport and its athletes.

For years, fans have been able to walk the racetrack and nab their favorite driver's autograph in the garage. Today, technology is also creating additional intimate ways to experience NASCAR. On television, computer and wireless screens, satellite radio, and even handheld devices at the track, fans can follow a race from the vantage point of a single driver, eavesdrop on driver-crew chief conversations, or "play director" to view the field from a preferred vantage point.

"Close access to the racing action and the stars of the sport is an important part of the fan experience, and the value NASCAR brings to sponsors," said Paul Brooks, President of NASCAR

Media Group. "Technology is playing an ever-increasing role in bringing fans closer to the racing action."

Here's how NASCAR is putting fans "inside the helmet":

- NASCAR Sprint Fanview: a next-generation scanner for fans at track, provides live in-car audio for all drivers, real-time race data and statistics, the live race broadcast and in-car camera channels for up to seven different drivers. *Time* named Fanview one of the most innovative new products of 2006.

- NASCAR HOTPASS on DIRECTV: Fans can follow five different drivers on fully produced channels during each Sprint Cup race. Each channel has its own announcing team, director and producer. Fans get multiple camera angles, real-time stats and telemetry, and in-car audio. HOTPASS marks the first TV service allowing fans to follow their favorite team for the entire "game."

- Sirius NASCAR Radio is an exclusive channel filling 24 hours a day with NASCAR news, in-depth analysis, and live talk shows. "Driver 2 Crew Chatter" offers 10 channels carrying the overall race call and the in-car audio of their favorite driver on a single channel throughout the race.

- TrackPass RaceView on NASCAR.COM is the first-ever live rendering of a major sporting event in 3-D. On screen race data shows drivers' positions and movements to within a few inches. Fans can select one driver or switch among the full field—following the cars around the track while listening to in-car audio feeds over their computer and getting information on track position, speed and time behind leader.

At a time when coaches and players cover their mouths with clipboards and gloves, there are no secrets in NASCAR. Fans are brought inside the action in every conceivable way. And that helps keep fans in the seats and sponsors logos on the race cars.

—Andrew Giangola, Director of Business Communications, NASCAR

CVA® Life Cycle

As defined previously, CVA® is the distance between perceived value per unit and unit cost (Exhibit 3.4). If perceived value falls below unit cost for any length of time, the organization may go out of business because the inputs to produce the product or service cost more than the outputs are worth—as *perceived* by the customers. If an organization is making inputs into something that is worth less, it is destroying the resources of society; and, if not subsidized, in a free market, that organization will go out of business.

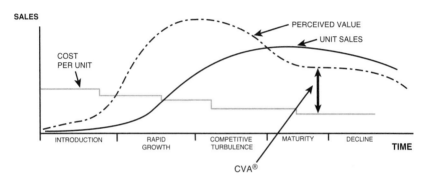

Reprinted with permission from "Managing through the Life Cycle," The Arrow Group, Ltd.®, New York, NY, 2008.

Exhibit 3.4   The competitive life cycle and CVA®

> *If perceived value falls below unit cost for any*
> *length of time, the organization may fail.*

It is important to note that it is the *perceptions* of customers as to the value of the product or service that have the impact. The *actual value* plays a role only in that it is likely the ceiling on perceived value. Few customers know the full value of any product or service they purchase. Moreover, if they somehow expect to receive more value than they actually do, they revise downward their evaluations of the perceived value of the product or service.

To the extent that CVA® is positive and sizable over time, then the financial performance of the organization improves. The job of every manager is to ensure that CVA® is as large as possible because that will maximize the shareholder value of the organization (Exhibit 3.5).

CVA®

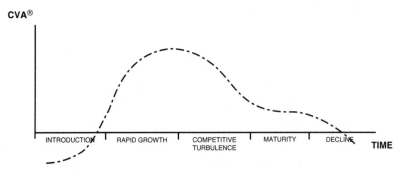

INTRODUCTION | RAPID GROWTH | COMPETITIVE | MATURITY | DECLINE   **TIME**
                               TURBULENCE

Reprinted with permission from "Managing through the Life Cycle," The Arrow Group, Ltd.®, New York, NY, 2008.

Exhibit 3.5   The CVA® life cycle

In the Introduction stage, CVA® may be negative because perceived value per unit may be below unit cost—the target customers do not yet understand or accept the value provided by the new product or service. The task of marketing, then, is to close any gaps between customers' perceptions of the benefits of the product or service with the actual benefits of the product or service and gain trial. Those communications costs—personal selling and media—are one of the reasons costs are often relatively high during this stage.

Notice the importance of forecasting CVA® over time. If decisions on new products or services were made based solely on the initial values of CVA®, then many businesses would be terminated before they have a chance to succeed. Often perceived value per unit is below cost per unit at the beginning of the life cycle.

During the Rapid Growth stage, CVA® typically is at its maximum. Customers appreciate the value being provided them by the product or service. Costs are beginning to fall. Competitors have not yet flooded the market with imitations that precipitate a price war. The task of marketing is to continually improve the product or service and to continually inform the customers of the benefits unique to their brand of the product or service.

The Competitive Turbulence stage is often known as *shakeout* because it is where many organizations struggle and sometimes disappear. Perceived value is often falling quickly as me-too competitors invade the market. If a firm is unable to decrease its costs, it finds itself crushed between the falling perceived value curve and the unit cost curve. If perceived value and costs are not effectively managed, CVA® may become negative and force the organization out of business.

During the Competitive Turbulence stage, the task of the manager is to make sure that costs are falling at least as rapidly as perceived value and to maintain perceived value as much as possible. These objectives can be accomplished, in part, by targeting market segments and ensuring that perceived value is kept steady or even improved for those key segments. Costs can be managed down by minimizing costs that are in common across segments—much as Chinese restaurants mix and match ingredients to create new dishes.

The CVA® marketing challenge during the Maturity stage is to keep perceived value per unit from falling. Usually, during this stage most of the ways to add value to the product or service have already been discovered and implemented. With that said, however, never take this for granted—one should always search for new sources of customer value. For marketing, that means reinforcing the brand position. During this stage, if CVA® is increased, it will be mainly through cost decreases; so emphasis must be placed on more efficient operations. For example, Spam® processed meat, which has been in the Mature stage for a long while, continues to earn increased profits due to cost efficiencies.

During the Decline stage, perceived value per unit may fall below unit cost because products or services have appeared that satisfy the customers' needs more effectively due to improved or different technology. This is the second time at which there are, typically, sizable pressures to decrease price. While some companies will survive the price wars of the Competitive Turbulence stage, the only companies that survive the price declines during this stage are those that have developed new products or services that satisfy the customers' needs and represent the next technological step associated with the market life cycle.

Dow Corning: Two-Brand Strategy Spells Success

It was called disruptive. It was called risky. But five years after Dow Corning Corporation reinvented itself with a two-brand strategy, the bottom line was called success. By changing the way it approached business—putting customer needs first by offering a choice in how to purchase materials and solutions—Dow Corning experienced double-digit sales growth from 2002 through 2007.

For its first 50 years, Dow Corning developed an industry with product innovation and technology leadership based on silicon science. But the business landscape shifted dramatically in the 1990s: product innovation alone could no longer drive or sustain the company's success.

The launch of its online business XIAMETER® was a bold step. The new business model, designed for a certain market segment—price-seekers—came with a risk of cannibalizing the traditional *Dow Corning*® brand, if current customers moved to the new offering. The first of its kind in the chemical marketplace, Xiameter has helped bring change to the industry. Designed for customers who can order in large volumes and know what they need, and how to use it, it complements the corporate brand which comes with expertise, advice, technical support, and scientists. So rather than cannibalizing the corporate brand as some feared, Xiameter has only made it stronger.

Offering customers choices and bringing new value propositions to the silicone marketplace, Xiameter was only one part of the company's larger global repositioning strategy, which was based on the results of Dow Corning customer feedback and segmentation studies. The Dow Corning brand was re-focused on providing a variety of solutions and services, in addition to the thousands of silicon-based materials the company offered. By making this change at the same time Xiameter was launched, the company was able to reinforce the value of its corporate brand.

—Scott Fuson, Chief Marketing Officer, Dow Corning
Reprinted with permission

Financial Performance over Time

The margin, cost, perceived value, and CVA® curves show the effects of marketing and branding on the financial performance of an organization.

Margin depends on the distance between the perceived value curve and the unit cost curve, CVA®. The wider the distance between the perceived value per unit curve and the unit cost curve, the more options for price and for margin.

If an organization prices to the maximum and allows no incentive for the customer, then the CVA® curve is the same as the margin curve. However, usually an organization allows some incentive to the target customer, which determines the number of units sold.

The CVA® curve is directly associated with contribution, as explained in Chapter 2, "How CVA® Affects Financial Performance." Contribution is usually a major component of profit, which, in turn, is usually a major component of cash flow.

Shareholder value consists of the sum of the properly discounted future cash flows of an organization for all its products, services, and markets. Overall, the CVA® curve for a specific competitive life cycle indicates the amount an organization's shareholder value is increased by the contribution generated in the specific market segment for which that competitive life cycle corresponds. In turn, that contribution can be decomposed into the portion due to the brand and the portion due to the benefits of the product or service.

As discussed in Chapter 4, "Perceived Value," *perceived value* consists of value from both the benefits the customer experiences with the product or service and the attributes the customer associates with the brand (Exhibit 3.6). Analyses such as conjoint analysis (discussed in Chapter 4) allow one to estimate the size of those two components of perceived value.[6]

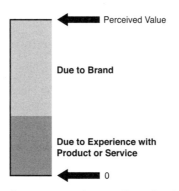

Reprinted with permission from "How Marketing Affects Shareholder Value," The Arrow Group, Ltd.®, New York, NY, 2008.

Exhibit 3.6 Brands and perceived value

For example, Interbrand has estimated the brand's portion of perceived value for various product categories (Exhibit 3.7). Not surprisingly, brands play a larger role in perceived value for products such as fragrances and a smaller role for products such as semiconductors.

Exhibit 3.7   Brands as a Percentage of Perceived Value

Product Category	Percentage of Perceived Value
Perfume	98
Cookies	90
Oil	85
Cars	75
Audit	60
Telephony	49
Hotels	40
Draft beer	30
Gasoline	14
Semi-conductors	5

Presented by Interbrand at the Columbia Business School in 2001.

The CVA® life cycle provides a basis for estimating brand equity as a percentage of shareholder value.

Brand Equity

Many companies have difficulty determining brand equity because they have not defined it precisely. At seminars on building and managing brand equity, participants are asked to define brand equity. Here are some of their answers:

- "Incremental value to consumer"
- "Measurable symbols and attributes that consumers use"
- "Brand's collateral"
- "Value added by name"
- "Market value of brand"

- "Asset that produces cash flows"
- "Added value that consumer is willing to pay for"
- "Goodwill"
- "Strength of brand in mind of consumer"
- "Value to shareholder"

These answers seem to vary considerably. However, when one looks them over, one finds that they fall into one of two categories, definitions concerning value imparted by the brand to the individual customer or consumer and definitions concerning value accruing to the company.[7]

The consumer-value definitions focus on the value a brand adds to a product or service and is sometimes described as a brand's price premium. This is erroneous because all added value does not show as a price premium unless one is pricing to the maximum. Several practitioners and academics endorse the consumer-value notion of brand equity. Such a definition does serve as a useful test of the power of a brand to an individual and provides an important component of brand equity. However, the consumer-value definition of brand equity is not complete from a finance or investment point of view and does not alone provide a rationale for the commonly accepted estimates of brand equity.

Brand equity is:

> *The net present value of the cash flows from a product or service with an established brand position minus the cash flows from a comparable product or service without an established brand position.*

This definition works very well as a practical and operational definition. It also has the advantage of being quite consistent with the way financial managers view the world, where any asset can be valued according to the cash flows it can generate.

To see brand equity, consider the perceived value curve as corresponding to a product or service that is an established brand. Compare that perceived value curve to the perceived value curve for a product or service without an established brand (Exhibit 3.8). That case would correspond to a commodity when an organization would price to the minimum—just above the variable cost per unit.

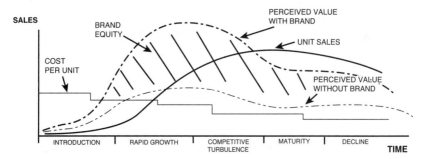

Reprinted with permission from "Managing through the Life Cycle," The Arrow Group, Ltd.®, New York, NY, 2008.

Exhibit 3.8   Brand equity

The distance between these curves is associated with the difference in their cash flows, adjusted also by any cost differences between the branded and unbranded product.

Hewlett-Packard: Assessing the Value of a Brand

Strong and relevant brands have inspirational *and* economic value. They are one of the most powerful connective forces to motivate and renew employees' engagement with their company.

Strong brands drive customer connections, foster the emergence and development of communities and open the door for new customers. A strong and relevant brand acts as a growth generator for customers to consider you and call you first; and builds loyalty with them. As a result, customer-valued brands drive higher margins which are a measure of a brand's preference over an unbranded offering.

Building a strong brand and keeping it fresh is a cross-company business concern and responsibility, guided by Marketing, but delivered by every facet of company operations.

In recent studies we conducted, brands can account for nearly 30% of what drives shareholder value.

The majority of brand value growth continues to come from improved financial performance, especially current and expected margin growth. On a combined basis, actual financial performance and historical growth have the greatest impact on shareholder value, but non-financial factors such as awareness, corporate reputation, culture, innovation, partnerships, and human capital have grown in importance.

Brand valuation is an economic measure that reflects actual customer behavior. This valuation can be broken down by business unit or division to better understand their contribution and potential. Brand valuation can also be a compelling metric to share with internal or external audiences such as analysts or shareholders.

Staying relevant in a world of increasing options and choice requires continual insight about customers and being able to act on these in *genuine* collaboration with your brand. Relevancy requires greater flexibility, and adaptability to appeal to customers' evolving needs; and requires knowing who you are, and aren't. Strong brands have passionate owners—internally and externally. Without this healthy community base, brands cease to be the relevant inspirational asset and financial growth engine they can be for a company.

—Gary Elliott, Vice President, Brand Marketing, Hewlett-Packard
Reprinted with permission

Valuing Brand Equity

Here is an inexpensive way to value the equity represented by an organization's brands—an approach that can be applied without the help of high-priced brand consultancies:

Sexton's Short-Cut to Estimating Brand Equity.

For companies with consumer products or services, the value of *all* their brands is typically 30 to 80 percent of the firm's market capitalization. For companies with industrial products or services, the value of all brands is usually about 15 to 30 percent of their market cap.

Why these percentages? For several years, a variety of published studies have presented estimates of the equity associated with many brands. Every year, *Business Week*, *Fortune*, and *Forbes* provide the market capitalization figures for numerous companies. The most recent figures available for the ten most valuable brands are shown in Exhibit 3.9.[8]

Exhibit 3.9   Brand and Company Values

	Brand Equity[*]	Market Capitalization[**]
Coca-Cola	$66.7	$135.9
IBM	59.0	157.6
Microsoft	59.0	253.2
GE	53.0	330.9
Nokia	35.9	145.7
Toyota	34.0	175.1
Intel	31.3	115.6
McDonald's	31.0	62.3
Disney	29.3	61.0
Google	25.6	147.7

Values in billions of US dollars.
[*] *Business Week*, "Best Global Brands," September 18, 2008.
[**] Forbes.com, "The World's Biggest Companies," April 2, 2008.

Over the years, if one compares the brand equity estimates to the market capitalization figures for the companies to which the brands correspond, most brand value estimates fall in the market cap percentage ranges mentioned above. Moreover, these percentages have been quite stable over time.

In performing this exercise, obviously one has to keep in mind that many companies, such as Disney, have more than one brand. To determine their total brand equity, all their brands must be summed.

In using these percentages, one must also consider the accuracy of the published brand equity estimates. Certainly they may be off the mark. However, for those brands on which the author has worked, the organization's own internal estimate of a brand's value is similar to the public estimates—say, within plus or minus 10 percent.

Not only have these percentages been relatively constant over the years, they also fall comfortably in line with major brand acquisitions such as those made in the late 1980s by Philip Morris (Kraft), Grand Met (Pillsbury), and Nestles (Rowntree), where purchase prices were four to five times the value of tangible assets—much of that outlay in excess of tangible assets likely due to brands.[9] These major acquisitions are widely thought to have created the current interest in brands and brand equity. Substantial outlays for established brands have been part of many other acquisitions such as Hilton's $4 billion purchase of Promus and its brands (including Embassy Suites and Hampton Inn) and InBev's $52 billion takeover of Anheuser-Busch and offers such as Microsoft's $44.6 billion bid for Yahoo![10] However, it should be pointed out that owning a brand is not the same as managing a brand well as various automotive companies have learned from their acquisitions of other automobile manufacturers.[11] In addition, maintaining a brand may not always be worthwhile.[12]

Estimating Brand Equity

Applying these concepts to estimating brand equity requires the following steps:

1. Forecast perceived value of the branded product or service over time.
2. Forecast unit sales of the branded product or service over time.
3. Forecast costs of the branded product or service over time.
4. Forecast perceived value of a comparable unbranded product or service over time.
5. Forecast unit sales of the unbranded product or service over time.
6. Forecast costs of the unbranded product or service over time.
7. Forecast the net cash flows of the branded and unbranded product or service.
8. Calculate the difference in net cash flows between the branded and unbranded product or service and discount appropriately.

Each of these steps utilizes established research techniques and does not rely on crucial subjective estimates as, for example, the multiple of cash flow techniques popularized by several consultancies usually do.[13]

Perhaps the most difficult steps are those involving forecasts of perceived value, but those estimates can be obtained through the use of research techniques such as constrained choice models and regression analysis (see Chapter 4).

To estimate the overall value of a brand, one must also consider the cash flows from possible brand extensions. That is why two companies may value a brand quite differently. Each may see different possibilities in the brand, and each may have different skills for exploiting the brand as an asset.

Estimating the Value of Brand Equity: Tetley Tea Acquisition

Tata Tea was considering purchasing Tetley Tea in 2000. Clearly, they would be purchasing not just production capacity for tea, but a valuable brand name in Tetley. The issue was how to estimate the value of the brand.

At the time, the overall tea market was growing at only 1 percent a year and was expected to plateau—zero growth per year—by 2005 and continuing in future years. The sales of Tetley Group in 1999 were $523,581,000, of which 85 percent were associated with the Tetley brand. The average gross margin was 55 percent. Tata's unbranded tea sales for the same year totaled $224,576,000. Tata's average gross margin on unbranded tea was 36 percent.

As a first approximation to the value of the Tetley brand, Tetley contributions forecast over time can be compared to those for unbranded tea. The relevant calculations are summarized in Exhibit 3.10.

In 1999, Tetley branded sales were $445,044,000 (85 percent of total sales for the Tetley Group). Assume those sales were growing by 1 percent each year from 2000 through 2004, then remained the same for years thereafter. Similarly, unbranded sales can be extrapolated with a 1 percent growth rate until 2004, then the same sales for the years afterwards.

Only gross margin figures were available, and these are biased low compared to variable margin figures. Gross margin is what remains after average costs have been removed, and average costs are always greater than variable costs because average costs include average fixed costs. This may cause estimation concerns if the variable costs for Tetley are much lower than those for unbranded teas, which may be true due to economies of scale.

Exhibit 3.10 Estimating Value of Tetley Brand Equity

		Actual 1999	2000	2001	Forecast 2002	2003	≥2004	Total
Tetley	Sales	$445,044	$449,494	$453,989	$458,529	$463,114	$467,746	
	Contribution	$244,774	$247,221	$249,694	$252,191	$254,712	$257,760	
	Discount Factor		.87	.76	.66	.57	3.31	
	Net Present Value		$215,082	$189,767	$166,446	$145,186	$853,186	$1,569,667
Unbranded	Sales	$224,576	$226,822	$229,090	$231,381	$233,695	$236,032	
	Contribution	$80,847	$81,656	$82,472	$83,297	$84,130	$84,972	
	Discount Factor		.87	.76	.66	.57	3.31	
	Net Present Value		$71,041	$62,679	$54,976	$47,954	$281,257	$517,907
							Difference	**$1,051,760**

Nonetheless, because gross margin estimates were the only margin estimates available, they were applied to predict the total gross margins for each year for sales of both Tetley tea and unbranded tea. An interest rate of 15 percent was assumed and the net present value of the Tetley gross margins compared to the net present value of the unbranded tea gross margins. The difference was approximately $1 billion, a rough estimate of the value of the Tetley brand. The actual price Tata paid for Tetley was $441,730,000. The disparity may reflect the simplifying assumptions made, such as the 15% discount rate and the average growth rate. Still, this easy-to-perform analysis would provide a valuable starting point for refining the brand equity estimates. It is possible that Tata may have obtained a bargain.

In addition to the use of gross margins instead of variable margins, reservations to this estimate include the distribution coverage of Tetley tea versus that of the unbranded teas and the assumption of the same growth rate for both.

Source: Rajsaday Dutt, Avin Dwivedy, Tze-Liang Chiam, "Tata Tea Ltd. and Tetley, PLC. (A)," Charlottesville, VA: Darden, 2004; Ulrike Wehr, "Tata Tea Limited (A)," Fontainebleau: INSEAD, 2004; and Passport GMID, "Tata Tea Ltd.: Company Factfile," Euromonitor International, 2008.

Conclusions

Tracking CVA® over time provides a framework for developing strategy. In particular, focusing on perceived value and costs directs attention to the two factors that determine an organization's financial performance. As shown in the various life cycles discussed in the chapter, the evaluation of competition may be similar in a variety of industries and in both products and services, even though the pace of change may vary considerably.

The CVA® life cycle and the other life cycles can also be used as a basis for forecasting financial performance—revenue, contribution, profit, cash flow, and brand equity.

In studies by the Conference Board and the American Productivity and Quality Center (APQC), one of the characteristics found to distinguish companies successfully managing their brands from those that were not was recognition of the need to monitor their brands by going beyond traditional measures, such as awareness, to focus on brand equity—the value of their brands.[14] For example, in the Conference Board study, 60 percent of the companies who were more successful in managing their brands claimed to have a system for measuring brand equity as compared to only 26 percent in the less successful group. In the APQC study, 31 percent of the firms selected as benchmark organizations with regard to managing brands said they had methodology for evaluating brand investments versus 4 percent for the other firms in the survey.

While their success in evaluating and monitoring brand equity varied, brand managers in those studies agreed that those efforts were necessary and deserved high priority. CVA® provides an approach to evaluating brand equity that is conceptually grounded in finance and economics.

Comments on Possible Methods of Valuing Brand Equity

Historic cost—All costs leading to current brand position. Historic costs may be difficult to unearth and are likely irrelevant to today's costs. There is no consideration of future cash flows.

Replacement cost—All costs required to replicate brand position today. Still a cost-oriented approach that does not consider future cash flows.

Customer satisfaction—Part of brand equity, but not the same as brand equity.

Price premium—Reflects only that part of the brand value for which one is charging, and then at only one moment in time to specific customers.

Market value—What someone is willing to pay for the brand. This method is economically sound, but difficult to identify in practice. Normally one would not want to put one's brand on the trading block just to see the price it brings.

Stock price—Possible for a one-brand company, not for a multi-brand company.

Multiple of cash flow—Brand cash flows estimated for a year multiplied by a *factor*. The key question for this method of valuation is: How does one determine the factor?

Discounted cash flow—Financially and economically sound and consistent with marketing theory and practice. This is the approach described in this chapter.

4

Perceived Value

Perceived value is the ceiling on price. It is the maximum the customer is willing to pay for the product or service and depends on what benefits the customer believes they are receiving from the product or service. It almost always can be expected to be below actual value just because a customer rarely understands all the benefits that they receive (Exhibit 4.1).

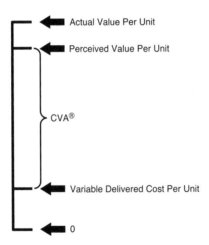

Reprinted with permission from "How Marketing Affects Shareholder Value," The Arrow Group, Ltd.®, New York, NY, 2008.

Exhibit 4.1   Customer Value Added

Managing perceived value is the purpose of marketing. This chapter focuses on how to manage and measure perceived value.

Expected, Actual, and Perceived Performance

There are three types of value in any marketing situation: expected, actual, and perceived. *Expected value* consists of the level of performance that the customer hopes to receive on any benefit provided by a product or service. *Actual value* consists of the level of performance that the customer actually receives on any benefit provided by a product or service. *Perceived value* consists of the level of performance that the customer believes that they have received on any benefit provided by a product or service.

Especially important in determining perceptions are the relationships between employees and customers.[1] As Roger Adams, former CMO of Home Depot observed, "We have to have a real emotional connection with customers."[2] At Verizon, the mobile telephone "churn rates" (percentage of customers leaving) are more than 40% lower than those of their nearest competitors because of the consistency with which they treat their customers—over many quarters the highest rating in the American Customer Satisfaction Index (ACSI) for their category.[3]

If actual performance on a benefit is below the level of performance expected by the customer, then the product or service has a *design problem* on that benefit because the customer expectations are not met. If the perceived performance on a benefit is below the level of performance actually provided, then the product or service has a *communications problem* because the customer does not realize the benefit performance they receive.

For example, suppose a passenger were evaluating an experience on an airline. Their expectation might be that the flight should be on time. In fact, the flight may have arrived 15 minutes late—a design problem in that there was a problem in operations. If the passenger feels that the flight arrived 30 minutes late, then there is also a communications problem—the airline has not clearly communicated its performance to the customer. In this illustration, the airline performed below expectations; but, in addition, the passenger perceived that the airline performed worse on punctuality than, in fact, it did.

The *perceptions* of the passenger as to what happens determine his or her future actions—not what actually happens.

Marketing Ratios

The relationship among expected, actual, and perceived values can be seen in *marketing ratios* (Exhibit 4. 2). To the extent that an organization designs a product or service that meets its customers' expectations, then actual value will correspond closely to expected value. If an organization communicates actual value to its customers, then perceived value will correspond closely to actual value.

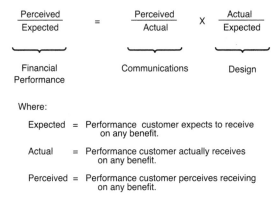

Reprinted with permission from "Marketing Strategy versus Marketing Tactics," The Arrow Group, Ltd.®, New York, NY, 2008.
Exhibit 4.2   Marketing ratios

If perceived value corresponds closely to expected value, then the organization will be rewarded in terms of its financial performance—through pricing, demand, and contribution.

> *Marketing managers need to manage expected value,*
> *actual value, and perceived value, in concert.*

When Hyundai was rated number 3 in J.P. Powers & Associates' automobile quality study, ahead of Toyota and Honda, only 23 percent of new car buyers considered a Hyundai compared to 65 percent for Toyota and 50 percent for Honda. In this instance, Hyundai's design ratio was strong but not its communications ratio. The actual value of its design was not being effectively communicated to its target customers.[4] Hyundai has had a strong design ratio and a weak communications ratio.

In contrast, when the infamous Edsel was introduced, the hype—intensive communications—was so extreme that perhaps no car could meet the expectations that had been built. The design of the Edsel came nowhere close to meeting the customer expectations and the automobile became synonymous with "marketing disaster."[5] The Edsel calamity resulted from very strong communications coupled with a very weak design ratio.

© Ashleigh Brilliant, 2008. Used with permission.

Determinants of Perceived Value

Overall, perceived value depends on many factors, such as the benefits the product or service provides, how important each benefit is to the customer, how well each is provided relative to competitors, and whether the customer correctly perceives how well each benefit is provided.[6]

Perceived value is not additive. Some benefits are necessary—such as safety for an airline—and, if they are not present, they have a substantial effect on perceived value. For example, if an airline is considered unsafe, no matter how good the movies are, they will not offset the low ranking on safety.

Perceived value is specific to each customer. To the extent that the customer consists of several individuals (the *decision-making unit*), perceived value must be considered for each individual.

If individuals view a product or service as having approximately the same perceived value, then those individuals may be grouped into a *market segment*.

Part of perceived value is due to the benefits directly experienced when the customer uses the product or service; the rest of perceived value is due to the benefits that have been associated with the brand itself (Exhibit 4. 3). To understand this distinction, suppose one were buying a piano. The product benefits would be those experienced when playing the piano in the showroom while the brand benefits would be those benefits one would have in mind *before* entering the showroom.

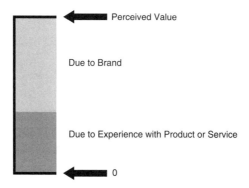

Reprinted with permission from "How Marketing Affects Shareholder Value," The Arrow Group, Ltd.®, New York, NY, 2008.

Exhibit 4.3   Brands and perceived value

The reason to build a brand is to create inertia in perceived value. To build a brand, one must associate the brand with certain benefits and certain levels of performance on those benefits. Those associations create perceived value inertia, which supports the value of a brand over time. Once those brand associations are built, the brand perceptions become dominant in affecting purchase decisions, which determine the cash flow from the brand.

Brands create inertia in perceived value.

Occasionally, as in the case of Harley-Davidson in the 1980s, brand inertia is exploited to hollow out a brand. When a brand is hollowed out, product and service investment are cut back to the detriment of value even while sales continue. In effect, managers who hollow-out a brand are selling off its brand equity. However, customers constantly compare their experiences with the product or service to their brand expectations and eventually realize that the performance of a hollowed-out brand has deteriorated. When that happens, the brand may die.

For new brands—brands before customers have experienced the brand through trial—most of the perceptions of the brand are based on brand communications such as mass media or word-of-mouth. Brand communications in the Introduction and Rapid Growth stages are especially crucial in building the brand position. After the customer tries the product or service, then those experiences are imprinted on the brand.

Citi: Drivers of Perceived Value

The value of branding as a strategic tool is increasingly being embraced by financial services. However, knowing how to identify the drivers of "perceived value"—then investing in them is not easy. Identifying where to invest to maximize customer appreciation requires long term tracking of many aspects of the customer experience and brand touch points. This type of tracking requires discipline and consistency of metrics, which can be tough to sustain in a dynamic market. But it is these metrics which are the window into how to grow your brand.

Making educated guesses regarding what is key is not a reliable approach as drivers vary according to category. Some are easy to estimate, we all know quality of customer service is key to the success of some brands e.g. hospitality brands, but is less important for others for instance, industrials. Others drivers are less transparent and more subtle, making identifying the correct measures a forensic science.

Trends in the financial services category indicate that there is renewed focus on improving two areas which drive higher long term rewards—customer service and communications. These are both strong drivers of customer value. Money and its management is an area where clients can require significant help in understanding the value they receive. Strong communications ensure a company is clear about what they have to offer therefore making the value more transparent.

Financial services have a different business model from many enterprises, often sustaining multiple relationships with one individual. Lending on one hand and investing assets on the other, so we strive for balance. We have an eye on maintaining long term relationships—this requires building and measuring your brand over many years. Significant improvements in how to measure have occurred, especially with respect to marketing forging strong partnerships with finance, collecting and analyzing data together. This type of teamwork gives better insights into what customers most care about and enables marketers to act on the information gathered. This is ultimately very beneficial for customers because we focus on what is valuable for them.

—Susan Avarde, Managing Director, Global Branding Citi
Reprinted with permission of Susan Avarde.

Branding and Perceived Value

Brands consist of three major components: identifiers, attributes, and associations (Exhibit 4.4).

> *An organization's brands are likely
> their most valuable single asset.*

Identifiers are all the symbols of a brand that are cues for customers. Identifiers include name, logo, spokesperson, color, shape, taste, aroma—anything that reminds a customer of the brand.[7] Whenever an identifier is changed, it has an impact on the brand in the customer's mind.

Attributes are the characteristics of the brand. They include the product or service category, features, benefits, needs, and the brand's expected, actual, and perceived performance on each of them.

If a brand identifier does not lead a customer to think of some attributes, then the brand has no presence in the customer's mind. Brands can be built on many different kinds of attributes, but the most powerful attributes are likely functional or emotional benefits or needs.

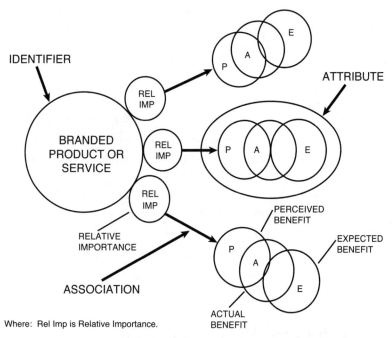

Exhibit 4.4   Components of a brand

The *associations* are the connections between the brand identifiers and the brand attributes within the customer's mind. The stronger the associations, the clearer the brand is to the customer. Associations become strong through *consistency*—continuously communicating the key attributes that make up the brand's position to the target customer by both word and deed. For example, MasterCard very effectively built associations with their long-running "priceless" campaign, constantly refreshing their creative while always staying on message.[8] As Roger Adams, CMO of Home Depot, observed, "The brands that win don't change what they stand for."[9]

Perceived value depends both on the product or service attributes linked to the brand and on the attributes as they are experienced by the customer. New brands need to rely on advertising, public relations, word-of-mouth, and other ways to communicate their advantages to target customers.[10] Well-known brands usually enjoy inertia in the customer's mind based on their past experience and knowledge of the brand. Unless technology is changing rapidly, the overall perceived value for established brands can be expected to depend more on those attributes associated with the brand and less on direct experience with the product or service.

Harrah's Entertainment: Synergistic Brands

Harrah's Entertainment is the world's largest gaming company, measured in revenue. With nearly fifty properties around the globe, including thirty-six in the United States, this size creates the opportunity for many scale-driven benefits. The flipside of the coin, however, is that size and distribution also create a unique set of challenges. Included in its portfolio are the Harrah's, Horseshoe, Caesars Palace, Rio, Bally's, Paris, Showboat, Flamingo, Harveys, Imperial Palace Las Vegas, and Grand Casino casino brands, many of which became part of the organization through a process of acquisition. As a result, Harrah's must market a disparate group of geographically dispersed casino brands to capitalize on the competitive advantage it enjoys by operating in every major gaming market in America.

Harrah's Entertainment relies on its Total Rewards program as a means of binding these unique brands together and rewarding its customers for their loyalty. Total Rewards is managed as a brand and positioned against a broad set of emotional and self-expressive benefits in addition to the more functional aspects of the loyalty program.

Originally developed as a program to track customer betting patterns and reward loyalty, Total Rewards has become much more ubiquitous at Harrah's, conspicuous in every marketing campaign to show customers how a relationship with the brand can provide access to a broad set of experiences, status, and a whole host of customer-selected opportunities. This aspirational, elevated, and liberating brand is rooted in the notion that playing at our properties leads to greater rewards than visiting our competitors. At the same time, the data we collect from our customers allows us to provide a more personalized set of experiences and offers. Not surprisingly, this cycle is reinforcing.

One of the key, differentiated benefits of the Total Rewards brand is its portability. This portability is essential and enables the Total Rewards brand to act as the glue that binds the portfolio of casino brands together.

—Mark Osterhaus, Vice President and Assistant General Manager, Harrah's Council Bluffs, Horseshoe Council Bluffs

Used with permission of Harrah's License Company, LLC.

Development of Perceived Value

Perceived value is formed as customers go through the process of buying. During the last 50 years, a considerable amount of research in universities, companies, and consultancies has focused on theories of buyer behavior or consumer behavior.[11] Much of this work is the application of psychological theory to understand how people buy.

In general, buyer behavior is thought to consist of several stages as shown in Exhibit 4.5. The main stages are:

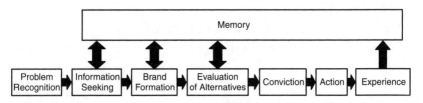

Reprinted with permission from "Understanding Customers," The Arrow Group, Ltd.®, New York, NY, 2008.

Exhibit 4.5   Buyer Behavior

As the customer proceeds through these stages, their memory is modified by the information they receive and their perceived value may be altered.[12]

Stages of Buyer Behavior

Problem recognition occurs when the customer realizes that their current situation is different from the situation they desire. For example, for a consumer, perhaps their television screen is not as large as they wish or, for a purchasing manager, perhaps the plastic a company is using in its fabrication is not sufficiently flexible for the designs they wish to produce. The discrepancy between the current situation and desired situation *motivates* the customer to solve their problem with a purchase.[13]

There appear to be three main types of buyer behavior.

What happens next depends on the significance of the problem and the knowledge the customer currently possesses about possible solutions. *Extensive problem-solving* takes place when how the problem is solved may have significant consequences and when the customer may not immediately know the optimal solution. *Limited problem-solving* covers those situations with moderate consequences when the customer is already familiar with some acceptable alternatives. *Habitual decision-making* describes how purchases of little import tend to be made.

Each of these three types of buyer behavior has implications for information seeking, brand formation, and evaluation of alternatives (Table 4.1). For example, during the extensive or limited problem-solving stages, the customer develops knowledge or feelings regarding the brand, then may eventually take action. (In Chapter 9, "Utilizing CVA® for Marketing Program Decisions," Exhibits 9.3 and 9.4, this pattern of behavior is described as Learn/Feel/Do or Feel/Learn/Do.) During habitual decision-making, the customer may simply try the product or service and develop knowledge or feelings afterwards. (In Chapter 9, this pattern of behavior is described as Do/Learn/Feel or Do/Feel/Learn.)

Extensive problem-solving tends to take place during the earliest stages of the competitive life cycle when customers encounter new product or services, limited problem-solving during the middle stages when customers consider known products or services, and habitual decision-making during the later stages when purchases may be routine. (See Chapters 3 and 7.)[14]

Table 4.1   Types of Buyer Behavior

Behavior	Problem Recognition	Information Seeking	Brand Formation	Evaluation of Alternatives
Extensive Problem-Solving	High signifi-cance High risk Low knowledge	Active/ extensive Multiple sources Continues throughout purchase process	Development of associations	Thorough Multiple criteria Compensatory evaluation
Limited Problem-Solving	Moderate significance Moderate risk Moderate knowledge	Passive/ convenient Supplementary sources	Adjustment of associations	As needed Primarily key criteria Non-compensatory evaluation
Habitual Decision-Making	Low significance Low risk High knowledge	Little or no search	Affirmation of associations	Inertia

Reprinted with permission from "Understanding Customers," The Arrow Group, Ltd.®, New York, NY, 2008.

Information seeking consists of all the ways a customer assembles the information on which they will base their purchase decision. Information seeking includes the overall effort devoted to obtaining information, the information sources utilized, and the processing of that information.[15]

If a customer is in the midst of extensive problem-solving, then their information seeking tends to be aggressive and comprehensive. Typically, multiple sources of information are utilized as the customer attempts to develop expertise with which to find solutions to the problem faced. During limited problem-solving, the customer tends to be more passive in accumulating information—absorbing whatever information happens to come their way.[16] In habitual decision-making, information is not usually sought although some information may register with the customer.[17]

Brand formation occurs when the customer is developing attitudes towards the product or service, including the brand identifiers, attributes, and associations. These comprise the awareness, knowledge, and liking stages of the hierarchy of effects model explained in Chapter 9 (Exhibit 9.2).[18] Attitudes include both cognitive components—beliefs about the brand—and affective components—emotional responses to the brand.[19] The customer also builds confidence in judging the brand—the strength of the associations between the identifiers and the attributes.[20]

During extensive problem-solving in the Introduction and Rapid Growth stages of the competitive life cycle, considerable brand formation takes place. During limited problem-solving in the Rapid Growth and Competitive Turbulence stages, perceived brand positions may also be changed. That is why the earlier stages in the competitive life cycle are often the crucial stages for developing a brand, as discussed in Chapters 3 and 7.

If the attitudes toward the brand are not developed correctly during these early stages, it may be difficult to change those attitudes later on when the customer is in the habitual decision-making mode and not seeking or considering new information. As mentioned earlier, Hyundai receives very high quality ratings for their automobiles but continues to face perceived value and CVA® challenges due to customer inertia stemming from their initial entry position of low price.[21]

During the *evaluation of alternatives,* customers focus on the brands in their *evoked set*—the products or services they are seriously considering. (Brands considered unqualified are the *inept set* and those left out are the *inert set.*)

There are many ways customers evaluate alternatives. The approach followed depends on the individual customer and the purchase situation. One approach involves *non-compensatory* rules to make decisions. In such cases, if a product or service does not meet at least minimum standards on all benefits, it is not considered. For example, if an airline is considered to be unsafe, no amount of courtesy by the attendants will compensate for that weakness. With *compensatory rules*, the customer evaluates a product or service on the basis of all the benefits in concert. When considering an automobile, a customer may not like the color of the car but may like its fuel efficiency so overall finds the car acceptable.[22]

Multi-attribute models attempt to sort out how all the benefits of a product or service work together to create value in the customer's mind. Such models range from simple additive models such as the Fishbein model to more elaborate ways of combining benefits and priorities.[23]

Whatever decision rules a customer uses or however the customer processes information, perceived value is the summary of what the customer believes a particular product or service is worth.

> *Perceived value summarizes what the customer*
> *thinks a product or service is worth.*

Conviction occurs when the customer believes they will make the purchase. *Action* is the purchase. Once they have purchased a product or service, the customer obtains *experience*. Their experience may be positive or negative or neutral. Those experiences enter sensory (or temporary) memory, short-term memory, and perhaps long-term memory and—through perceived value—influence the customer's behavior in the future.[24]

MySpace: Friend-to-Friend

Five years ago, MySpace did not exist.

Today MySpace reaches more than 76 million people every month in the United States and more than 120 million people worldwide. And each of them spends on average more than 4 hours per month on the site.

For marketers, first and foremost, you have to fish where the fish are. And MySpace has become a ridiculously well-stocked pond. On any given day, it's even bigger than American Idol.

As a pure reach play, MySpace is a no-brainer. But it offers a lot more. The oldest form of marketing isn't caveman drawings, it's friend-to-friend. MySpace has become the most powerful word-of-mouth marketing platform in the digital space.

Researchers have coined a term for what happens on MySpace. It's called the Momentum Effect. That's where your customers generate exponentially greater value than you actually spend in media dollars.

In the Summer of 2008, McDonald's ran a campaign bringing back the Big Mac Chant. If you're old enough, you remember: "Two all-beef patties, special sauce, lettuce, cheese…." McDonald's enlisted emerging MySpace bands to cut their own versions and engage their fan bases. We supported the campaign with a media push and the audience took it from there.

Thousands of people entered the contest and millions touched the campaign as awareness spread through networks of friends. Someone would discover the contest and enter it, blog it, comment on it, or message their friends. Some set of their friends would thereby discover, self-express, and communicate to their friends. And so on. And so on. And so on.

McDonald's took advantage of a viral virtuous cycle that literally did not exist just a few years ago. They created a campaign that empowered the audience and provided value in their lives. Everybody won.

It's just one of many good examples of what happens millions of times every day on MySpace. We don't employ legions of editors to decide what's cool or relevant. Our audience does it for their own groups of friends. When brands tap into those networks with something compelling, the value is astronomical—for everyone.

—Jeff Berman, President of Sales & Marketing, MySpace

Reprinted with permission of Jeff Berman.

Managing Perceived Value

There are many ways to manage perceived value by utilizing design and communications to affect buyer behavior.

Make Customers Aware of a Problem That One's Product or Service Can Solve

The phenomenal success of Apple's iPod is due to their meeting customers needs for seemingly infinitely accessible portable music.

Their initial communications educated the customer to the experiences iPod made possible.[25]

In Australia, Kellogg's has advertised their ready-to-eat cereals as a source of energy for children going off to school and a healthy start for the day for seniors. Such a message is designed to stimulate sales of all ready-to-eat cereals. However, because Kellogg's often has nine of the top ten selling cereals in Australia, it makes sense for them to increase overall demand for cereals by informing customers about the problems that cereals can solve.[26]

Ocean Spray has entered many markets outside the United States by positioning cranberry juice as offering an entirely new taste to experience—what Ocean Spray's president, Stewart Gallagher, has described as the "cranberry mystique"—combining the taste, health, and heritage of cranberries.[27] L'Oreal caught the eyes of young Japanese women by making them aware of a mascara that would make their eyes more attractive by thickening and curling their lashes.[28]

Make Information Easily Accessible to the Target Customers

Organizations need to make inventories of their current and potential contact points with customers. Often these points are identified with a customer contact map—a diagram of all the places and times during the day when the customer receives information. The organization then needs to select contact points where their information will escape message clutter and reach the customer. For example, during their growth phase, Altoids mints made relatively heavy use of outdoor advertising such as bus station posters to gain the attention of customers.[29]

Communicate Those Benefits of Most Concern to the Target Customers

One airline flying the routes between the United States and Europe touted their fine food and wine—even though at the time they had the worst safety record for transatlantic airlines. Fine food and wine—though appealing in the right circumstances—cannot off-set concerns about safety.[30]

Focus on Just a Few Benefits

Trying to communicate more than two or three benefits can be counterproductive—customers may simply not be able to absorb all that information. Likely to be much more effective is concentrating on just a few benefits that are important to the target customers. Miller Lite initially focused on "tastes great" and "less filling" in an advertis-ing campaign that ran for only a few years in the 1970s. Still, so power-ful was that simple two-benefit message, most people remembered "tastes great" and "less filling" more than 30 years later.[31]

Be Consistent in Communications to Strengthen Associations

In the mid-1970s, Miller Lite abandoned their "tastes great/less filling" campaign to attempt several other advertising campaigns, none of which seemed to gain traction with the customer—what noted brand guru Al Ries called the "zig-zag problem."[32] In the past, Burger King often changed advertising campaigns.[33] To build a solid position for a product, service, or brand, one must employ messages that are consistent over time and over all contact points. For several years MasterCard used a variety of positions such as the "Future of Money" until they settled on the powerful "Priceless" campaign.[34]

Consistency is Branding 101. Campaigns as diverse as those from IBM, Visa, Foster's, GE, Mountain Dew, Samsung, Dow Corning, Pfizer, the Hallmark Channel, and Nokia have employed consistency in their benefit messages over time and across varied markets to build strong brands.

Strong brands are built by consistently communicating a few benefits of high importance to the customers.

If Necessary, Associate the Product or Service with a Strong Brand

Brands with positive attributes can increase the perceived value of a product or service. Associating powerful brands with a product or service can increase the revenue and contribution from that product or service. For example, the Wharton School and Financial Times brands add perceived value to Pearson books.

However, the brand must stretch sufficiently to have a positive effect on the product or service. For example, Levi's attempted to stretch their brand to shoes but the venture failed.[35] In contrast, the international chain of exercise facilities for women, Curves, used their name to brand a cereal produced by General Mills—an effective stretch for the Curves brand.[36]

Add Benefits and Then Inform the Customer about Them

The publisher of a well-known magazine once changed their magazine's format in a very striking and attractive way. When the author asked how and when they informed customers about the change, they replied that they thought the customer would see the changes when they purchased the magazine. Such thinking, of course, is backward—one needs to inform customers about new benefits so that they might be persuaded to make a purchase.

Publishers of software often update their software but fail to effectively inform their customers as to why these changes are important—or even needed—and why the new version of the software should be purchased.

Close Gaps Between Customer Perceptions of Benefit Performance and Actual Performance

Considered one of the most effective advertising campaigns ever, the initial introduction of the Volkswagen Beetle to the United States in the 1950s, faced the problem of customer skepticism about foreign cars (rather difficult to believe today, but true). Volkswagen closed the gaps between perceived and actual benefits with fact-based ads about availability of spare parts, engine reliability, and resale value.[37]

Improve Performance and Then Tell the Customer— in That Order

In the telecommunications industry, sometimes companies have done this backwards, telling customers that their service has improved before the improvements have happened. Banks and fast food chains sometimes have made the same mistake—boasting about their customer service before the service was improved. In contrast, both British Air and Continental Airlines improved their customer service, then communicated the improvements to customers with great positive impact on sales.[38]

Jaguar automobiles had many serious performance problems during the 1980s. After Ford acquired the brand and fixed many of the problems, they ran a print advertisement which read: "The greatest challenge we've faced in sixty-two years of auto making. Changing your perception of Jaguar."[39]

Persuade the Customer That Certain Benefits Are Especially Important

The highlighted benefits would be those that the company does well. To persuade customers to change their priorities is not always easy. When Land Rover introduced the Discovery, they focused on the family market and emphasized the Discovery's seating capacity (at the time greater than most of their competitors). Seating capacity may not have been a priority benefit until Land Rover pointed it out.[40] Eastman Chemical has promoted their Spectar plastic by showing how its flexibility can be used to advantage in many fabrication situations.

Make It Easier to Purchase the Product or Service

There are many ways to make purchasing easier, making times or locations more convenient. For example, in many locations McDonald's outlets are open 24 hours a day, 7 days a week.[41] For many customers, purchasing on-line provides the most convenience. Nieman Marcus, among others, designs the home page the customer will see based on the customer's past purchases.[42] Expedia and Travelocity place considerable effort into making their Web sites both friendly and efficient.[43]

Be Sure Customers Know What Benefits They Receive

Heublein once introduced a product called Wine & Dine, an upscale easy-to-prepare pasta dish. One side of the package showed the pasta, the other side was cut out to show a bottle of chianti. The wine was intended to be used as part of the sauce for the pasta and was salted and spiced. Unfortunately, it seemed that many purchasers thought the wine was to be drunk with the pasta—and it tasted very bad due to the seasoning that had been included for the sauce. What was supposed to be a benefit became a liability because the customers did not understand what they were to do.[44]

If a benefit is not easy to see, for example, if equipment has high reliability, customers may need to be reminded of that benefit. For many years, Maytag employed an advertising campaign featuring the lonely Maytag repairman—lonely because "those darned Maytag appliances never break down."[45]

Ensuring the Customer Experience Is Positive

Focus on how customers are treated pays off in higher retention rates—the key parameter of the life-time customer value models discussed in Chapter 2, "How CVA® Affects Financial Performance." At Verizon, the mobile telephone "churn rates" (percentage of customers leaving) are more than 40 percent lower than those of their nearest competitors because of the consistency with which they treat their customers—over many quarters the highest rating in the American Customer Satisfaction Index (ACSI) for their category.[46]

Some studies have shown that in general approximately 60 percent of perceived value may be due to the experience with people associated with the product or service.[47] When employees and customers are satisfied, a "virtual circle" leading to higher profits is created.[48] Mini purchasers are made to feel part of a large, friendly community, including rallies and personalized service attention.[49] At HP, customer loyalty is developed by providing employee training in customer experience. A voice-of-the customer process stores all customer complaints on a company-wide data base and all complaints are handled within a few hours. Employees are rewarded for successes in satisfying customers.[50]

Bundling Perceived Value

When a customer buys a combination of products and services, it is called *bundling*. CVA®, then, depends on the customer value added associated with each product or service in the bundle. However, determining the CVA® of the bundle may require more analysis than simply adding the CVA® values associated with each product or service in the bundle. The act of bundling (for example, arranging for one-stop shopping) may add to the perceived values of the products or services and may lower the costs associated with providing them.

The Boeing 777: Managing Perceived Value

The Boeing 777 airplane family has captured the majority of the 300–400 seat commercial airplane market having sold more than 1000 airplanes since it first went into service in 1995.

Maximizing the perceived value of a product that has a list price starting at $200 million dollars is challenging as there are many variables that affect how the 777's value is perceived by airlines. At Boeing, we traditionally quantify the value of the 777 by determining how well the airplane fits in the airline's fleet and the value that it can bring to the airline in its operation over the life of the asset. This also involves comparing it to alternative fleet solutions available to the airline. This process involves detailed technical and economic evaluation.

- The evaluation begins with defining interiors and configurations that match the airline's brand and define the mission capability on the airline's specific network.
- The airline will typically have very detailed ground rules on how to evaluate fleet investment and new airplanes in terms of technical, technology, performance and maintenance

characteristics. Various technical briefings are used to convey these aspects to the airline and differentiate them from alternative solutions.

- Complex analytical models are used to simulate the revenue the 777 can bring to an airline and to quantify the 777 characteristics in operating and ownership cost.

Like other high-tech businesses, the global commercial aviation business is a very complex environment. At Boeing, we must think well beyond traditional marketing communication tactics, technical product comparisons, and detailed economic analysis. Though these are all critical aspects of the airline's evaluation process, many other areas must be considered that have a very real impact on the product's value in the mind of customers. Things like:

- **Design:** Did we include our customers early enough in the design process to ensure we meet or exceed their requirements? Are we offering the right features that will help the airline maximize their use of the product? Are we designing the brand into the product such that it represents the standard of excellence to differentiate our product from the competition?

- **Acquisition**: We may have the preferred product but do we have production capacity to satisfy the timing of the airline's network and fleet growth plans? What alternative lift solutions can we offer in the mean time? Can we assist the customer in obtaining more favorable financing terms? Can we offer to take older aircraft as trade-in to help facilitate the airline's transition to a more modern fuel efficient fleet?

- **Build**: Can we make the airplane configuration process easier? Does the customer feel engaged and informed throughout the production process? Are we delivering a quality product on-time that meets or exceeds customer expectations?

- **Introduction**: Can we offer training or other services to help mitigate the impact of introducing a new technology platform to the airline? Can we offer supply chain solutions to minimize inventory costs associated with introducing a

new airplane type? Can our on-site expert support team provide additional help to make the introduction into service
smoother?

- **In-Service:** Does the product perform as promised generating good revenue at a reasonable cost? Is the customer
  delighted with the airplane's introduction and in-service reliability such that they are willing to exercise follow-on
  orders? Are we continuously investing to improve the product to enhance its perceived value into the future?

These are just a few examples among many other variables that
affect the customer's perceived value in our business. More than
just marketing, managing perceived value is something that the
entire company has to understand and support because maintaining strong customer relationships is vital to Boeing's long-term success. It is critical at all levels of the organization to create an
awareness that every interaction the customer has with Boeing,
and our products, either adds to or detracts from the value the customer perceives they are receiving from our relationship.

—Steve Haro, 777 Brand Manager, Boeing

Reprinted with permission.

Measuring Perceived Value

"If one cannot measure it, one cannot manage it."

There are several possible ways to estimate a customer's perceived
value per unit:

- Value-in-Use
- Direct customer response
- Indirect customer response
- Judgment

Value-in-use is based on an economic comparison between the product or service the customer is using (or thinking of using) and the product or service for which perceived value needs to be estimated. First, the costs associated with the product or service currently being used are calculated. Next, the costs of utilizing the product or service under consideration are analyzed, where the unit price of that product or service is left as an unknown. Then that price for the product or service under consideration is calculated such that the costs of the current product or service and the new product or service are equal. If that price were charged, then, in economic terms, the customer would be indifferent between the two products or services. Therefore, that price would represent the perceived value per unit for that customer because at any price above that value, the customer would not purchase.

The value-in-use approach is especially useful when purchase decisions are made on the basis of functional and economic reasons and when the costs and benefits of using a product or service can be computed. When other reasons are involved in the purchase, such as emotional reasons or any reason that is difficult to quantify in monetary terms, the value-in-use method is less effective. Although, even in situations where purchase reasons are difficult to quantify, the value-in-use method does provide useful information in the form of a lower bound on the value of perceived value per unit.

One reservation to the value-in-use method is that the comparison is made to an existing product or service. The outcome depends on the choice of that product or service. In addition, for a totally new product or service, there may not be an appropriate product or service to which to make the comparison.

Value-in-use employs economic comparisons
to estimate perceived value.

Value-in-Use Calculation: Valve Case

Suppose a company uses a standard valve in their production line (Exhibit 4.6).

Currently they are paying $5 per valve and, for preventive maintenance, need to change the 200 valves in the production line six times per year. Each time they change the valves costs $5,000. Their total current costs for value for this production line is $36,000 per year.

A new valve needs to be changed only three times per year. If the unit price of that new value is $35, then the annual costs of using the old valve and the new valve would be identical. Thirty-five dollars is the estimate of the perceived value per unit or the maximum price for the new valve. Notice, however, that that estimated perceived value does not include the impact of the brand of the company making the new valve. If that company were new to the field, then the impact of their brand reputation on the perceived value of the valve would likely be low; but if the company were well-known in the valve industry (or even in a related industry) and had a positive reputation, for a benefit such as reliability, then the perceived value per valve would very likely be higher than $35 per valve.

Current Situation

Need to change every two months
at cost of $5000 per change.
Price per valve is $5.
Purchase consists of 200 valves.

Current Cost

200 x 6 x $5 + 6 x $5000
     = $36,000

Cost with New Product

200 x 3 x (?) + 3 x $5000
     = 600 x (?) + $15,000

Implies Max price = $35

Reprinted with permission from "Managing the ROI of Pricing," The Arrow Group, Ltd.®, New York, NY, 2008.

Exhibit 4.6   Value-in-Use analysis—Valve case

One can ask customers directly what they are willing to pay for a product or service. That is known as *direct customer response*. Examples of such questions are shown in Exhibit 4.7.

"How much are you willing to pay? _____

"Which of the following prices would you be willing to pay?

$5 ___ $7___ $10 ___ $12 ___

"How likely would you be willing to pay $10?

Not at all likely 1 2 3 4 5 6 7 Very likely

Reprinted with permission from "Managing the ROI of Pricing," The Arrow Group, Ltd.®, New York, NY, 2008.

Exhibit 4.7   Direct response example

The problem with asking customers directly what they are willing to pay is that most, if not all, customers realize that the reason the question is being asked is to help an organization set their price. Under such circumstances, it is difficult to imagine that a customer would be completely honest in answering the question. They would be much more likely to give a low price for their answer in order to influence the organization to charge a lower price.

Indirect customer response methods try to avoid the bias of direct customer response methods by asking questions in a more realistic way. With constrained choice methods, for example, the respondent cannot simply choose the lowest price available as there are consequences for selecting the lowest price—the benefits of the product or service change depending on the price chosen.

Constrained choice methods include both conjoint analysis and discrete choice modeling. Both are similar in concept.[51]

In *conjoint analysis*, a respondent is presented with several alternative bundles of benefits for the product or service—different price levels, different brand names (including a generic brand), different benefits, and different performance levels for benefits. The respondent is asked to designate the bundle of benefits that would be his or her first choice. Typically researchers learn very little from this first question, as customers will choose the most benefits at the cheapest price.

The second and succeeding questions, however, can provide a lot of insight into how the customer makes his or her decision. The respondent is told that his or her first choice has now been removed from the list and he or she must give a second choice. At this point, if the respondent wants to stay at the same price level, he or she will need to give up one of the benefits. The respondent, then, will have to make a trade-off; and so, sometimes conjoint analysis is known as *trade-off analysis*.

As the respondent makes successive choices, those alternatives are removed from consideration. This process reveals the order of preference among the alternatives for the customer. In turn, that allows estimates of the overall perceived value to that customer for any bundle of benefits.

In such an analysis, both functional and emotional benefits can be included. Of special importance, the brand can also be included so one can estimate the impact of the brand—even the separate impact of a corporate brand and a product or service brand. Such estimates can play a major role in estimating the value of a brand as explained in Chapter 3, "CVA® over Time."

Besides overall perceived value, constrained choice methods also provide estimates of the change in perceived value corresponding to changes in the bundle of benefits offered the target customer. The changes in perceived value represent marginal revenue to the organization. They can be compared to the cost of providing the benefits associated with the perceived value changes, the *marginal cost*. As long as the change in perceived value per unit is greater than the change in costs per unit, then CVA® is increased.

The comparison of changes in perceived value per unit and costs per unit is at the heart of *value-engineering*. Product or service changes should be considered if they increase CVA®. That includes both changes that increase perceived value per unit more than they increase costs per unit and changes that decrease costs per unit more than they decrease perceived value per unit.

Remember that to monetize perceived value, one of the attributes in the analysis must be price.

Discrete choice modeling is similar in approach. However, with that technique, it is not necessary to provide the respondent with every possible combination of benefits and prices.

Constrained choice methods have all the usual reservations of any statistical technique, both random error and systematic error (or bias). Nonetheless, such methods are essential to understanding and monitoring perceived value over time.

Constrained choice methods allow the monetization of perceived value.

Conjoint Analysis: Motel Room Case

Suppose a motel chain is attempting to estimate perceived value for a one-room stay. Included in the analysis are the possibility of a free breakfast and the brand name of the chain (Table 4.2).

Table 4.2   Conjoint Analysis—Motel Room Case

Order of Preference	Well-known Chain Brand	"Free" Breakfast	Room Rate per Night	Utility Value
5	Chain brand	Free	$300	4
7	No brand	Free	300	2
6	Chain brand	Not free	300	3
8	No brand	Not free	300	1
1	Chain brand	Free	200	8
3	No brand	Free	200	6
2	Chain brand	Not free	200	7
4	No brand	Not free	200	5

Reprinted with permission from "Managing the ROI of Pricing," The Arrow Group, Ltd.®, New York, NY, 2008.

Initially, the respondent is presented with eight choices: two price levels ($200 or $300), two branding levels (with and without the chain brand name), and two breakfast levels (free or not).

Suppose the respondent's first choice is: Chain brand, free breakfast, and $200 per night. That choice is then removed from the list and the respondent asked to select from the remaining seven alternatives. In this illustration, the respondent chooses to stay at the $200 price level but trade-off the free breakfast in order to keep the price at that level. The respondent would select in order all the alternatives. The order of the choices would provide the information to estimate the respondent's perceived value for the motel room.

As shown in Table 4.2, the respondent's ranking of the alternatives are converted into utilities by assigning the first choice the utility value of *8*, the second choice the utility value of *7*, and so forth. The utility associated with each level of an attribute is estimated by finding the difference between the total of the utilities for one level of an attribute and the total of the utilities for the other level of that attribute (Exhibit 4.8). For example, the total of the utilities for all combinations including a free breakfast is *20*, while the total utilities for all combinations not including a free breakfast is *16;* so, the number of utility units associated with the free breakfast is the difference of 20 and 16 or *4*.

Chain Brand versus No Brand = (22 – 14) = 8 utility units

Free Breakfast versus No Free Breakfast = (20 – 16) = 4 utility units

$200 versus $300 = (26 – 10) = 16 utility units

So one utility unit = ($300 – $200) / 16 = $6.25

Converting utility units into money:

Chain Brand is worth $50 to this customer since

8 X $6.25 = $50

Free Breakfast is worth $25 to this customer since

4 X $6.25 = $25

Reprinted with permission from "Managing the ROI of Pricing," The Arrow Group, Ltd.®, New York, NY, 2008.

Exhibit 4.8   Motel room example utilities

To convert the utilities to dollars, notice that the difference in utilities between a price of $200 and a price of $300—a $100 difference—is *16* utility units, or $6.25 for one utility unit. The value of a free breakfast to this customer would then be estimated at the monetary equivalent of four utility units or $25. If it costs less than $25 to provide the free breakfast, then adding the free breakfast would increase CVA® to this customer and should be considered.

The *relative* utilities can also be estimated with regression analysis, where the dependent variable is the utility value of each combination, and the independent variables are the attributes coded as binary variables (1 for Chain Brand, 1 for Free Breakfast, 1 for $200 Room Rate, 0 otherwise). The relative utilities are given by the estimated regression coefficients in Table 4.3. Notice that they have the same relation as the utilities calculated earlier—for example, the value of a free breakfast is one unit compared to the four units for the $100 price difference, suggesting the breakfast is worth one-quarter of the price difference or $25.

Table 4.3   Motel Room Example Using Regression Analysis to Estimate Utility Units

	Regression Coefficients (Relative Utility Units)	Standard Error of Regression Coefficient
Intercept	1	2.81004E-16
Chain	2	2.81004E-16
Breakfast	1	2.81004E-16
Price	4	2.81004E-16

Reprinted with permission from "Managing the ROI of Pricing," The Arrow Group, Ltd.®, New York, NY, 2008.

Perceived value can also be estimated with *judgment*. Such estimates may be more likely to be inaccurate than those from approaches such as value-in-use or constrained choice methods. However, if there are budget or time pressures, it may be necessary to employ judgment methods.

The judgment approach begins by surveying the current products or services and their market prices. Then, the product or service under consideration is systematically compared to the other products with respect to benefits provided and performance on those benefits, much like the perceived value analysis described in Chapter 6, "Managing CVA®." Finally, an estimate of perceived value is made subjectively based on those product-to-product or service-to-service comparisons.

Dangers to the judgment approach include making estimates without consulting customers. Most of the major marketing disasters of all time, such as Polavision instant home movies, the RCA VideoDisc for recording video, or the Tigershark fighter aircraft, were designed with minimal input from customers. Organizations proceed without some form of customer input at their peril.

The judgment approach also has the same limitation of the value-in-use approach, namely, that the estimates are being made in comparison to a selected set of products or services. If these products or services do not represent the appropriate comparisons, or if there is no appropriate product or service to compare to the product under consideration, then the judgment-derived perceived value estimates may not be relevant to the situation.

Charles Schwab: Back to Basics: Test Markets Inform and Validate Marketing Investment

Going into 2005, the brokerage firm Charles Schwab was in turn-around mode, focused on cutting expenses and restoring our customer value proposition. The marketing budget was cut significantly, with only a small allocation for retail advertising. The company needed to grow, but the risk of spending ineffectively was one that nobody wanted. With a refreshed brand positioning and a new advertising platform, but no advertising running nationally, we made the decision to go back to basics: an integrated marketing test using three sets of matched markets to determine the impact and return of a competitive level of marketing investment.

Within six months, we saw significant impact on key business metrics—notably new accounts and net new assets from new households—and on Schwab brand perceptions and preference. We launched "Talk to Chuck" nationally in the fall of 2005. We built an econometric model and continued local market testing to inform spending strategies and monitor returns. With renewed focus on clients, consistent financial discipline and a rigorous approach to marketing investment, Schwab's net income grew from $286M in

2004 to $2,407M in 2007, while our pretax profit margin* grew from 16 percent to 37.1 percent. Profitable growth was back.

—Becky Saeger, Executive Vice President and Chief Marketing Officer, Charles Schwab

*Results have been adjusted to reflect the divestiture of U.S. Trust.

Reprinted with permission of Becky Saeger.

Estimating Demand Curves

Recall a demand curve reflects the perceived value per unit for a given product or service for all those customers in a market (Exhibit 4.9). Therefore, perceived value per unit can be estimated by estimating the relevant demand curve. Demand curves are well-known in theory but less so in practice. A 2008 Interbrand survey of senior marketing executives found that fewer than 50 percent claimed that they "quantitatively" understood how their brand impacts demand.[52]

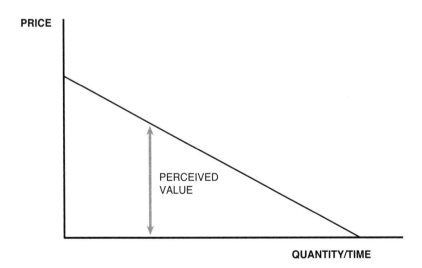

Reprinted with permission from "Managing Pricing ROI," The Arrow Group, Ltd.®, New York, NY, 2008.

Exhibit 4.9   The demand curve

There are several ways to estimate a demand curve:

- Customer value research
- Historical analysis
- Experimental analysis
- Judgment

Customer value research consists of applying techniques such as conjoint analysis and discrete choice modeling. If perceived value for a specific product or service, such as was done in the motel room example, is estimated for each of several customers in the target market, then those perceived value estimates, coupled with estimates of the numbers of customers for each perceived value level, can produce a demand curve.

Historical analysis employs econometric methods to estimate the parameters of a demand curve (Exhibit 4.10). Notice that in the typical analysis, the dependent variable is quantity of units sold, while the independent variables include price. That means that to compute CVA®, it may be necessary to rewrite the estimated relationship between quantity and price as the relationship between price and quantity.[53]

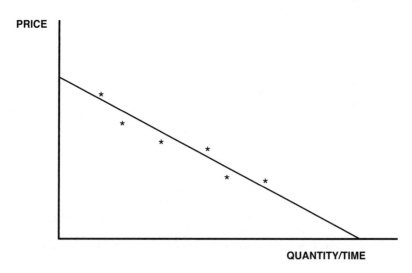

QUANTITY/TIME

* Price and quantity observations

Exhibit 4.10   Estimating the demand curve

Demand Curve Estimation Men's Shaving Cream

The data for this example includes unit sales and price for various market segments of men who use shaving cream as well as customer evaluations on a scale of 0 to 5 of the brand's attributes with respect to benefits such as close shaving and moisturizing.

Ordinary least squares regression analysis was used to estimate the relationship between unit sales and price and the various brand attributes as perceived by the customers. Partial results (disguised for reasons of confidentiality) are shown in Table 4.4.

Table 4.4   Regression Results—Men's Shaving Cream

Variable	Estimate	Standard Error	t-value	p-value
Intercept	126,483	24,512	5.16	<.0001
Price	-9,674	3,120	-3.10	.0024
Close-shaving	8,223	3,302	2.49	.0140
Moisturizing	6,846	727	9.42	<.0001

The quantity-price relationship is estimated as:

$Q = 126{,}483 - 9{,}674\,P + 8{,}223\,CS + 6{,}846\,M$

Where:

Q = Quantity
P = Price
CS = Close-Shaving Performance
M = Moisturizing Performance

Rewriting the relationship as a demand curve produces the following:

$P = 13.0745 - .000103\,Q + .85\,CS + .71\,M$

The Y-intercept—value of price when unit demand is 0—is $13.07. That would estimate the maximum perceived value for a specific bundle of brand attributes (minimal performance or 0 scores on the close-shaving and moisturizing variables). As benefit performance is improved, or benefits are added, or the bundle of benefits is more effectively communicated to the target customers, the demand curve shifts to the right and the maximum perceived value increases.

The y-intercept estimate, such as $13.07, would be used in the calculations of CVA®.

With *experimental design*, prices are manipulated so that the impact of different price levels on unit demand can be seen. There are various approaches to experiments—the two extremes being a fully controlled experiment and a randomized experiment.[54]

In a fully controlled experiment, all factors that may have an influence on sales, such as price, advertising, packaging, and promotion, are explicitly manipulated in order to isolate the effect of the variable of interest, for example, price. Almost the opposite occurs in a randomized design, where only the variable of interest, price, is explicitly altered. The experiment is arranged so that the levels of all other variables, such as advertising, can be assumed to be equal for each of the different price levels.

In experiments conducted outside laboratories in the real word, randomized designs are much more feasible than completely controlled experiments because there may always be factors beyond the experimenter's control, such as competitors' actions or the weather, which can lead to systematic bias in the results. In fact, sometimes competitors may deliberately alter their marketing mix to confound the results of an experiment.

Judgment is also a viable way to estimate demand curves. While judgment estimates cannot be evaluated with statistical tests, they can still be useful in practice. The Groupe Le Soleil case in Chapter 2 was based on a judgmentally estimated demand curve.

Demand curves show perceived value per unit
for all customers in a market.

Conclusions

Perceived value is the heart of how marketing and branding affect financial performance. Perceived value *can* be estimated in monetary terms a variety of ways.

Design and communications provide ongoing control over perceived value. Branding creates long-term perceived value and long-term financial results.

While perceived value determines the upper bound of CVA®, cost per unit determines the lower bound. The next chapter discusses costs relevant to CVA®.

5

Costs

For many organizations, how they classify and report costs makes it very difficult, if not impossible, to determine the impact of their marketing and branding activities on financial performance. While more and more organizations have moved to some form of activity-based accounting, where costs can be more easily separated into categories such as variable and fixed costs and indirect and direct costs, there remain many organizations that continue to struggle by using average costs for marketing decision-making.

Especially pernicious is the widespread use of average full costs, where overhead is spread over all units of the product or service—almost always arbitrarily. Use of average full costs can distort decision-making for nearly all marketing decisions.

To utilize the concept of CVA® most effectively requires the capability of identifying incremental costs per unit. This chapter examines what costs are relevant to CVA® and to sound marketing decision-making.[1]

The Income Statement in Custodial Format

Exhibit 5.1 is an income statement, deliberately simplified to focus on how costs need to be classified for application of CVA® concepts. The presentation is in what is called *custodial format*—an accounting presentation of *past* performance. Unfortunately, with revenue and costs presented in the custodial format, there is no way for a manager to answer a question such as, "What happens to contribution and to profit if unit sales increase by 10 percent?"

Sales (500,000 units @ $5)		$2,500
Costs of Goods Sold		
Materials	500	
Direct labor	400	
Manufacturing		
overhead	400	
Total		1,300
Gross Margin		1,200
Expenses		
Advertising	100	
Selling	300	
Management	250	
General and		
administrative	350	
Total		1,000
Profit before taxes		200

Reprinted with permission from "Financial Analysis for Marketing," The Arrow Group, Ltd.®, New York, NY, 2008.

Exhibit 5.1   Income statement in custodial format (000)

Managers need to be able to use accounting information to look forward, not backward. By classifying costs into variable and fixed costs, the custodial format can be transformed into *contribution format*, which enables a manager to develop forecasts of future financial performance. (A contribution accounting format is very similar to the approaches followed in activity based accounting.[2])

Many accounting systems look backward.
What they should do is help managers look forward.

The custodial income statement shows total revenue is $2,500,000 from sales of 500,000 units at a unit price of $5. *Costs of goods sold* include material, direct labor, and manufacturing overhead (depreciation, utilities, property taxes, etc.) Revenue minus the cost of goods sold is *gross margin*.

The expenses assigned to this business consist of advertising (both for the product and for the corporation), selling (salaries plus commissions), management, and general and administrative (G&A). The G&A is the corporate overhead and includes items such as various corporate departments (such as accounting, human resources, and marketing research), expenses associated with headquarters, and the salaries of C-level executives.

Profit before taxes is gross margin minus expenses or $200,000.

Types of Costs

To convert the custodial accounting statement to one in contribution format requires classifying costs into fixed and variable.

A *fixed cost* is any cost that does not change with unit sales (Exhibit 5.2). Typical fixed costs are rent, property taxes, plant and equipment, salaries without any bonus component, and most kinds of advertising. *Average fixed costs per unit* is simply fixed costs divided by units.

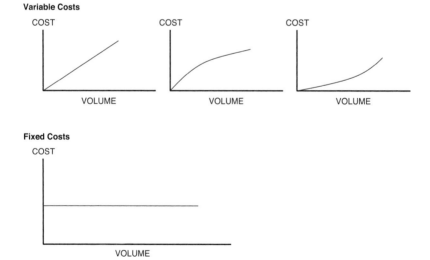

Exhibit 5.2   Types of costs

A *variable cost* is any cost that changes with unit sales (Exhibit 5.2). Typical variable costs include raw material costs, component costs, energy costs, sales commissions, promotion costs, and the costs of certain kinds of advertising such as cooperative advertising, where allowances are given to resellers on the basis of units.

Variable costs are commonly assumed to increase linearly with unit sales, but may increase in a nonlinear fashion. However, even if variable costs are nonlinear functions of volume, they can often be approximated with a set of linear functions (Exhibit 5.3).

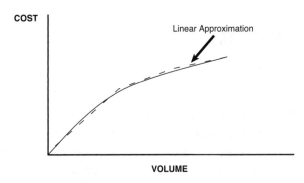

Exhibit 5.3   Nonlinear variable costs

Clearly, there is a grey area in classifying costs as variable or fixed. In the long run, any cost will increase with volume because new capacity becomes necessary. Usually one classifies costs over a given volume range, indicating which costs are variable and which costs are fixed within that volume range. If sales are beyond that range, then the variable cost per unit and the fixed costs are changed (Exhibit 5.4).

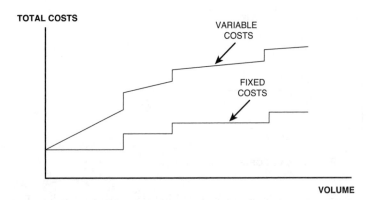

Reprinted with permission from "Financial Analysis for Marketing," The Arrow Group, Ltd., New York, NY, 2008.

Exhibit 5.4   Costs over time

THERE ARE
NO
REAL
BARGAINS ~

THE FULL COST
OF EVERYTHING
IS ALWAYS PAID
BY SOMEBODY.

© Ashleigh Brilliant, 2008. Used with permission.

The Income Statement in Contribution Format

To convert an income statement from custodial format to contribution format, all costs and expenses are divided between those that are variable and those that are fixed.

In Exhibit 5.5, variable costs consist of material, direct labor, variable manufacturing overhead costs such as utilities, and sales commissions. Revenue minus variable costs is the *contribution* or *variable margin* of this business—the incremental profit from sales.

Fixed costs consist of advertising, selling, management, and G&A. Contribution minus fixed costs is the profit before taxes.

In both the custodial and the contribution format, profit before taxes remains $200,000. Changing the presentation format of the income statement, of course, does not change the financial results! Changing the format does, however, allow more insight into costs and their impact going forward.

Sales (500,000 units @ $5)		$2,500
Variable Costs		
Material	500	
Direct labor	400	
Manufacturing overhead (variable)	350	
Commission (10%)	250	
Total		1,500
Contribution (or Variable Margin)		1,000
Fixed Costs		
Advertising	100	
Selling	50	
Management	250	
Manufacturing overhead (fixed)	50	
General and administrative	350	
Total		800
Profit (before taxes)		200

Reprinted with permission from "Financial Analysis for Marketing," The Arrow Group, Ltd.®, New York, NY, 2008.

Exhibit 5.5   Income statement in contribution format (000)

For example, the question, "What happens to contribution and profit if unit sales increase by 10 percent?" can now be easily answered with the information presented in Exhibit 5.5.

If sales increase by 10 percent, or $250,000, then variable costs increase 10 percent, or $150,000, resulting in a 10 percent increase in contribution, or $100,000. Because fixed costs do not change when sales increase, profit increases by the entire change in contribution—$100,000. A 10 percent increase in sales leads to a 50 percent increase in profit!

Zappos: Evaluating Costs and Creating Value for Customers

At Zappos.com, we take a very different approach to marketing. We believe that our best form of marketing is through repeat customers and word of mouth, so most of the money that we would have spent on paid advertising we instead put into the customer experience. Here are some of the things we do:

- Free shipping
- Free return shipping
- 365-day return policy

By offering free shipping both ways, many customers will order 10 pairs of shoes, try them on with 10 different outfits in the comfort of their living room, and return the ones that don't fit or don't look good—with Zappos.com paying the shipping back to us.

We run our warehouse around the clock, which actually isn't the most efficient way to run a warehouse, but it gets the orders out to our customers as quickly as possible. Combined with our surprise upgrades to expedited shipping, many customers order as late as midnight Eastern and are surprised to find their order on their doorstep 8 hours later.

We also run our Customer Loyalty Team (our call center) 24/7, and unlike most web sites, we put our 1-800 number at the top of every single page of our web site, because we actually want to talk to our customers!

Our call center is run very differently from most call centers. We don't measure call times like most call centers do, because it causes the reps to try to get the customer off the phone as quickly as possible. We also don't have scripts, because we want our customers to feel like they have a personal, emotional connection with us. And we don't try to upsell customers like a lot of call centers do.

In fact, if a customer is looking for a specific pair of shoes and we're out of stock of their size, every rep is actually trained to look on at least 3 other web sites, and if they find the shoe on another web site, to direct the customer to that web site. We'll lose that sale, but we're not interested in trying to maximize every transaction. Instead, we're interested in building a life-long relationship with each of our customers.

We started out with almost no sales in 1999, and we are currently on track to do about $1 billion in gross merchandise sales in 2008.

> The #1 driver of that growth has been from repeat customers and word of mouth, and we intend that to be our strategy moving forward. By putting most of the money that we would have spent on paid advertising into improving the customer experience instead, we believe that we can continue to grow for the foreseeable future.
>
> All of the things that I've described are not free. But our belief is that even though they cost more, they result in much higher value for our customers and bring us closer to our goal of having the Zappos.com brand be about the very best customer service and the very best customer experience.
>
> —Tony Hsieh, CEO, Zappos.com
> Printed with permission

Identifying Costs for CVA®

Determining CVA® requires knowing the variable or incremental delivered cost per unit—the lower bound of CVA®, *Variable cost per unit*, is calculated by dividing variable costs by unit sales (Exhibit 5.6).

Average Cost Per Unit	= All Costs/Unit Sales
Average Cost Rate	= All Costs/Dollar Sales
Variable Cost Per Unit	= Variable Costs/Unit Sales
Variable Cost Rate	= Variable Costs/Dollar Sales
	= Variable Cost Per Unit/Price
Gross Margin Per Unit	= Gross Margin/Unit Sales
Gross Margin Rate	= Gross Margin/Dollar Sales
Contribution or Variable Margin Per Unit	= Contribution/Unit Sales
Contribution or Variable Margin Rate	= Contribution/Dollar Sales
	= Contribution Per Unit/Price

Exhibit 5.6   Accounting concepts

Variable cost per unit is always less than *average total cost per unit* because average total cost per unit is the sum of variable cost per unit and average fixed cost per unit (Exhibit 5.7). That means that calculating CVA® with average total cost per unit instead of variable cost per unit will always underestimate CVA®.

Exhibit 5.7 Example of Costs

Unit Volume (000)	Variable Costs (000)	Fixed Costs (000)	Total Costs (000)	Variable Cost per Unit	Average Fixed Cost per Unit	Average Total Cost per Unit
100	$300	$800	$1100	$3.00	$8.00	$11.00
200	$600	$800	$1400	$3.00	$4.00	$7.00
300	$900	$800	$1700	$3.00	$2.67	$5.67
400	$1200	$800	$2000	$3.00	$2.00	$5.00
500	$1500	$800	$2300	$3.00	$1.60	$4.60
1000	$3000	$800	$3800	$3.00	$0.80	$3.80

Reprinted with permission from "Financial Analysis for Marketing," The Arrow Group, Ltd.®, New York, NY, 2008.

Using average cost per unit in place of variable cost per unit underestimates CVA®.

If the income statement is in contribution format, it is possible to find variable cost per unit. If the income statement is in custodial format, it is not possible to find variable cost per unit—and therefore not possible to determine CVA®. With an income statement in custodial format, often average total cost per unit is employed in place of variable cost per unit, biasing CVA® low, which, in turn, may result in underspending on marketing activities.

Price minus variable cost per unit is the *contribution per unit* or the *variable margin per unit*. Contribution per unit can also be found by dividing contribution by unit sales.

Both variable cost per unit and contribution per unit can be expressed as percentages of price—the *variable cost rate* and the *contribution or variable margin rate*, respectively. The contribution rate represents the incremental profit as a percentage of incremental sales and is constant within any interval for which the variable cost per unit is constant.

The contribution or variable margin rate allows managers to evaluate marketing decisions incrementally.

The contribution or variable margin rate can be very useful for evaluating marketing and branding decisions. The *gross margin rate*—gross margin per unit as a percentage of sales—differs from the contribution or variable margin rate and cannot provide estimates of incremental profit due to marketing or branding decisions.

Employing the Variable Margin Rate

Consider the income statement shown in Exhibit 5.5. Currently, sales are $2,500,000 at $5 per unit.

Suppose price is decreased or increased. How must unit sales change if contribution is to remain constant at $1,000,000?

Note that any price decrease proportionately decreases contribution per unit even more, while any price increase proportionately increases margin per unit even more.

For example, suppose a product is priced at $5 with a variable cost per unit equal to $3 and a contribution per unit of $2 (Exhibit 5.8). If sales are currently 500,000 units, then the total variable margin is $1,000,000. If price is decreased by 20 percent, then contribution per unit falls by 50 percent from $2 to $1 per unit (and the contribution rate goes from 40 percent to 25 percent). After such a price cut, unit sales must double to 1,000,000 units just to maintain the current contribution. If unit sales do not at least double, contribution falls.

On the other hand, if price is increased by 20 percent, then contribution per unit increases by 50 percent, from $2 to $3 (and the contribution rate goes to 50 percent). Then, if unit sales do not fall more than one-third (below 333,333 units), contribution increases.

The changes in unit sales needed to compensate for various price changes for a given variable margin rate is shown in Exhibit 5.9. For example, if the current variable margin rate is 40 percent (as in the example above), then if price is decreased by 20 percent, unit sales must double if total contribution or variable margin is to be maintained, as can be seen in the body of the table. Similarly, if the current variable margin rate is 40 percent and price is increased by 20 percent, then if unit sales are 67 percent of current sales, contribution or variable margin rate is maintained.

Exhibit 5.8   Maintaining Contribution with Price Changes

	Present	Price Decrease	Price Increase
Price	$5	$4	$6
Variable Cost per Unit	$3	$3	$3
Contribution or Variable Margin per Unit	$2	$1	$3
Unit Sales	500,000	1,000,000	333,333
Contribution or Variable Margin	$1,000,000	$1,000,000	$1,000,000
Contribution or Variable Margin Rate	.40	.25	.50

Reprinted with permission from "Financial Analysis for Marketing," The Arrow Group, Ltd.®, New York, NY, 2008.

Necessary percentage of current unit sales to maintain current contribution margin.

Proposed Price Change (%)	Current Contribution Rate or Variable Margin Rate																		
	10	15	20	25	30	35	40	45	50	55	60	65	70	75	80	85	90	95	100
+ 25	29	38	45	50	55	58	62	64	66	69	71	72	74	75	76	77	78	79	80
+ 20	33	43	50	56	60	64	67	69	72	73	75	76	78	79	81	81	82	83	83
+ 15	40	50	57	63	67	70	73	75	77	79	80	81	82	83	85	85	86	86	87
+ 10	50	60	67	72	73	78	80	82	83	85	86	87	88	88	89	89	90	90	91
+ 5	67	75	80	83	86	88	89	90	91	92	92	93	93	94	94	94	95	95	95
0	100	100	100	100	100	100	100	100	100	100	100	10	100	100	100	100	100	100	100
- 5	200	150	133	125	123	117	114	113	111	110	109	108	108	107	107	106	106	106	105
- 10		300	200	167	150	140	133	129	125	122	120	118	117	115	114	113	113	112	111
- 15			400	280	200	175	160	150	143	138	133	130	127	125	123	121	125	119	118
- 20				500	300	233	200	180	167	157	150	144	140	136	133	131	129	127	125
- 25					600	350	267	225	200	183	175	163	156	150	145	142	138	136	133

Reprinted with permission from "Financial Analysis for Marketing," The Arrow Group, Ltd., New York, NY, 2008.

Exhibit 5.9   Price Changes, Variable Margin Rate, and Unit Sales Change

Using average total costs as the basis for pricing does not allow one to see the substantial effects that may be associated with price changes.

Graphing Contribution

Contribution is simply revenue minus variable costs as shown in Exhibit 5.10.

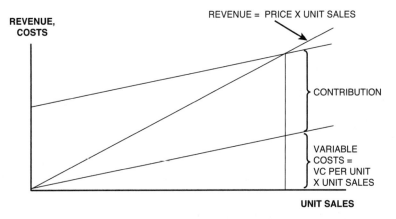

Reprinted with permission from "Financial Analysis for Marketing," The Arrow Group, Ltd.®, New York, NY, 2008.

Exhibit 5.10   Contribution

Revenue is the product of price and unit sales, while *variable costs* are the product of variable cost per unit and unit sales. Because price is assumed to be greater than variable cost per unit, contribution—the difference between revenue and variable costs—increases with unit sales. In the example used in the chapter, at unit sales of 500,000 units, contribution is $1,000,000.

Fixed Costs

Fixed costs have no impact on maximizing contribution because fixed costs exist regardless of what marketing and branding decisions are made. Fixed costs *do* have an impact on *profit*, which is calculated as contribution minus fixed costs. In general, the role of fixed costs is to determine net financial performance (including whether to stay in business) and whether or not a fixed outlay should be made on advertising or some other marketing activity that might affect CVA®.

Breakeven Sales Level

Total fixed costs determine the *breakeven sales level* of an organization. The breakeven sales level is that level of sales at which revenue covers all costs or where contribution is exactly equal to the fixed costs (Exhibit 5.11).

Breakeven Level	=	Sales Level When Revenue Equals Variable Costs and All Fixed Costs
	=	Fixed Costs/Contribution Rate
Shutdown Level	=	Sales Level When Revenue Equals Variable Costs and All Direct Fixed Costs
	=	Direct Fixed Costs/Contribution Rate

Exhibit 5.11   Benchmark sales levels

The fixed costs in the income statement presented earlier in Exhibit 5.5 are $800,000. The breakeven sales level is calculated by dividing fixed costs by the contribution rate of 0.40. When sales are $2,000,000 or 400,000 units, contribution is exactly equal to fixed costs; and so, sales are at the breakeven level (Exhibit 5.12).

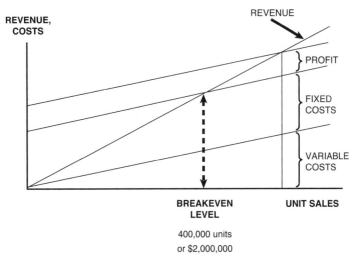

Exhibit 5.12   Breakeven sales level

Using the Right Cost Information: The Atlantic versus Pacific Case*

The Atlantic Company sells a commodity product through distributors. There is no close substitute for the product, so total industry demand is price insensitive. However, within the industry, demand for each competitor's product is price sensitive.

There are ten companies in the industry. Eight are local suppliers, each with a market share of 2% or less. The Atlantic Company is the market share leader. The Pacific Company is second in share and is Atlantic's strongest competitor.

Over the past six months, Pacific has increased its share by 2%, primarily from Atlantic's share of the market. New managers have recently taken control of Pacific and have declared their intention to continue to increase Pacific's share aggressively.

The current financial situation for each company is shown in Exhibit 5.13.

Exhibit 5.13 Atlantic Versus Pacific current situation (in millions)

	Atlantic	Pacific
Share	64%	18%
Sales	$320.0	$90.0
Variable Costs	176.0	54.0
Variable Margin	144.0	36.0
Fixed Costs	64.0	26.0
Profit	80.0	10.0
Variable Cost Rate	55%	60%
Variable Margin Rate	45%	40%
Capacity Utilization	85%	75%

Reprinted with permission from "Atlantic Company Case," The Arrow Group, Ltd.®, New York, NY, 2008.

The Pacific Company managers want to increase share. What should the managers of the Atlantic Company do?

In a world where there is no opportunity to target customers or to differentiate one product from another, the main weapon for increasing share is price. Incidentally, this situation is described by economists as *perfect competition*, but is not so perfect from the viewpoint of marketing managers.

If they cut price, the Pacific Company can increase its share. The first question for the Atlantic Company managers is: How much damage can a Pacific price cut do to their business?

Because the Pacific Company is currently at 75% capacity, in the short run the most sales it could achieve would be the sales that would fill its capacity. In the longer run, Pacific can expand its capacity; but in the short run the most sales it can garner is $120 million at current prices. Therefore the most damage that the Pacific Company can do to the Atlantic Company is to cut Atlantic's sales by $30 million at current prices.

The next question for the Atlantic Company managers concerns how should they respond to a Pacific Company price decrease? The Atlantic Company can ignore the price cut, follow it, or cut price even more, itself.

The effects of the scenarios on the financial performance of each company are shown in Exhibit 5.14. As an example, for Scenario I, assume that the Pacific Company decreases its price by 5%.

Exhibit 5.14   Atlantic versus Pacific Scenario I (in millions)

Atlantic Does Not Follow	Atlantic	Pacific
Sales	$290.0	$114.0
Variable Costs	159.5	72.0
Variable Margin	130.5	42.0
Fixed Costs	64.0	26.0
Profit	66.5	16.0
Atlantic Follows	**Atlantic**	**Pacific**
Sales	$304.0	$85.5
Variable Costs	176.0	54.0
Variable Margin	128.0	31.5
Fixed Costs	64.0	26.0
Profit	64.0	5.5

Reprinted with permission from "Atlantic Company Case," The Arrow Group, Ltd.®, New York, NY, 2008.

If the Atlantic Company ignores the Pacific Company 5% price cuts, then Atlantic's sales decrease by $30 million and its profits by $ 13.5 million. If it matches the price cut, its sales decrease by $16 million and its profits by $16 million. Note that if Atlantic, in turn, cuts price an *additional* 5% for an overall price decrease of 10%, then its sales decrease by $32 million and its profits decrease by $32 million.

All of these scenarios result in much lower financial performance for the Atlantic Company. Sometimes there is hope that an aggressive response and further price cutting might discourage a company like the Pacific Company—but at what cost to the Atlantic

Company? Moreover, even if the Atlantic Company succeeds in putting the Pacific Company out of business (and there may be legal issues in doing so), the Pacific Company capacity still remains; and another group of investors might decide to enter the market and continue the pressure on the Atlantic Company.

A totally different way to respond to the Pacific Company is to adopt a proactive strategy rather than a reactive strategy. The Pacific Company managers have declared their intention to increase market share. Why not give them what they want—without waiting for them to cut prices?

Suppose the Atlantic Company increases its price before the Pacific Company cuts the price. The possible effects of such a scenario are shown in Exhibit 5.15. As an example, for Scenario II, suppose that the Atlantic Company price increase is 5%.

Exhibit 5.15   Atlantic versus Pacific Scenario II (in millions)

Pacific Does Not Follow	Atlantic	Pacific
Sales	$304.5	$120.0
Variable Costs	159.5	72.0
Variable Margin	145.0	48.0
Fixed Costs	64.0	26.0
Profit	81.0	22.0

Pacific Follows	Atlantic	Pacific
Sales	$336.0	$94.5
Variable Costs	176.0	54.0
Variable Margin	160.0	40.5
Fixed Costs	64.0	26.0
Profit	96.0	14.5

Reprinted with permission from "Atlantic Company Case," The Arrow Group, Ltd.®, New York, NY, 2008.

If the Pacific Company does not increase its prices in response, then the Atlantic Company's sales are $ 304.5 million and its profits are $81 million. If the Pacific Company raises its prices as well, then the Atlantic Company's sales are $336 million and profits are

$96 million. Either case leads to financial returns that are superior to the case in which the Pacific Company cuts price first, regardless of the Atlantic Company's response to the price cut.

By pre-empting the price change, the Atlantic Company achieves stronger financial results. Those results are lower than what the company enjoyed before the Pacific Company made clear its intentions to expand market share; but, if a company is targeted by a price-cutter and there are no ways to compete other than price, then it is certain the company's financial results will suffer. The issue is to maintain as much of sales and profits as is possible during such an encounter.

To effectively cope with a price-cutting competitor, it is essential to know one's variable and fixed costs. If the Atlantic Company were basing their decisions on average costs, it would be very likely that it would not be able to evaluate accurately the effects of the various scenarios on its financial performance.

The broader lesson is that perceived value and CVA® play a very limited role in what are commonly referred to as *commodity markets*. Such competitive environments may be unavoidable; but, when they occur, often the low-cost producer is the only winner. In turn, that reinforces the need to target customers and innovate continually to add value for the target customer—and then use branding and other marketing tools effectively to ensure that the target customer appreciates the value that is being provided.

° All names are fictitious and any similarities to real organizations or people are coincidental.

Source: "The Atlantic Company," © The Arrow Group, Ltd., New York, NY, 2008. Used with permission.

Direct and Indirect Fixed Costs

The classification of fixed costs as direct or indirect is at the core of decisions to carry on with a business or to stop the business. Direct fixed costs determine when a business should be shut down.

A *direct fixed cost* is any cost that disappears if the activity under consideration disappears. For example, if an advertising campaign promotes only one specific product or brand and that product or brand ceases to exist, then there is no reason for the advertising campaign—and it would disappear. In that case, the advertising campaign is *direct* to the product or brand.

An *indirect fixed cost* is any cost that persists even if the activity under consideration disappears. Corporate advertising campaigns would be indirect to all products and services because if they disappeared, the corporate campaign would continue—until there was just one product or service left. Then the corporate campaign would be direct to that final product or service. Similarly, the compensation of a Chief Executive Officer is indirect to all the products and services of his or her organization—until there is just one product or service remaining. Generally, indirect fixed costs consist of overhead.

Exhibit 5.16 shows costs classified as direct and indirect fixed costs.

Sales	(500,000 units @ $5)		$2,500
Variable Costs			
	Material	500	
	Direct labor	400	
	Manufacturing overhead (variable)	350	
	Commission (10%)	250	
	Total		1,500
Contribution (or Variable Margin)			1,000
Fixed Costs			
	Advertising (product)	50	
	Selling	50	
	Management	250	
	Manufacturing overhead (fixed)	50	
	Total direct fixed costs		400
	Advertising (corporate)	50	
	General and administrative	350	
	Total indirect fixed costs		400
	Profit (before taxes)		200

Reprinted with permission from "Financial Analysis for Marketing," The Arrow Group, Ltd., New York, NY, 2008.

Exhibit 5.16   Income statement with direct and indirect costs (000)

Shutdown Sales Level

Direct fixed costs determine what is called the *shutdown sales level* (Exhibit 5.17) which, in this example, is $1,000,000. If the contribution from a business does not cover its direct fixed costs, it is operating at a volume such that it is using up resources of the organization and normally would be shut down.

The shutdown level is always below the breakeven level.

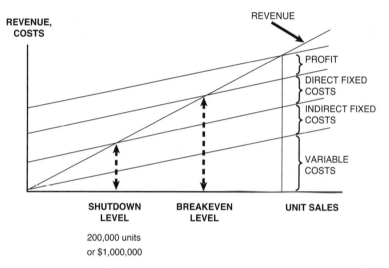

Reprinted with permission from "Financial Analysis for Marketing," The Arrow Group, Ltd., New York, NY, 2008.

Exhibit 5.17   Shutdown level

Overhead Allocation: The NVT Case

As discussed in Chapter 1, "Marketing and Financial Performance," NVT was a British company that produced famous motorcycles such as the Triumph. The company went bankrupt in the 1980s in part due to its misunderstanding of the effects of overhead allocation on decision-making. Their product line consisted of a few large motorcycles. They began to delete models from their product line because they were "unprofitable" under full-costing. Each time they deleted a model, the overhead that had been assigned to that model had to be reallocated to the remaining models. Eventually there were not enough models selling enough units to cover the company's overhead—and they went bankrupt. Happily, the company was purchased, and the brand name was revived so that Triumph motorcycles live on.

Evaluating Contribution

In deciding whether or not to continue to operate a business, contribution must be compared to various costs and targets in this order:

1. Contribution > Direct Fixed Costs? If not, the business is below shutdown level.
2. Contribution > Direct Fixed Costs + Indirect Fixed Costs? If not, the business is below breakeven level.
3. Contribution > Direct Fixed Costs + Indirect Fixed Costs + Target Profit? If not, the business is below target profit level.

All indirect fixed costs must be covered for an organization to stay in business in the long run. However, if those costs are hidden, as they are in an average cost calculation, they can easily distort decisions.

Enterprise: Creating Value by Executing Operations and Marketing with Discipline and Harmony

Unlike other well-known car rental brands, Enterprise "sprouted" away from airports, so instead of serving out-of-town rental situations, it grew up serving the in-town variety. In a good portion of these situations, consumers were renting cars for temporary substitute transportation while their personal vehicles underwent body or mechanical repairs.

Then, as now, when consumers were renting cars for temporary substitute transportation:

- Selection of car rental brands was frequently determined by employees of auto insurance companies and repair facilities;

- Getting to the rental facility required considerably more effort than merely walking from an airport's gate area to its ground transportation area.

Consequently, Enterprise's first marketing efforts almost exclusively targeted employees of the auto insurance and repair industries. And given the obvious benefit of the company's pick-up service, it successfully compelled many of them to select Enterprise for their customers.

Growth followed; yet, after nearly three decades of highly effective business marketing, the company's quest for greater success eventually led to the consideration and implementation of a consumer-marketing initiative. During the decade that followed, Enterprise experienced 10x growth and evolved from a virtual unknown to category leader.

At the consideration phase, however, senior management was divided on whether or not the value derived from a consumer-marketing initiative could justify the cost of the initiative...not to mention the cost of serving increased demand, the cost of setting public expectations, the cost of inviting competitive examination, and more. And at the implementation phase, senior management remained divided on whether or not the company's pick-up service should be featured in its mass communications. Clearly, Enterprise's pick-up service was its most differentiating and relevant attribute; but many feared that promoting a pick-up promise would escalate personnel costs and operational stress to the breaking point.

The company's president (now, chairman), a true leader and visionary, settled the division by reminding all that picking people up—physically and emotionally—is what we do and who we are, so it's what we're going to say we do in our advertising. And with this simple reminder, he launched an alignment of operations and marketing that resulted in a creation of value that led to Enterprise's leading brand and market positions.

—Steven T. Smith, Chief Marketing Officer,
Enterprise Rent-A-Car

Printed with permission of Steven Smith

Conclusions

Understanding costs is central to applying CVA®. In particular, variable cost per unit is the floor of CVA®. Many accounting systems employ a custodial format to present financial performance. Unfortunately, custodial systems look backward and do not provide information for looking forward. Contribution accounting systems allow managers to evaluate their marketing and branding decisions on a going-forward basis. Contribution accounting systems are based on classifying costs between variable and fixed costs and between direct and indirect costs. Contribution accounting systems support the use of CVA® concepts.

One manages CVA® with marketing and branding strategies, as explained in the next chapter.

6

Managing CVA®

CVA® should be the focus of all marketing strategies. Successful marketing strategies manage CVA® effectively over time. This chapter examines the process of developing marketing strategy—including targeting and positioning—to manage CVA® to maximum effect.

Marketing Strategy Versus Marketing Tactics

Unfortunately, many marketing strategies seem focused on tactics to the detriment of strategic thinking. Arguably, the two components of a marketing plan that reflect strategic thinking are the choice of target market and the determination of the positioning of the product or service. The author has been asked by many companies—all well-known—to review their marketing plans. Approximately 50 percent of those marketing plans do not have thoughtful and fact-based discussions of target market and positioning! Instead, those plans consist only of business objectives and action steps.[1]

Why are the target market and positioning decisions given scant attention in so many marketing plans? Perhaps short-term pressures do not allow time for evaluation of alternative markets and alternative positions through careful consideration of customers and competitors.

In June 2008, 96 percent of the members of the ANA's Marketing and Media Committees thought their senior management considered short-term profits extremely or very important (versus 60 percent for long-term brand equity).[2]

© Ashleigh Brilliant, 2008. Used with permission.

Due to short-term pressures, customer opinion may not be brought into the strategic planning process—a risky practice often accompanied by disastrous results. Most of the greatest disasters in marketing, such as the Tigershark fighter aircraft and Polavision instant home movies, were due to failures to incorporate customer information into strategic thinking.[3]

Inertia may be the culprit—staying with customers and designs that are known—thinking they are "safe" when, in fact, keeping everything the same may be the most risky option. As Peter Drucker observed, "Defending yesterday is far more risky than making tomorrow."

Or some managers may think these decisions are not worth much time because they feel it is tactics such as pricing and communications that will govern their success. Those are often the opinions of newcomers to marketing. However, tactics may have only short-term effects. Promotions, for example, have often been found to simply transfer future sales to the present.

In fact, if the target customer and positioning choices are incorrect, then there is little tactics can do to save the day. If an organization targets the wrong customers against the wrong competitors with the wrong product or service at the wrong time, terrific deals and terrific advertising may lead to short-term sales, but will not lead to long-term success. As mentioned earlier, there is a saying in advertising that, "Great advertising makes weak products fail even faster." In other words, people may be persuaded to try the product but will not repurchase it once they discover its shortcomings.

Target customers and positioning represent the organization's destination—pricing, advertising, and other tactics are the details of how one gets there. If the destination is wrong, the tactics may well be wasted resources.[4]

Strategic marketing decisions determine the destination;
tactical marketing decisions determine how one gets there.

Motorola: Building a Powerful Marketing Strategy with Business-to-Business Customer Value

Corporations large and small deploy Motorola's mobile communication solutions to enhance their own value to customers. Motorola recognized that such enterprises possessed unique needs that must be fundamentally comprehended in the marketing process. In recent years, Motorola took on this challenge as they reorganized business-to-business marketing efforts around customer segments rather than traditional product lines. To capitalize on the move required a change in the mindsets of the various individual departments, from product developers and product marketing to marketing communications and regional marketing. The entire language of communication had to shift from the product's attributes to the customer's requirements in a real-world environment far removed from the development lab.

To establish this common language, product managers and solutions marketing teams develop a handful of real-world scenarios describing the daily needs of a market segment such as Government & Public Safety and Enterprise Mobility (updating them over time). For instance, in the local and state government segment, disaster planning and prevention is an operational and conceptual process that is never-ending. The combined marketing and field teams flesh out those scenarios with an eye to the design, usage and ultimate communication of a product's attributes. As product engineers bring new products to life, product marketing applies that same customer input to position those creations within the solutions framework. This same scenario-driven language links the marketing communications teams who design targeted marketing campaigns. The goal is that the same customer input that spawned the product idea guides its marketing efforts, even as those products roll out around the globe through regional marketing organizations. Working with the customer's needs in mind animates this entire process as the product moves through the pipeline toward launch.

The goal of marketing leadership is always to speak with one voice around the world. Motorola strives to take a step beyond that. They speak with one global voice, but it is the customer's voice.

—Eduardo Conrado, Corporate Vice President, Global Marketing and Communications, Motorola

Reprinted with permission

Components of a Marketing Strategy

A marketing strategy consists of four main components[5]:

- Target market
- Business objectives
- Positioning
- Programs (or Tactics)

The *target market* consists of those customers on which the organization will focus. This choice is made in conjunction with the positioning decision.

The *positioning* consists of the key benefits the organization will provide to the target customer and that they will communicate to the target customer. Note that for maximum effect, positioning should be developed with an *individual* decision-maker in mind—not an entire segment as many marketing textbooks suggest.

The individuals targeted by the marketing plan may not even be the person who makes the decision but instead key influencers. For example, Steve Wynn, creator of the Mirage, Bellagio, and the Wynn Las Vegas hotels focuses on taxi drivers. Wynn observes, "Visitors to Las Vegas will ask a cab driver about a place and believe everything he says. I have never built a hotel without having special bathrooms and vending machines set up for cab drivers."[6]

The target market and positioning decisions are made through analyzing the needs of the potential customers, as well as evaluating the organization's capabilities versus those of their competitors. These decisions are made through an *iterative* process in which decision-makers examine various target market and positioning alternatives until it is clear—which target market/positioning pairing offers the highest potential for success. Over the years, for example, tequila has been repositioned in the US from just a down-market beverage for the college crowd to include super-premium versions for high-income drinkers resulting in sales growth of over 30 percent per year since 2002.[7]

Business objectives comprise the financial results the organization hopes and expects to achieve from the business. They may include market share, revenue, contribution, profit, and cash flow.

Programs consist of all the ways an organization manages its relationship with its target customers and include personal selling, advertising, Internet activities, pricing, promotion, customer service, and distribution. Often programs are referred to as the *tactics* of the marketing strategy.

Developing a marketing strategy consists of four major steps (Exhibit 6.1). The *situation analysis* consists of gathering information on customers, competitors, the organization itself, and the overall competitive environment (for example, demographic or economic trends). *Segmentation analysis* involves identifying possible market segments, then choosing the segment on which to target the marketing efforts. *Assembly of strategy* consists of defining the business objectives for the product or service, determining the positioning for the product or service, and formulating programs such as advertising and pricing to implement the strategy.

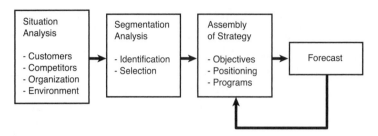

Reprinted with permission from "Formulating Marketing Strategy," The Arrow Group, Ltd., New York, NY, 2008.

Exhibit 6.1   Developing a marketing strategy

Targeting and Positioning Low-Calorie Beers

In the 1960s, the beer industry in the United States was mature—growing at a few percentage points per year. Miller Brewing changed that with a strategy for low-calorie beer that combined precise targeting and positioning.

The first low-calorie beer introduced in the United States was Gablinger's Beer, introduced in 1966, six years before Miller Lite. Gablinger's was positioned for dieters as a "Great tasting premium beer 100 percent fat free, less calories than skim milk." Anyone on a diet is likely not drinking a lot of beer—Gablinger's failed quickly.[8]

As mentioned in Chapter 4, "Perceived Value," the Miller Brewing Company introduced Miller Lite as a "Great tasting/Less filling beer." The target segment was not dieters, but beer drinkers who liked to drink a lot of beer without feeling bloated. The low-calorie beer market took off with a growth rate of 35 percent per year—reflecting the powerful marriage of targeting and positioning and the consequent impact on CVA®. From 1972 to 1979, Miller Brewing went from the number 7 United States brewer to the number 2.

Identifying Possible Target Markets

After a thorough situation analysis, the first step in constructing the marketing strategy is to assess the possible target markets for the product or service. All potential customers are assigned to smaller groups known as *market segments*. A *market segment* is a group of customers or potential customers who have similar needs or seek similar benefits.

There is no single correct way to segment a market—there may be hundreds of ways to segment a market. That means the identification of possible target market segments is a key step in the process of developing a strategy. If one segmentation scheme does not lead to a promising marketing strategy, then it may be necessary to re-segment the market another way. Even if a particular segmentation scheme does lead to a promising strategy, one might choose to re-segment the market in case there might be an even more promising strategy associated with a different segmentation scheme.

Market segmentation is based on the association between descriptors of customers (such as demographics for business-to-consumer markets or industry for business-to-business markets) and the needs of those customers.

The four steps to segment a market comprise the *Segment Identification Analysis*:

1. Define the possible market segments by their characteristics.
2. List the benefits sought by customers.
3. Estimate the relative importance of each benefit to customers in each market segment.
4. Consolidate the market segments as appropriate.

In the Segment Identification Analysis, various market segmentation schemes can be examined. The key to the analysis is the *Market Segment Chart* (Exhibit 6. 2). Each column corresponds to a different possible market segment, which is identified with descriptors (for example, high income families with young children or large manufacturers of computer components).

Each row corresponds to one of the benefits a customer might seek from the product or service. Within the chart, the scores represent the importance of each of those benefits to the typical customer in each proposed market segment. Note that, of course, there may not be a typical customer. As a result, the analyst is using an average for each segment. There may be much variation within a segment as to how important a benefit might be. That variation means that

another market segmentation scheme might produce more clearly
focused market segments.

Benefits	Possible Segments				

Reprinted with permission from "Segment Identification Analysis," The Arrow Group, Ltd.,
New York, NY, 2008.

Exhibit 6.2   Market Segment Chart

It is also possible that if several market segments that have been
assumed to be different show similar priorities for many of the benefits. Then it may be useful to consolidate them into one market
segment.

The Segment Identification Analysis simply enables discussion of
market segmentation. It is also possible to utilize various statistical
techniques such as cluster analysis or factor analysis to develop systems for segmenting markets. For example, one can find clusters of
customers with similar benefit priorities and then determine the key
descriptive measures that identify them. The Segment Identification
Analysis is especially useful for spotlighting issues during a discussion
among members of a marketing team. Statistical tools are helpful
when dealing with large sets of data and may validate the ideas that
surface during the discussion surrounding Segment Identification
Analysis.

Segment Identification Analysis: Airlines

Suppose an airline has identified three possible segments (Exhibit
6.3): business travelers, vacation travelers with children, and vacation travelers without children. For simplicity, assume that only

four benefits are considered: punctuality, courtesy, baggage handling, and food.

Benefits	Possible Segments		
	Business Traveler	Vacation Traveler with Children	Vacation Traveler without Children
Punctuality	9	7	8
Courtesy	7	10	8
Baggage handling	6	7	7
Food	3	5	4

Where: 10 – very important, 1 – not important.

Reprinted with permission from "Segment Identification Analysis," The Arrow Group, Ltd., New York, NY, 2008.

Exhibit 6.3   Market Segment Chart—Airlines

The chart shows how important each benefit is to members of each market segment. It is very important to note that these priorities are obtained by asking the *customers* their opinions.

The benefit priorities for the three segments do vary somewhat. For example, the business travelers value punctuality the most, while the vacation travelers with children value courtesy the most. These market segments can be thought of as distinct groups of customers.

Evaluating Possible Positions for the Product or Service

Positioning consists of just a few key benefits provided by the product or the service. The reason for selecting a few is that the brand needs to be built on benefits to the customer; and it is difficult for most customers to remember more than two or three benefits. That is why the choice of those benefits comprising the position can be crucial.[9]

The benefits can be economic such as Wal-Mart's everyday low prices; functional such as "fast actin" Tenactin foot powder; or emotional such as Harley-Davidson's freedom. Becton Dickinson continued their success in the hypodermic needle market with safety.[10] What is important is that the benefits are high priorities for the target customers *and* that the organization can provide those benefits at levels superior to what competitors provide.[11]

The *benefit advantage* consists of one or more benefits that an organization provides at a level superior to what its competitors provide. The Ted Bates advertising agency used to call the benefit advantage "The Unique Selling Proposition."

> *Customers pay for benefit advantages.*
> *Benefit advantages affect revenue.*

The *competitive advantage* consists of one or more capabilities that an organization possesses that allows the organization to provide benefit advantages. At the corporate level a competitive advantage is often called a *core competency*.[12] For example, optics technology is at the heart of Canon's success and would likely appear as a competitive advantage for all their key products such as cameras, copiers, and printers.[13]

> *Managers pay for competitive advantages.*
> *Competitive advantages affect costs.*

Many of the author's clients have found the *Competitive Advantage Analysis*, initially developed by the author and two colleagues and later refined by the author, to be very helpful with their positioning decisions. In fact, some of them use this analysis as a test for their new products and services—to determine if they are ready for the marketplace.

Steps in Competitive Advantage Analysis:

1. Select the market segment and the members of the decision-making unit.
2. List the benefits sought by the customer.
3. List the capabilities that any organization would like to have in order to serve that customer.
4. Evaluate the capabilities in comparison with the target competitor.
5. Identify competitive advantage and benefit advantage.

The Competitive Advantage Analysis relates costs (capabilities) to value provided customers (benefits), and therefore is directly relevant to managing CVA®. However, the output of the analysis is *not* perceived value, but actual value. To finally connect the results to CVA® requires another analysis, the Perceived Value Analysis described later in this chapter.

The main focus of the Competitive Advantage Analysis is the Capabilities Chart (Exhibit 6.4). The chart is completed for each target segment and, if possible, for each member of the decision-making unit within that segment. If the target segment or target decision-maker changes, then the chart needs to be changed. However, it is not that difficult to handle changes in segment or in decision-maker because if one has completed the chart for one segment or one decision-maker, one most likely has most of the information needed for all the other segments or decision-makers.

Relative Importance	Benefits	Capabilities				

Reprinted with permission from "Competitive Advantage Analysis," The Arrow Group, Ltd., New York, NY, 2008.

Exhibit 6.4   Capabilities Chart

Generally, the Segment Identification Analysis will have been completed prior to the Competitive Advantage Analysis. One of those segments is selected and the benefits listed in the left-hand side column in the Capabilities Chart. Across the top of the chart, the various capabilities that an organization needs to succeed with the product or service are placed as column headings. These should be the capabilities that *any* organization would want—regardless of how strong or weak one's own organization is on any of those capabilities. If one does not list all the necessary capabilities, then one may bias the analysis for (or against) one's organization.

Capabilities usually fall into one of three categories: Skills—which are provided by people, resources—which are inanimate such as technology or materials, and features including attributes associated with one's brand.

Next, for each benefit, the capabilities that are involved in providing that benefit are identified by squaring the cell at the intersection of the row for that benefit and the column for that capability. These should be first-order relationships between the capabilities and the benefits. For example, for a piano manufacturer, piano tuners are essential to producing the sound of the pianos and so the cell corresponding to sound and tuners would be squared. An automated assembly line may reduce the piano costs, which would allow more money to hire more tuners—who would help produce a better sound; but, that would be too many links in the relationship between automated assembly line and sound, so the automated assembly line cell in the sound row would not be squared. Cells should be squared only if there is a *direct* relationship between the capability and the benefit.

There should be at least one cell squared in each row. If none are squared, then it may be possible that one or more capabilities have been left out of the analysis and should be inserted. For example, in the airline example shown in Exhibit 6.5, there is no cell squared in the food row because no capabilities related to food, such as a competent caterer, were included in the analysis.

| | | Capabilities | | | | | | |
| | | | | | | Brand | | |
Relative Importance	Benefits	Attendant Training	Mechanics	Young Aircraft	Information System	Punctu-ality	Courtesy	Baggage Handling
9	Punctuality		1,0	1,1,1		1,1,1		
7	Courtesy	1,0					1,1,0	
6	Baggage Handling				1,0			0
3	Food							

Exhibit 6.5   Capabilities Chart—Airline business traveler

The payoff step is the evaluation of the organization's capabilities with respect to delivering the benefits. The strength or weakness of an organization's capabilities will vary depending on the target competitor. Therefore it is necessary to define the target competitor when evaluating the organization's capabilities. Usually one should start by choosing the most powerful competitor; however, it is valuable to perform the analysis for other competitors as well. If some of the competitors are very similar—for example, a number of small competitors—then select one of them to represent that entire group of competitors.

For each cell that is squared, there are three important questions:

1. **Sufficient.** Is the organization's capability sufficient to provide the benefit at an acceptable level of performance? If yes, score a *1*. If no, score a *0*.

2. **Superior.** Is the organization's capability superior to those of competitors in providing the benefit? Note: The capability must be superior—matching the capability of a competitor does not signify superiority. If yes, score a *1*. If no, score a *0*.

3. **Sustainable.** Is the organization's superiority in the capability sustainable over a specific time period? For service industries, typically the time period used is one year. For consumer packaged goods, two or three years may be used. For capital goods, 5 years or more may be used. If yes, score a *1*. If no, score a *0*.

Only if the first question is answered with a yes (*1*) should the next question be asked. For example, if the capability is not sufficient to provide a benefit, it is not necessary to ask if it is superior. Similarly, if the capability is not superior, then it is not necessary to ask if it is sustainable.

If a cell has only a *0*, that represents a *veto* for the product or service. If that product or service is marketed as is, then one can expect failure because the organization's capabilities are not sufficient to provide the target customer with acceptable value.

If a cell has a *1,0*, that is *neutral*. That capability for that benefit is neither helpful or harmful.

One hopes to find *competitive advantages* in the Capabilities Chart. A *competitive advantage* is a capability that allows the organization to provide one or more benefits to the target customers at a performance level higher than its competitors. Benefits associated with a competitive advantage are the *benefit advantages* for the product or service.

> *There are two types of competitive advantages—one is short-lived, the other is sustainable over some period of time.*

A short-lived competitive advantage is identified by *1,1,0* in a cell. A *1,1,0* in a cell means that the benefit is being provided at a level higher than those of competitors but that the capability that provides that performance can be copied soon by one or more competitors. The implication is that if one is going to use that benefit in the positioning of the product or service, it should be done quickly and announced quickly in all the product or service communications. It may also be wise to try to improve that capability to stay ahead of imitating competitors.

A sustainable competitive advantage is identified by a *1,1,1* in a cell. A *1,1,1* signifies that the capability is such that performance on that benefit is being provided at a level higher than those of competitors and that superior performance can be sustained over some time interval. Benefits associated with sustainable capability advantages should be considered for the positioning of the product or service.

Ideally, any benefit in the positioning of a product or service should be *both* a benefit of high priority to the target customer and one that is associated with sustainable competitive advantages for one or more capabilities. In reviewing the Capabilities Chart, one hopes to find sustainable competitive advantages (*1,1,1*). If they are present, the competitive advantages are most powerful if they correspond to benefits of high importance to the target customer.

If there are no sustainable competitive advantages in the rows corresponding to the most important benefits, that is not necessarily fatal. The competitors may also not have sustainable competitive advantages on those benefits. That is why it is usually useful to do this analysis—even roughly—for the competitors of most concern.

This analysis can also be projected over time, for each stage of the life cycle. Usually one expects to see vetoes—cells with *0*—only in the first stage of the competitive life cycle (the Introduction Stage) or in the final stage (the Decline Stage)—for entirely different reasons.

Cells with *0* may be expected in the Introduction Stage when considering new products or services that are not yet ready for market. Cells with *0* may be expected in the Decline Stage because the organization's capabilities to provide benefits may have decreased relative to those of competitors—quite possibly because there is a new technology that provides benefits at a higher level of performance.

For those products or services introduced in the Introduction Stage, one should see sustainable competitive advantages *(1,1,1)* or, in some industries such as financial services, short-lived competitive advantages *(1,1,0)*. The author's clients often use this analysis as a test of whether they should proceed to market with a product or service, whether they need to improve their capabilities first, or, sometimes, whether they should abandon plans to go ahead with the product or service. For example, at one point Corning used this analysis to evaluate requests for capital expenditures for new products.

For products or services in the Rapid Growth Stage, there will be sustainable competitive advantages, but also short-lived competitive advantages, as new competitors enter the market. There will also be more neutral cells *(1,0)* as capabilities are copied.

During the Competitive Turbulence Stage, most of the cells will be neutral because all the slow followers come into the market and imitate all the existing capabilities. Generally, value to the customer relative to the values provided by other competitors falls during this stage, sometimes rapidly. It is imperative to have built a strong brand position during the Rapid Growth Stage and to manage costs down if one is to survive shakeout during this stage. Target marketing is also crucial.

In the Maturity Stage, there are many neutral cells. The competitive advantage capabilities tend to be associated with either the brand or with costs.

In the Decline Stage, the cells are usually neutral or veto cells because a new technology is bringing a new product or service into the market—one with benefit performance levels that cannot, perhaps, be matched by the old technology.

The Competitive Advantage Analysis can be used for customer value engineering–evaluating changes in actual value to the customer in relation to corresponding changes in costs.

One way to evaluate such changes is to bisect those cells corresponding to the proposed changes (Exhibit 6.6). Let the lower part of the cell correspond to the current evaluation of the organization's capabilities. The upper part of the cell can be used to express the evaluation of capabilities that the organization would like to have—perhaps a *1,1,1*. Then the manager can evaluate whether or not it is worth the time and money to change the current evaluation to the one that is desired by considering the effect of the changes on CVA®. Note that both increases and decreases in capabilities can be analyzed this way.

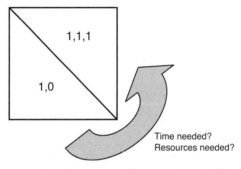

Reprinted with permission from "Competitive Advantage Analysis," The Arrow Group, Ltd., New York, NY, 2008.

Exhibit 6.6   Evaluating changes in Competitive Advantage Analysis

Competitive Advantage Analysis: Airlines

Suppose an airline has tentatively decided to target business travelers (Refer to Exhibit 6.5). Key capabilities have been identified as training for their attendants, availability and skill of mechanics, the ages of their aircraft, and their baggage information system. In addition, their brand reputation on the benefits of punctuality, courtesy, and baggage handling represent key capabilities.

They choose a leading airline as their target competitor. Compared to that airline, their training programs, mechanics, and baggage information system are not superior. However, the average age of their fleet is lower—and that may provide a competitive advantage. In particular, age of aircraft has a direct relationship to punctuality—a relatively important benefit for their business traveler.

For the business traveler segment, the airline's position would consist of the benefit advantage of punctuality supported by the competitive advantage of the relatively young age of their aircraft.

However, the airline does have problems that must be addressed. Their brand reputation for baggage handling is unacceptable, and their baggage information system is rated just average. They may wish to upgrade their baggage handling capabilities; otherwise, their low brand ranking on baggage handling may cancel their advantage of punctuality. Customers may be happy to arrive on time, but not if their baggage does not arrive with them.

Determining Design

The Competitive Advantage Analysis indicates actual value—the benefits the organization can provide now at a level superior to their competitors and that the customer will receive. While those benefits may be superior to those the target customer can find from other organizations, they may not fully meet the customer's expectations. One can employ the *Design Analysis* to find out whether the customer's expectations are met.

Steps in Design Analysis:

1. Select the market segment and the member of the decision-making unit.
2. List the benefits sought by the customer.
3. Estimate the performance level desired by the customer on each benefit.
4. Evaluate performance on each benefit.
5. Identify design gaps.

The main purpose of the Design Analysis is to compare what the organization provides—actual value—to what the customer wants—expected value—as discussed in Chapter 2, "How CVA® Affects Financial Performance." The key chart is the Actual Value Chart (Exhibit 6.7).

Benefits	Organization		Competitors							
	A	E	A	E	A	E	A	E

Where: A – Actual performance.
         E - Expected performance.

Reprinted with permission from "Actual Value Analysis," The Arrow Group, Ltd., New York, NY, 2008.

Exhibit 6.7   Actual Value Chart

All the benefits sought by the target customer are listed in the rows in the left-most column on the chart. The columns represent the organization for which the analysis is being done and the key competitors. The entries in each column are the level of performance customers actually receive on each benefit and the level of performance expected by the customer on each benefit.

If the expected performance level is higher than the performance actually received, then that represents a *design gap*. Design gaps may have a large impact on purchase decisions if they correspond to benefits that are high priorities for the target customer.

Whether or not the organization closes a design gap depends on whether it is technologically feasible and, if so, the time and cost needed to do so. Whether the investment is warranted also depends on the competitors' positions and their possible actions with respect to the same benefits.

Design Analysis: Airline Case

The Actual Value Chart for the punctuality, courtesy, baggage handling, and food benefits for the business traveler segment is shown in Exhibit 6.8.

Benefits	Airline X		Competitors					
			A		B		C	
	A	E	A	E	A	E	A	E
Punctuality	8	10	6	10	5	10	6	10
Courtesy	7	10	8	10	5	10	3	10
Baggage handling	3	10	5	10	7	10	6	10
Food	4	6	3	6	2	6	3	6

Where: A – Actual performance.
         E - Expected performance.

         1 - Poor, 10 – Excellent.

Reprinted with permission from "Actual Value Analysis," The Arrow Group, Ltd., New York, NY, 2008.

Exhibit 6.8   Actual Value Chart—Airlines

The customer has high expectations—*10* for punctuality, courtesy, and baggage handling. Airline X does relatively well on punctuality, not badly on courtesy, and poorly on baggage handling. There are design gaps on all three benefits. For example, the design gap on punctuality is 10 minus 8 or *2*.

The design gap can be seen with a perceptual map (Exhibit 6.9). Expected performance and actual performance are shown for the punctuality and courtesy benefits. The design gaps are the distances between the expected and actual values.

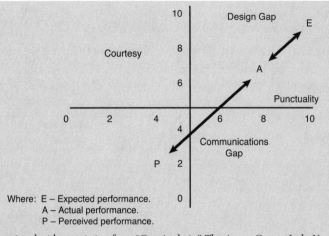

Where: E – Expected performance.
        A – Actual performance.
        P – Perceived performance.

Reprinted with permission from "Gap Analysis," The Arrow Group, Ltd., New York, NY, 2008.

Exhibit 6.9   Perceptual map—Airline X

Airline X could increase CVA® by improving its performance on benefits and then communicating those changes to the target customers.

Selecting Target Segments

Many consultancies have developed methodologies for selecting business opportunities. However, many of those methods are expensive and time-consuming to employ. The approach suggested here, the *Segment Selection Analysis*, is based on those methodologies, but is much simpler (and cheaper) to utilize.[14]

Steps in Segment Selection Analysis:

1. List the market segments under consideration.
2. Evaluate each with respect to the organization's relative ability.
3. Evaluate each with respect to the attractiveness of the opportunity.
4. Select the target market segment.

There are two major dimensions in all methods for selecting business opportunities. All consultancies use these same two dimensions—their approaches differ only in the specific measures used for each dimension.

The two dimensions are the same two dimensions a person would think of when walking into a room with many poker games and attempting to select a table at which to sit. One dimension would be the abilities of the players at the table; the other, the amount of money in play. The first dimension is *relative ability*; the other is *attractiveness*. Relative ability concerns whether or not one can win; attractiveness determines whether it is worth winning.

When selecting target markets, relative ability depends on the capabilities of one's organization, versus those of the competitors, to provide value to the target customers. In general, capabilities include skills such as operations and marketing and resources such as plant and equipment.

Evaluating relative ability is the focus of the Competitive Advantage Analysis, so the output of that analysis can be used to evaluate an organization's relative ability to win a given market segment.

Attractiveness of a market depends on such characteristics as its size, growth potential, and ease of access. Managers always have a set of criteria in mind that signify a market to be attractive. For example, the US telecommunications market may be very attractive to SK Telecom due to its size while the US appliance market may have lost its appeal to GE due to the competitive environment.[15]

To select a target market, it is necessary to take the list of market segments from the Segment Identification Analysis and evaluate each one in terms of the organization's relative ability to succeed in that market and the attractiveness of that market with respect to the organization's future financial performance.

These evaluations can be made on a scale of 1 to 5, where 1 means weak ability or a very unattractive market, and 5 means strong ability or a very attractive market. The markets under consideration can then be located on a Segment Selection Chart (Exhibit 6.10).

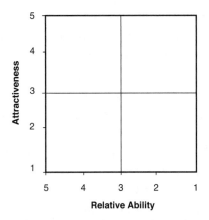

Reprinted with permission from "Segment Selection Analysis," The Arrow Group, Ltd., New York, NY, 2008.

Exhibit 6.10   Segment Selection Chart

Those market segments that have the most appeal are found in the upper left quadrant of the chart—indicating markets in which the organization has strong relative ability and the financial prospects are very attractive.

However, each quadrant poses a specific challenge. For market segments in the upper left quadrant, the challenge is how much growth to pursue: As one is growing share, generally profits are not strong. For market segments in the upper right quadrant, the challenge is which segments might have promise and be worth investment. Chasing too many market segments in the upper right quadrant can be ruinously expensive because the organization's resources may be spread over too many opportunities. Market segments in the lower left quadrant often represent markets in the Mature Stage of the competitive life cycle and are often related to political power within their organization due to their size. The challenge for these markets is to be wary of over-investment. Finally, market segments in the lower right quadrant may play a variety of roles. The challenge is to understand whether those segments should be pursued for special reasons, such as providing a technological or market window, or whether they should be ignored.

There is no simple formula for selecting target market segments. However, focusing on the dimensions of relative ability and attractiveness helps keep managerial attention on CVA®.

Segment Selection Analysis: Airlines

The three segments the airline is considering—business travelers, vacation travelers with children, and vacation travelers without children—are shown in the Segment Selection Chart (Exhibit 6.11). All the segments are relatively attractive. However, the airline's relative strength on punctuality—an important benefit for the business travelers—leads to relatively high ability to target that market segment.

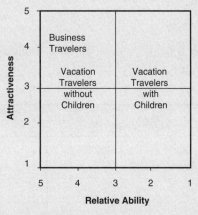

Reprinted with permission from "Segment Selection Analysis," The Arrow Group, Ltd., New York, NY, 2008.

Exhibit 6.11   Segment Selection Chart—Airlines

Developing Communications

Managing CVA® requires managing perceived value. Even if the design of a product or service is close to what the target customer expects, it is necessary to communicate the performance of the product or service, especially on those benefits of high importance to the target customer.

Perceived value can be examined with a *Perceived Value Analysis*. Note that this analysis should be used to examine how to develop communications to *manage* perceived value, not to *calculate* perceived value. Methods to estimate perceived value are described in Chapter 4.

*A perceived value analysis helps a manager find gaps in an
organization's communications with the customers.*

Steps in Perceived Value Analysis:

1. Select the market segment and the member of decision-making unit.
2. List the benefits sought by the customer.
3. Evaluate the performance on each benefit.
4. Estimate the performance level perceived by the customer on each benefit.
5. Identify the communications gaps.

The main chart for the Perceived Value Analysis is the Perceived
Value Chart (Exhibit 6.12).

Benefits	Organization		Competitors					
	P	A	P	A	P	A	P	A

Where: A – Actual performance.
        P – Perceived performance.

Reprinted with permission from "Perceived Value Analysis," The Arrow Group, Ltd., New
York, NY, 2008.

Exhibit 6.12   Perceived Value Chart

As in working with the Actual Value Chart, consider a market
segment and, if possible, a member of the decision-making unit. For
each benefit, determine the actual performance of one's organization.
These evaluations may come from the Competitive Advantage Analysis.

For each benefit, learn from customers what their perceptions
are of the performance the organization has provided. It is very
important that these evaluations come from customers—not from
managers trying to think like customers.

Comparing the actual and perceived levels of performance reveals any communications gaps. Most common are communications gaps in which the perceived level is below that of the actual level. In such cases, the organization may develop communications to close those gaps on those benefits of relatively high priority to their target customers.

Sometimes perceived levels of performance are higher than the actual levels. Those situations may become problems for an organization. If a customer thinks a performance level is higher than it actually is, they may be disappointed when they use the product or service. Such disappointment may eventually damage the brand. Whenever perceived levels of performance exceed actual levels, an organization should try to improve its performance to match customer expectations. If that is not possible, then the organization should attempt to use communications to manage customer expectations so that the customers will not be disappointed with the product or service.

Perceived Value Analysis: Airlines

Perceived and actual evaluations for the airline example are shown in Exhibit 6.13.

Benefits	Airline X		Competitors					
			A		B		C	
	P	A	P	A	P	A	P	A
Punctuality	4	8	3	6	5	5	4	6
Courtesy	2	7	6	8	4	5	1	3
Baggage handling	1	3	3	5	5	7	3	6
Food	1	4	1	3	2	2	2	3

Where: A – Actual performance.
P – Perceived performance.

1 - Poor, 10 – Excellent.

Reprinted with permission from "Perceived Value Analysis," The Arrow Group, Ltd., New York, NY, 2008.

Exhibit 6.13   Perceived Value Chart—Airlines

Airline X has a communications problem. The target passenger believes that the airline's performance on each of the three benefits was even lower than it actually was. The communications gaps on these benefits can also be seen in the perceptual map in Exhibit 6.9.

To meet customer expectations, Airline X must both improve their performance on the benefits and then communicate those improvements to their target customers.

Managing the Brand

The target market and positioning developed for the marketing strategy are the basis for the branding strategy. In particular, one or two—or perhaps three—benefits from the positioning should be used in building the brand. Generally, more than three benefits are difficult for customers to remember, so the brand communications need to concentrate on those benefits central to the marketing strategy (such as punctuality in the airline illustration). If one tries to communicate too many benefits, it is possible that none of them will register with the target customer.

Even if a Competitive Advantage Analysis suggests that there are several benefits that could be benefit advantages for the product or service, choose only a few benefits for the branding strategy. This is the *discipline* required by branding.

Over many years, Burger King constantly changed the tag line of their advertising. While a tag line is not the brand position, it is related to the brand position—and changing it frequently does not help build the brand. Only recently, according to the CEO of Burger King, did they stabilize their brand by focusing on iconic brand attributes such as "Have It Your Way."[16]

It is possible to change a brand position over time, but it should not be done frequently nor should it be done abruptly. Shortly before they were purchased by Footsmart, Thom McAn was trying to change its brand position from inexpensive, sturdy shoes to fashionable shoes—in just a few months. That was an extreme change that would have been difficult over a long period of time, and they tried to make the change in just a short period—not easy.

To be effective, branding strategies need to be *consistent* over time and over space. All points of contact with the target customer should communicate and reinforce the benefits chosen for the position.

> *Brands often represent a significant portion of perceived value so they must be managed carefully.*

Bombay Sapphire: Deviating from the Competitors

I have managed premium and super premium spirits for almost 20 years. I remember many events where otherwise well mannered and fairly wealthy consumers would try to smuggle bottles of liquor out under their jackets. I even recall a particular movie star who uttered, "Wow, I can't believe you sent me a bottle of Dewar's 12 year old scotch—that is amazing! I mean, people send me suits and tennis shoes, but 12 Year old scotch?!?" Forget that the price of the bottle of scotch—even in a special gift pack—wasn't anywhere near the cost of these other goods—his perceived Customer Value was extremely high. Indeed, it was far higher than the *actual price* on the shelf.

I am intrigued about how to create such value in the mind of consumers. In the case of Bombay Sapphire gin, a brand I managed globally, we concentrated on *deviating* from the conventional approach to create a successful, consistent program that communicated this value to customers. We tried to ensure that nothing about Bombay Sapphire was like other gins—a fact that allowed it to grow volume in an otherwise declining category and re-invent the gin category globally. (And—it also doubled the Brand Value!)

Deviation vs. Differentiation

Bombay Sapphire didn't simply differentiate from competitors, but it *deviated* from the gin and industry norm—in its concept, strategy and marketing.

Concept

- The liquid is lighter and more delicate than its "ginnier" competitors—and therefore "mixable" for a gin due to a highly unique production process. The package is square and blue vs. the standard round green gin bottle.

- All communication of usage indicated classic martinis and modern new cocktails vs. old fashioned gin and tonics to communicate higher quality and therefore higher value than the typical brand

Brand Strategy and Visual Identity

The entire brand strategy and brand visual identity needed to deviate from other gin brands—unique core values, the distinct Sapphire Blue, the square shape, and even the overall method and style of marketing.

Marketing

- The brand connected with the cutting edge design community from the beginning with Martini glass design print advertisements and continued through experiential events, a foundation supporting new designers and several global design competitions.

- Utilization of PR and experiential marketing vs. the typical advertising and in-bar promotions like other brands.

- Emphasizes quality communications including media channels, high quality materials, higher price (a communication to consumer!) and even brand partnerships.

Take it to Markets—Product and Brand Education

Bombay Sapphire is in 114 countries around the world. To communicate this value consistently, how could all those people coming in contact with Bombay Sapphire understand why the consumer *should* perceive a higher value and is therefore willing to pay a higher price? On Bombay Sapphire we utilized experiential brand summit meetings—attendees received production training, experiential events and even Sapphire Blue IPODs. We had a brand ambassador that traveled to each country year round educating internal personnel and the trade. We created a translucent Sapphire blue cube "brand manual" that was a work of desk art coupled with an intranet to explain the unique product and brand characteristics to each and every marketer who worked on the brand.

So, there are many elements that must come together to communicate this value. It must be known to the entire value chain to ultimately create a higher perceived value at the end consumer—so that they can be wowed when they come in to contact with your product.

—Marshall Dawson, Strategic Brand Consultant and Cofounder, Deviate Marketing, and former Global Brand Director, Bombay Sapphire gin and Grey Goose vodka

Reprinted with permission

Conclusions

The role of marketing in an organization is to manage perceived value—an important component of CVA®. Marketing strategies need to be developed that efficiently increase perceived value. That means that target markets must be chosen with CVA® in mind; and positioning needs to be determined with CVA® in mind. Design and communications must be formulated to maximize CVA®.

As markets move through time, competitive conditions change, and strategies to manage CVA® must change—the topic of the next chapter.

7

Managing CVA® over Time

Competitive conditions change over time, and as they change, CVA®—especially perceived value—must be managed if an organization is to maintain top financial performance. CVA® must be managed as technologies, other trends, and the behaviors of customers and competitors change.

In this chapter, winning CVA® strategies are described for each stage of the competitive life cycle.

Managing CVA® Through the Market Life Cycle

Perceived value consists of three major components: the portions due to the corporate brand, product or service brand, and the benefits of the product or service (Exhibit 7.1). Generally, the corporate brand helps sustain perceived value and CVA® during times of changing technologies, while the product or service brand and the product or service benefits can be used to manage perceived value and CVA® during the different stages of the competitive life cycle.

Recall from Chapter 3, "CVA® over Time," that there are different levels of sales life cycles (Exhibit 7.2). The market life cycle shows unit sales corresponding to a particular customer need, such as an individual's need to travel great distances or a business' need to maintain its buildings. The product or service life cycle refers to sales of a specific way to meet that need, such as ocean-going ships or aircraft for long-distance travel or general or specialized services for building maintenance.

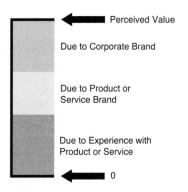

Reprinted with permission from "How Marketing Affects Shareholder Value," The Arrow Group, Ltd., New York, NY, 2008.

Exhibit 7.1   Brands and perceived value

Long-term CVA® health depends on many factors, but one that is especially important is the power of the corporate brand. For some organizations, such as IBM or Kodak, much of brand equity is associated with the corporate brand because much of the perceived value is due to the corporate brand. Especially for those organizations, care must be taken in developing the associations for the corporate brand and managing them over time.

For other organizations, such as Procter & Gamble and Unilever, where most of the brand equity is associated with product or service sub-brands, the corporate brands still have an impact on CVA®, but not as great.

Conceptually, the *corporate brand life cycle* falls between the market life cycle and the product or service life cycle (see Exhibit 7.2). The corporate brand *must* be associated with the market life cycle—with a need, and not with a specific product or service. If the corporate brand is associated with a product or service life cycle, then when and if that technology becomes obsolete, the corporate brand will struggle.

For example, Xerox has been a dominant brand associated with a specific technology—photocopying. As that technology becomes obsolete, Xerox needs to broaden the associations of its corporate brand to allow the organization to move more easily into new product categories. From 2003 through 2006, Xerox revenues were flat, although net income did increase. Sales increased in 2007 and net income fell. Going forward, for revenue and income increases, a major CVA® challenge for Xerox remains broadening the associations of their corporate brand.[1]

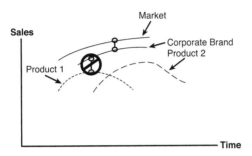

Reprinted with permission from "Managing through the Life Cycle," The Arrow Group, Ltd., New York, NY, 2008.

Exhibit 7.2   Levels of life cycles

To manage CVA® effectively, the corporate brand must be sufficiently broad to support all current products and services as well as allow any desired extensions to other product or service categories.

Air Products: Managing the Corporate Brand

"All the world is a stage, and all the men and women merely players. They have their exits and entrances." What Shakespeare didn't add was that brands can remain on the stage much longer than humans, and if properly nurtured, can last for generations. The world is now truly a stage for global brands, and in particular those that successfully manage the natural tension that exists between the role of a company's product brands and corporate brands.

Product brands are, by their nature and creation, clearly defined offerings in the market place with sustainable product advantages and a promise of performance delivered for the user that provides strong business results for the company. Even a commodity can be successfully branded such as Dow Corning's offering in the silicon sector, Xiameter® to differentiate it from the company's value product offering, adding significant profitability overall.

The corporate brand, on the other hand, has become an altogether more complex being, sharing the stage with corporate reputation and in many cases serving as the global standard bearer of what makes a company "special."

In a digital world, where there is increasing scrutiny from a wide range of corporate stakeholders including purchasing departments, potential investors and new recruits all of whom may be interested in the company's position on a range of issues such as sustainability and diversity, what constitutes being "special" has never been more demanding or more closely connected to the role of product brands.

In a world drowning in information and starved of knowledge, where it is estimated that an individual is subjected to over 10,000 messages a day, the drive for simplicity has become a stampede. Companies such as Air Products have taken a masterbrand approach, linking global leadership in key businesses closely to their reputational values.

I believe that there are five questions that Marketing Directors and Corporate Brand Directors should answer as they plan for the future.

1. Have I truly considered the values of my corporate brand and how it can leverage and protect my product brand in the market?

2. Do I know enough about my company's product portfolio so that I can create sources of sustainable differentiation for my corporate brand?

3. Can I use the unique properties of our key products as sources of corporate reputation enhancement?

4. How can I view The Corporate Brand Director/Marketing Director as an ally—not a foe—in the battle for budget, resources, and voice?

5. How can I leverage the relationship between corporate and product brands as a source of inspiration and not conflict, creating a win/win for both?

There is an old advertising saying "interrogate the product until it gives up its secret." This has never been more appropriate in understanding the true value and relationship between a company's product and corporate brands.

—John R. F. Dodds, Global Marketing Communications Officer, Air Products and Chemicals, Inc.

Reprinted with permission.

Financial Objectives Throughout the Competitive Life Cycle

As discussed in Chapter 3, there are four types of life cycles that indicate how competitive conditions change over time (Exhibit 7.3). The unit sales life cycle shows the growth in total demand for the product or service (or for the branded product or service). The margin per unit life cycle shows how profitability may be expected to change over time. The cost per unit cycle corresponds to the lower bound of CVA®, while the perceived value per unit cycle corresponds to the upper bound of CVA®.

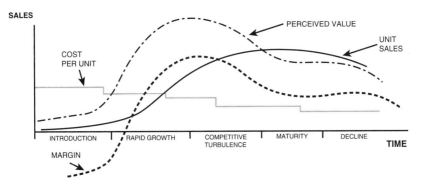

Reprinted with permission from "Managing through the Life Cycle," The Arrow Group, Ltd., New York, NY, 2008.

Exhibit 7.3　The competitive life cycle

The sales, margin, perceived value, and cost life cycles show why it is difficult, if not impossible, to achieve both growth objectives and profitability or cash flow objectives at the same time from the same market segment. Rather, a manager must set priorities for which objectives are most important in a given market segment at a given time (Exhibit 7.4).

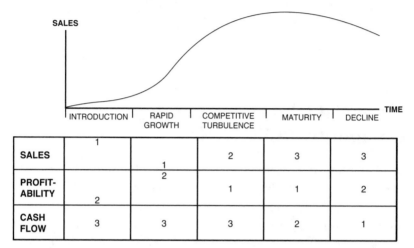

	INTRODUCTION	RAPID GROWTH	COMPETITIVE TURBULENCE	MATURITY	DECLINE
SALES	1	1	2	3	3
PROFIT-ABILITY	2	2	1	1	2
CASH FLOW	3	3	3	2	1

Reprinted with permission from "Formulating Marketing Strategy," The Arrow Group, Ltd., New York, NY, 2008.

Exhibit 7.4   Setting priorities for objectives

It is typically difficult—if not managerially and mathematically impossible—to achieve both growth and cash flow objectives at the same time from a specific market segment.

For example, usually the main objective for the Introduction stage is sales growth, with profitability a distant second, and cash flow an even more distant third, because growth typically costs money. During the Rapid Growth stage, growth in sales might still be the most important goal, but profitability would be a closer second because profits become more feasible. In the Competitive Turbulence stage, maintaining profitability in the midst of a likely price war might be the first concern of the manager, while growth might fall to the second place. In the Maturity stage, focus might shift to profitability, with cash flow the second priority. Finally, for an organization still competing during the Decline stage, cash flow might be the main priority.

This is not the only scenario for the prioritization of financial objectives, but it is a plausible scenario. The most important point is that it is generally not possible to get all three objectives—sales growth, profitability, and cash flow—at the same time from the same market segment.

However, a manager can obtain all three objectives at the same time from the same product or service by assigning different market segments different roles. Some segments might be the segments that provide growth in sales, some the segments that provide profitability, and some the segments that provide cash flow.

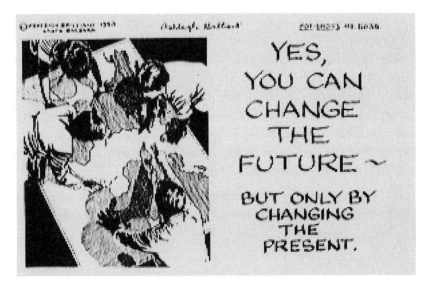

© Ashleigh Brilliant, 2008. Used with permission.

Managing CVA® Throughout the Competitive Life Cycle

How perceived value is built over time has a major impact on CVA®. There has been considerable research concerning how perceived value is developed from organizations such as the Strategic Planning Institute, CoreBrand, Bates Worldwide, and Young & Rubicam.[2]

For example, Young & Rubicam (Y&R) has studied how brands change over time with their BAV® model (Brand Asset Valuator) based on a data base spanning many countries and many years.[3] The implications of this work are quite consistent with what are considered sound marketing practices, namely, communicating value to the target customer.

Exhibit 7.5 summarizes these findings. What follows is the author's interpretation of the BAV and does not necessarily represent Young & Rubicam's past or current interpretations of their results. The vertical axis can be considered to represent Customer Value (what Y&R has called *Brand Strength*) and the horizontal axis can be considered to represent Association (what Y&R has called *Brand Stature*). In the BAV study, *Customer Value* depends on the answers to two questions—how differentiated is a brand, and how relevant is that difference to the customer. Differentiation and relevance are two major components of perceived value. *Association* depends on the answers to two other questions—how admired is a brand, and how familiar is the respondent with the brand. Those two questions are related to perceived value via the strength of the association between the attribute differentiation and the brand.

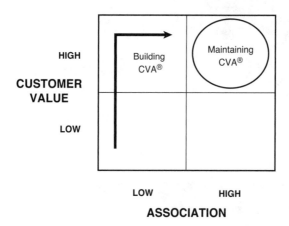

Adapted from Brand Asset Valuator®, Young and Rubicam. Kevin Keller, *Strategic Brand Management*, Englewood Cliffs, NJ: Prentice-Hall, 1998.

Exhibit 7.5   Managing a brand over time

A new brand starts life in the bottom left-hand corner of the grid. Generally, an organization begins the life of a successful brand by communicating value to the target customer—not by just building name association or brand awareness. Brand awareness without specific value attributes is like empty calories—it will have little effect on the target customer's purchasing behavior. In 2000, many new dot-com companies spent considerable amounts of money on advertising on the broadcasts of the US professional football championship, the Super Bowl. Most of those ads were designed to build brand name awareness, but few were designed to build value knowledge in the mind or heart of the target customer. Many of those embryonic dot-com companies went out of business during the following year; and many reneged on their Super Bowl advertising expenses.[4]

Once value is built in the perception of the target customer, then associations are strengthened. The optimal location on the grid is the upper right-hand corner, and that is where all the powerful brands in the world live. They all have extraordinarily high perceived value. The main objective for brands in the upper right is to maintain CVA®.

All marketers want to avoid the failure route—when resources are cut back from successful brands, and either their communications are decreased or—even more dangerous—their production values decline due to inferior operations and lack of effective quality control. Such brands are being *hollowed out*.

Often brands may be hollowed out to improve financial performance but those improvements are typically short-lived. Cutting costs that cut perceived value in the long-run decreases CVA®. Cutting costs may succeed in the short-run in increasing financial performance because there is inertia in perceived value. However, once customers realize that the product or service is no longer providing the benefits they expected at the levels they expected, they will revise their perceived values and consequently CVA® will fall.

Brand awareness is a trailing indicator of brand health.

While a brand is hollowed out, it may have high awareness or name recognition. That is because brand awareness is a trailing indicator of the health of a brand, not a leading indicator. Brand awareness is usually the last measure to fall when a brand fails. When a brand is about to fail and has high awareness, the customers are saying, "I know you, and I don't like you." Many organizations use brand awareness to track their brands even though it is a trailing indicator and likely a misleading measure (see Chapter 10, "Building the Marketing Accountability Scorecard").

Hollowing out of a brand often occurs because of the short-term pressures on managers and the fact that it can succeed in improving financial returns in the short-term, helping a manager to be promoted and leave the weakened perceived value situation for his or her successor to handle.

These principles for building and maintaining perceived value and the strength of a brand guide the management of CVA® during the five stages of the competitive life cycle (Exhibit 7.6). For example, during the Introduction and Rapid Growth stages, the wiring of a brand to its distinctive properties is imperative.

Exhibit 7.6   Stages of the Competitive Life Cycle and Strategy

Stage	Introduction	Rapid Growth	Competitive Turbulence	Maturity	Decline
Key Characteristic	Competitor is old technology	Direct competitors enter	Segments emerge	Purchase routine	Competitor is new technology
Strategy	Educate customer as to value	Differentiate from competitor	Target market segments	Reinforce brand position	Associate brand with need°

°Must be done in the early state of life cycle
Reprinted with permission from "Managing Brand Equity Over Time," Donald E. Sexton, *Quarterly Review of Canada China Business Council*, Summer, 2004, pp. 9-11.

Nortel: Building Brands in the 21st Century

If there were a *"It was the best of times. It was the worst of times"* moment for marketing in the last 100 years then surely we are living it now. The traditional goals of brand building and marketing generally remain unchanged. It's still all about creating market demand and selling stuff, but virtually everything else has changed. And it has changed radically and forever.

Consider this. Today's buyers are the most connected, sophisticated, and well informed in history.

We are living a tectonic shift in the flow of information to buyers. And the buyers are now driving the agenda. Some facts. Eight hours of video gets uploaded to YouTube every minute. Eighty million people visit Facebook daily and if MySpace were a country it would be the 7th biggest, ahead of Russia. Eight hundred million people now access the Internet from their mobile phones. In fact, buyers interact with media via their mobile devices more than any other source. And we're just feeling the breeze before the storm. By 2020, it is projected that there will be nearly 1 Trillion (that's right, trillion with a "T") connected devices on the planet.

For decades marketers have successfully "pitched" a one way message to customers and enjoyed tremendous results. But the rules of the game are changing right under our feet.

During the 90s I was part of the corporate marketing team at IBM. I led worldwide advertising at a time when IBM's reputation had been badly bruised around the globe. How did we set about rebuilding the IBM brand? Our tools were largely television and print. We invested aggressively and portrayed a more relevant, accessible image of the company. Over time, the company's performance improved, the value of the brand was restored and IBM's market value increased in the billions.

In a sense we were able "pitch" a new IBM without actually developing any real interaction or dialogue with our target audiences. Nothing we claimed was ever really contested. There was no viral video, no blogging, no social networks.

Today, I work for Nortel. Like IBM in the 90s, Nortel's reputation has suffered and we've been working to strengthen perceptions, regain trust and create the momentum needed for growth. But the tools and the approach to brand building today stand in sharp contrast to the decade before. Today's marketing is two-way not one-way—it's about creating an experience. And for brand builders it's ultimately about developing the kind of trust that one can't just claim. Earn it, prove it and you can count on millions to enthusiastically advocate you in their blogs, their videos and posts. Betray the trust and the word spreads like wildfire.

All the current market data points to shifts in the media landscape and we at Nortel are living proof of that phenomenon. Digital, viral video, mobile, blogging, and experience marketing are just some of the tools enabling us to build the brand and our market value on the customers' terms not just ours.

It's a challenging and exciting time for marketers. A strong brand is still essential to the creation of market value but our buyers and target audiences are now becoming true influencers and stake-holders in the brand building process. If these last few years are any indication of what the future holds then strong buyer and cus-tomer advocacy will become the ultimate tools of brand building and market value creation.

—Lauren Flaherty, Chief Marketing Officer, Nortel

Reprinted with permission.

Introduction Stage

At the beginning of the competitive life cycle, the competition for a new product or service is represented by those products and serv-ices produced with older technologies, for example, digital imaging versus film or digital audio versus analog. Target customers may not yet appreciate the benefits associated with the new product or serv-ice. In addition, resellers may not appreciate the benefits of the new product or service, and so may not give it support.

For the pioneering firm—the first in the market with the new product or service—the primary task for managing CVA® during this stage is to communicate to the target customers and to any necessary resellers the reasons the new product or service is superior to the products or services currently on the market. Apple's initial ads for the wildly successful iPod showed the physical beauty of the device— a level of design expected from Apple, then moved quickly into a sec-ond phase of communications showing people experiencing the *joy* of their music through iPod.[5] The Introduction stage is the stage during which the perception of value must be developed in the minds and hearts of the key decision-makers who will determine the eventual success of the product or service.[6]

There are two major types of strategies for doing this: skimming and penetration (Exhibit 7.7).

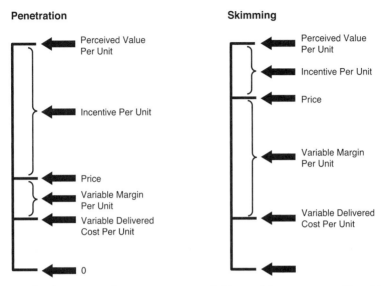

Reprinted with permission from "Pricing, Perceived Value, and Communications," Donald E. Sexton, New York, NY, 2008.

Exhibit 7.7 • Introduction strategies

In a skimming strategy, the organization focuses on just those customers who will be very appreciative of the differences in benefits provided by the new product or service and are willing to pay for those differences. For example, among the first purchasers of digital cameras were photojournalists who immediately perceived the value of being able to send images back to their offices—digitally. Usually a skimming strategy utilizes distribution channels such as specialty stores that are targeted to these high-interest users.

A skimming price is relatively high because it is supported by the relatively high value per unit perceived by the target customers that still allows a customer incentive. However, a high price often becomes an invitation beckoning others into the market. Therefore, successful skimming strategies require entry barriers. In the long run, there are no entry barriers, but skimming strategies succeed the longer competitors are kept out of the market.

Entry barriers can be based on patents or copyrights, but they can also be based on resources or even on a strong brand. For example, Stainmaster carpet fiber from DuPont was protected primarily by the strength of its well-designed and well-executed branding communications.[7]

In a penetration strategy, the organization attempts to win over most of the potential customers before new competitors enter. Many segments are targeted simultaneously. Penetration strategies typically require considerable resources for building initial production capacity and for communicating to customers. Distribution for a penetration strategy would usually saturate the market.

Penetration strategy prices are set relatively low to provide great incentive to all possible customers. Low prices also make it more difficult for others to enter the market because it lowers their potential margin per unit.

The danger of the penetration strategy is that the penetrating organization expends considerable resources to develop the market, and then a fast follower improves the product or service sufficiently to persuade the customers to shift to their product or service. To counter that, the first organization, the one employing a penetration strategy, needs to develop loyalty among the customers they win— perhaps with loyalty programs or with products or services that work only with their components or materials (such as razor blades in a shaver). That is rather like building entry barriers around each individual customer.

From the perspective of CVA®, the perceived value relative to that for the old product or service must be increased as quickly as possible—either for the target market of a skimming strategy or for the multiple markets of a penetration strategy. The sooner that perceived value is maximized, the more revenue, contribution, and profits.

Increasing perceived value requires understanding of customers, especially their needs, so that the organization can make clear why the new product or service meets their needs better than the products and services currently available. Understanding customers is basic marketing, yet nearly all the well-known major product failures, such as the Tigershark aircraft and Polavision instant home movies, had minimal communication with target customers regarding their needs in common.[8] As Gene Simmons, legendary rock star and successful entrepreneur, has cautioned "Never throw money at what you don't know."[9]

In contrast, Harrah's success in the casino industry derives in large part from their use of data bases to understand their customers and increase their perceived value by, for example, providing personal attention and lowering waiting times that develop customer loyalty. Does such customer knowledge pay off? Harrah's data show that customers happy with their Harrah's experience increase their spending on gambling at Harrah's by 24 percent per year. As Gary Loveman, CEO of Harrah's Entertainment explained, "Let the neighbors lure tourists with knights on horseback, fiery volcanoes, pirate ships, and mini-Manhattans. We'll just keep refining what we're already pretty good at: drilling into our data and making sure our regular customers are more than satisfied."[10]

Increasing perceived value requires
understanding of customers

At the same time, efforts need to be expended on lower costs per unit. The faster those costs are managed down, the more revenue, contribution, and profits. Often lowering costs is associated with the later stages in the life cycle. In fact, lowering costs in the early stages of the life cycle may have even more effect on the long-run financial performance of the product or service.

Introduction Stage—Pets.com

Pets.com was one of the many dot-com companies that advertised on the 2000 Super Bowl. They raised more than US$130 million for their start-up. Much of that, however, went for Super Bowl ads that cost approximately $2 million for a thirty second spot. Pets.com allowed people to order pet food and other pet supplies on the Internet. Their ads, featuring a sock-puppet, created a lot of buzz, won awards, and apparently enticed many people to visit the site. Unfortunately, these visitors did not make enough purchases to keep pets.com in business. During the last quarter of 1999 and the first two quarters of 2000, they lost US$125 million on sales of less than US$23million (Exhibit 7.8). Their stock price went from US$11 to US$1.38 in just six months.

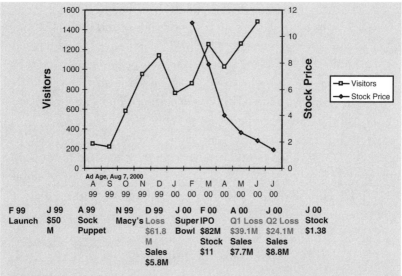

	F 99	J 99	A 99	N 99	D 99	J 00	F 00	A 00	J 00	J 00
	Launch	$50 M	Sock Puppet	Macy's Loss	D 99 $61.8 M Sales $5.8M	Super Bowl	IPO $82M Stock $11	Q1 Loss $39.1M Sales $7.7M	Q2 Loss $24.1M Sales $8.8M	Stock $1.38

Source: Debra Aho Williamson, "A Dog's Life," *Advertising Age*, August 7, 2000, p. S10,
and Patricia Riedman, "Sock Puppet Joins Homeless," *Advertising Age*, November 14, 2000, p. 86.

Exhibit 7.8   Pets.com

Apparently they were unable to persuade their target customers to perceive that buying pet supplies from them provided sufficient value in terms of convenience or selection. The pets.com tag line was "because pets can't drive." While that was true, it was also true that the pets' owners could drive to the supermarket and pick up pet supplies. When pets.com failed, likely their most valuable asset was the sock-puppet—a tribute to building awareness, but not perceived value.

Source: Debra Aho Williamson, "A Dog's Life," *Advertising Age*, August 7, 2000, p. S10, and Patricia Riedman, "Sock Puppet Joins Homeless," *Advertising Age*, November 14, 2000, p. 86.

Rapid Growth Stage

There are two main characteristics of the Rapid Growth stage: The market is starting to grow quickly, and now there are direct competitors in the market providing a similar product or service. The faster growth rate means that whatever one does in this stage is magnified by its effects in the long run. This is typically the most cru-cial stage in the competitive life cycle—where the eventual winner often emerges. The presence of direct competitors means that the perceived value of the product or service may start to fall because there are alternatives for the target customer.

For the pioneer, the CVA® challenge is to maintain perceived value despite the entrance of direct competitors. That can be accom-plished, in part, by careful market focus to avoid head-to-head con-frontations with the new entrants. However, that strategy will work only as long as each organization pursues separate markets. Sooner or later the competitors will meet each other.

A longer-term solution to managing CVA® is for the pioneer to continue to evolve the product or service by adding value—either by adding benefits or improving the level of performance of existing benefits and then communicating those improvements to the target customer. One of the main reasons pioneers fail during the Rapid Growth stage is that they continue to use only a communications strategy suited for the Introduction stage. That is, they continue to communicate the benefits of the product or service versus the old products or services, but neglect to communicate why their benefits are superior to those of the direct competitors that have entered the market.

During the Rapid Growth stage, the pioneer needs to manage CVA® with a dual-focus communication strategy. They can continue to develop the basic market for the product or service; but, in addi-tion, they need communications that emphasize why their brand of the product or service is superior. DuPont implemented such a strat-egy very effectively with their Stainmaster carpet fiber. As they were developing the market, they also improved the product and touted those improvements versus the imitators that were beginning to enter the market.

For the fast-follower—the competitor attacking the pioneer—to manage CVA®, they need to introduce a product or service that has more benefits or performs at a higher level than that of the pioneer. And, they need to communicate those benefit advantages to the tar-get customers. Microsoft tried to overtake Apple's iPod with their Zune, in part by focusing on emerging bands, but that benefit may not be sufficient for success. As Michael Gartenberg of Jupiter Research observed at the time, Microsoft is "going to have to find a crossover strategy really fast. If you're not a fan of independent bands no one has heard of, this isn't the device for you."[11]

Both pioneer and fast-followers need to monitor and evolve their products during the Rapid Growth stage, so they need continued product or service research and development skills to manage CVA®. They need to associate tightly their benefit advantages to their brands. This stage may be the point at which there is the greatest degree of separation among all the brands in the market. Rapid Growth is a propitious time to build brand positions. Both groups also need to apply continuous pressure to push their per unit costs down.

Rapid Growth Stage—Taster's Choice Versus Maxim

One of the most dramatic fast-follower success stories involved Kraft (formerly General Foods) and Nestles. From marketing research, Kraft learned that coffee-drinkers were looking for a coffee that was both convenient and rich-tasting. At the beginning of the story, the late 1960s, coffee was available only as brewed coffee—perceived to be rich-tasting, but messy to prepare—and instant coffee—perceived to be thin-tasting, but convenient to prepare.

Kraft was the pioneer in developing freeze-dried coffee, which was as convenient to prepare as instant coffees and had a richer taste. Their brand of freeze-dried coffee, Maxim, attained a 10 percent share of the instant coffee market in about two years. Initial Maxim television ads featured a scientist who explained what freeze-dried coffee was and why it was convenient and tasted richer than existing soluble coffees.

Kraft's mistake was not moving beyond that message to build perceived value specifically for their brand, for example, rich taste. Nestles introduced their own freeze-dried coffee with television ads that said, "You know what freeze-dried coffee is, now taste the best, Taster's Choice." Less than two years later, Taster's Choice became the share leader in freeze-dried coffee and Maxim never caught up (Exhibit 7.9).

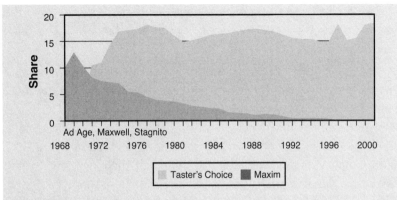

Exhibit 7.9   Soluble coffee

During those two years, pricing and dealing were similar for Taster's Choice and Maxim, but less money was expended on Taster's Choice advertising. By the late 1990s, the Taster's Choice market share was 20 times that of Maxim, and Maxim disappeared from the market.

Nestle's demonstrated the classic fast-follower strategy: Focus on the perceived value of the brand—not just the product category. Kraft stayed too long with a product-oriented communications strategy and did not build the perceived value of Maxim in time to stop Taster's Choice. Taster's Choice seized the attribute of rich taste, made it their own, and took a commanding lead in perceived value.

Source: Peter Flatow, "Beyond 'Me Too'–ism: Being Second Isn't All Bad," *Adweek*, September 22, 1986.

Competitive Turbulence Stage

This stage is often characterized by price wars and advertising wars. The reason is that now there may be many entrants in the marketplace. The product or service technology may be well-known and available to many organizations. The consequence is that there may be many products or services that are very similar with regard to benefit advantages.[12]

Hopefully, organizations have built their brands by the time the slow-followers arrive on the scene. If not, then they are at the same disadvantage as all other competitors.

Assuming that the organizations present during the Rapid Growth stage—pioneer and fast-followers—built their brands then, their CVA® management tasks are to maintain perceived value as much as possible while driving costs down faster than perceived value is falling. During difficult competitive times in the airline industry, Continental Airlines has decided to maintain their perceived value while other carriers, such as the airline described in Chapter 1, "Marketing and Financial Performance," have lowered their perceived value by cost-cutting apparently without regard to customer value.[13]

Usually maintaining perceived value requires precise targeting of market segments. During the Competitive Turbulence stage, market segments proliferate as customers become more knowledgeable about the product or service category—and they make their specific needs known. If an organization tries to meet the diverse needs of all these market segments with a single product or service, then it will probably not meet the needs of anyone.

Targeting market segments may require a different model of the product or service tailored to each segment. The CVA® problem for management is that several different models may increase costs. It is necessary to have engineering skills that allow model differences, which satisfy market segment differences but which will not increase per unit costs more than they increase perceived value per unit for customers in each market segment.

Similarly, targeting market segments may require a different communications approach tailored to each segment. The communications strategy must allow for individual market differences but not increase per unit costs more than they increase perceived value per unit for customers in each market segment.

Note that if the organization can target new market segments— and succeed in each of them. It is possible to increase revenue, contribution, and profits during this stage even while price wars occur in some markets.

If CVA® is not defended during the Competitive Turbulence stage, then the product or service may fail. If perceived value per unit is allowed to decrease faster than cost per unit, then CVA® shrivels and perhaps even becomes negative. At that point the net value the organization produces, as perceived by society, may be too small to encourage the organization to continue.

Competitive Turbulence Stage—Mountain Dew

Mountain Dew was positioned in their advertising for outdoor-loving teenagers in suburban and rural areas. In the late 1980s, Mountain Dew managers decided to reposition the brand with an edgier image for urban teenagers. They gave the Mountain Dew manager seven years to complete the repositioning—which she did very successfully.

Each year, the advertising was changed slightly to move the brand toward the desired brand position. The ads had often showed a number of clean-cut teenagers frolicking at a lake. Each year the creative was changed—to bicycles, to motorcycles, to extreme sports, to urban venues—but in any one year the change was never so much that it was not credible. Seven years later Mountain Dew was the third largest selling soft drink among 18-25-year olds, after Coke and Pepsi.

By focusing the brand on a specific target segment—18-25 year olds in urban areas, Mountain Dew was able to concentrate its efforts and increase the perceived value of the brand to these particular customers, thereby achieving the share objectives (Exhibit 7.10).

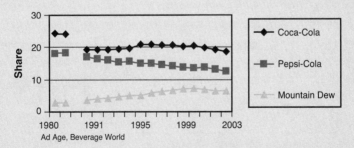

Source: Anne Glover, "Rejuvenating Brand Equity," presented at the Building and Managing Brands Program, Columbia University, 1994.

Exhibit 7.10   Soft drinks

Maturity Stage

During the Maturity stage when most or all functional benefits have been copied, a powerful brand provides differentiation. During this stage, perceived value per unit is often stable for a while. There may be no new slow-followers and no new technologies entering the market. Per unit costs may be decreasing due to economies of scale or continued value-engineering.

During this stage, it may be difficult to increase perceived value because many of the benefits and benefit performance levels have been copied. Often much of perceived value depends on brand-related attributes.

Managing CVA® during this stage usually consists of monitoring perceived value per unit and reinforcing brand attributes as needed to maintain perceived value per unit while at the same time finding ways to reduce costs without detracting from perceived value or, at the least, without detracting from CVA®.

Maturity Stage—Automotive Insurance

Automobile insurance represents a mature market in which increasing or maintaining market share can be expensive. Progressive and GEICO have both increased their market shares by finding ways to add to their perceived values (Exhibit 7.11).

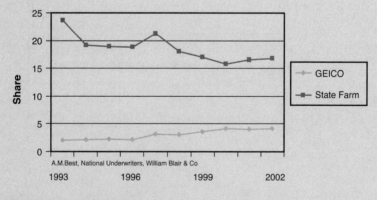

Exhibit 7.11   Auto insurance

Progressive utilizes vans to go directly to the locations of accidents and settle claims on-site at that moment. GEICO invites policy-holders to contact them and learn if they might save money on their car insurance if they switch to GEICO. Both companies doubled their market shares by finding ways to add to perceived value even in a mature market situation where ways to add value are usually difficult to find.[14]

Decline Stage

The key decision for successfully managing CVA® during the Decline stage typically must be made long before the start of the Decline stage. Well before the revenue from a product begins to decline, managers must make the decision to develop a product or service for the competitive life cycle that is just beginning if they are to remain successful with customers in the market by continuing to meet their needs with new technologies. Product and service technologies change but customer needs persist.

The key decisions for the Decline stage—namely to develop new products or services—typically must be made long before the Decline stage begins.

Typically, a Decline stage occurs because of a product or service that appears due to a new technology and satisfies the customers' needs at levels superior to the current products or services. If an organization has such a product or service, then they can continue to serve the customers in their market and continue under the market life cycle. If they do not have such a product or service, or if they are late introducing such a product or service, then they may face difficulties continuing in that market.

Therefore, the main CVA® challenge, here, is to look continually for new products or services that might replace what is currently being provided.

As regards the current product or service, it is difficult in this stage to increase CVA® by increasing perceived value because there is likely a new product or service that has perceived value per unit potentially far above that of the current product or service. The main way to increase CVA® during this stage is to continue to lower per unit costs.

At some point, CVA® will decline so much that the business falls below the shutdown level. At that point, it should be closed. The operation may be closed earlier should there be higher return uses for resources available.[15]

Decline Stage—Film and Digital Cameras

The advent of Canon's initial digital camera signified that the days of photographic film as the image-making choice of the mass market were numbered. The long-time global leader in photographic film, Kodak, was slow to move to the digital technology. The time to move to the life cycle of a new product is before it begins—not well after the new product has been accepted in the market.

While Kodak has fought back in the US with its own brand of digital camera, the delay in moving to digital technology was costly in terms of impact on the company's profits, brand equity, and stock price (Exhibit 7.12 and Exhibit 7.13).

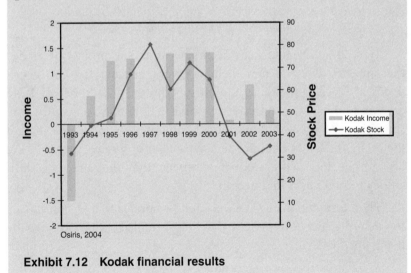

Exhibit 7.12   Kodak financial results

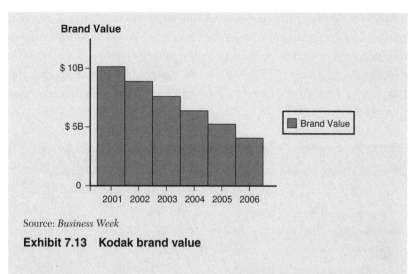

Source: *Business Week*

Exhibit 7.13   Kodak brand value

Polaroid—synonymous with instant film photography—was also damaged by digital imaging technology. Although they did eventually produce and sell their own brand of digital camera, it was too little too late, and the company went bankrupt in 2002.

To manage CVA®, one must anticipate changes in technology and the consequent effects on the product or service life cycle. Perceived value depends on effective communication; but, foremost, it depends on the design of the product or service. If a new technology leads to a product or service with superior design, then, if an organization is to stay with the market (the market life cycle), they must move to that new technology with dispatch. Both Kodak and Polaroid were slow off the mark and paid the consequences in terms of a diminishing of their CVA® for imaging products.[16]

Optimizing Financial Performance over Time

At least in theory, it is possible to make marketing decisions such as design, branding, pricing, and communications that optimize CVA® throughout the competitive life cycle. These would be the marketing decisions that would maximize the net present value of the product or service contribution over time.

Dynamic programming is an optimization method that is used for optimizing decisions over time—especially when there are a series of decisions to be made—such as annual marketing plans. With dynamic programming, one starts at the end of the problem by analyzing the last decision period (when the product or service is likely to be phased out).

Dynamic Programming and CVA®

Initially, one considers the last period and determines the contributions for different possible levels of CVA® (Exhibit 7.14). Then one looks at the possible levels of CVA® and the corresponding contributions. For example, if the perceived value in the last period is 8 and variable cost per unit is 4, then the contribution for that period is estimated to be 80.

Then one considers the period just before the last period and determines the optimal decision for that period. Suppose in that period the perceived value per unit were 11 and the variable cost were 4. To examine the impact of moving perceived value per unit from 11 in this period to 8 in the final period, one adds the contribution for this period (240) to the contribution in the last period (80) that was associated with a perceived value per unit of 8.

In addition, the decision to lower perceived value will result in lower fixed costs such as advertising. For illustration, suppose that if the decision is made to decrease perceived value per unit, then there is a savings in advertising of 30 per perceived value unit decreased. So, if perceived value per unit was 11 and was decreased to 8, then the fixed cost savings due to decreased advertising expenditures is 3 times 30 or 90. Those savings are also added to the contribution for this period and the last period so the total contribution is 410 (240+80+90)—given that the perceived value is 11 in the next to last period and the optimal CVA® decision is made.

Note that 410, obtained by decreasing perceived value per unit from 11 to 8 in the last period, is the maximum contribution for that situation. Lowering perceived value per unit to 10 in the last period gives a total contribution of 390 (240+120+30) and keeping perceived value per unit at 11 yields a total contribution of 340 (240+100).

Exhibit 7.14

CVA® Decision: Last Period

Perceived Value Per Unit	Variable Cost Per Unit	CVA®	Period Contribution	Total Contribution
8	4	4	80	80
10	4	6	120	120
11	6	5	100	100

CVA® Decision: Last Period Minus One

Perceived Value Per Unit	Variable Cost Per Unit	CVA®	Period Contribution	Fixed Cost Saving	Last Period Contribution	Total Contribution
11	4	6	240	90	80	410
13	4	8	320	150	80	550
15	7	8	320	210	80	610

Note: Cost savings equals at 30 times decrease in perceived value.

Reprinted with permission from "Managing through the Life Cycle," Arrow Group, Ltd.®, New York, NY, 2008.

For each perceived value per unit level in the period before the last one, the optimal final period decision can be determined by comparing the total contribution (this period contribution plus last period contribution plus fixed cost savings) for each alternative change in perceived value per unit. In this example, the optimal decision for each level of perceived value per unit in the next to the last period happens to be to decrease perceived value per unit to 8 in the final period.

Similarly, a table can be constructed for the CVA® decisions in the period immediately before, then the period before, and so on, until the first decision period is reached. In such a way, a sequence of optimal decisions for CVA® can be built up.

The optimal CVA® decisions would be determined for that final marketing plan. That is, marketing decisions would be made that would lead to the optimal value of CVA® for the last time period. Then the year immediately before would be considered, and the CVA®-optimizing marketing decisions made for that year given the optimal decisions made for the final year. The process would continue year by year until it reached the present. The result would be a series of decisions over time that would optimize CVA® through the life of the product or service.

While a dynamic programming analysis of CVA® marketing decisions is feasible in theory, in practice it would likely be much more difficult. There is always the challenge of linking marketing decisions to outcomes such as perceived value per unit and unit sales. In addition, the competitive environment is not quiet, but noisy. Technologies change, competitors change, and customers change. Any series of "optimal" marketing decisions would depend on assumptions about technologies, competitors, and customers, as well as all other aspects of the competitive environment. If those assumptions needed to be modified, then that would alter the series of optimal marketing decisions.

Nevertheless, managerial thinking similar to the thought process followed in a dynamic programming analysis—which starts at the final stage and works back to the present—might provide overall guidelines for how a product or service might be managed over time to optimize CVA®. At the least, such an analysis might spotlight the dangers of hollowing out a brand and the need to consider future consequences for CVA® due to decisions made today.

Lincoln Financial Group: What Happens When You Don't Support Your Brand

Perhaps the point to ponder isn't what you can gain by investing in your brand, but what do you risk losing if you don't? This is especially challenging in the b2b service sector where cause and effect has a long tail and it is tough to correlate brand investments to specific product sale gains. One thought is to sell your brand *investment* as brand *insurance*, i.e. not based on what you gain but mitigating your risks.

Let's consider an example. Company A is a major employee services organization who needs to build their brand to employers and through to their employees. Due to extreme business pressures external brand building programs were brought to a halt. The prevailing thought was that brand equity would likely remain stable over two years and could be reinvigorated when the company was ready.

This company's tracking study showed that the percentage declines for consideration remained stable while awareness levels dropped (Table 7.1). When applied against the universe of employed Americans (170 million), those consideration scores translated to 5 million less people who might consider the brand.

Table 7.1 Company A: Halts Brand Support in Year 1 Universe: 170 Million Employed Consumers

Measure	Year 1	Universe Impact	Year 3	Universe Impact	Net Effect
Awareness	70%	119M	60%	102 M	17 M less aware
Consideration	37%	43 M	37%	38 M	5 M less will consider
Strong Consideration	12%	14 M	12%	12 M	2 M less will strongly consider

However, its main rival, Company B maintained their brand investment during this same period and as a result garnered considerably more people who would consider their brand over Company A than the percentages might indicate (Table 7.2).

Table 7.2 Company B Maintains Brand Investment and Expands Prospect Pool At Expense of Company A

Measure	Year 3 Company A	Year 3 Company B	Company B Market Advantage
Awareness	60%	78%	31 M more people aware
Consideration	37%	41%	16 M more who would consider
Strong Consideration	12%	14%	7 M more who would strongly consider

Moral: your loss is your rival's gain, consider your brand investment as brand insurance!

—Edward A. Faruolo, VP Brand Development and Advertising, Lincoln Financial Group

Reprinted with permission

Conclusions

Managing CVA® as technologies change requires a brand that is associated with the customers' needs, not with a specific technology. Such brand-building must be done soon to allow the organization to continually introduce products and services that meet the ongoing needs of their customers.

Managing CVA® throughout the competitive life cycle involves both strategic decisions and tac\tical decisions. Strategically, target markets and positioning must be employed with their impact on CVA® in mind. Tactically, communications must be focused to increase perceived value—at reasonable cost—so that CVA® is increased when possible and maintained when under pressure from competitors or from other technologies.

During the Introduction stage of the competitive life cycle, benefits relevant to a customer are communicated through the sales force and media with the objective of gaining trial. The Rapid Growth stage is the time during which these benefits are wired to the brand because the functional benefits will likely be imitated during Competitive Turbulence. Products and services in the Maturity stage may have little functional differentiation but, will, it is hoped, have great brand distinction. During the Decline state, even a powerful brand may not survive if its technology is obsolete.

CVA® informs specific strategic decisions—more on that in the next chapter.

8

Utilizing CVA® for Strategic Decisions

The two key strategic decisions in marketing are selecting a target market and the determining of the positioning of the product or service for the customers in that market.[1] Both these decisions, in turn, affect branding—how one builds a brand for customers in a specific target market by selecting benefits from the positioning of the product or service.

As Kevin Clancy has correctly observed, improving marketing measures alone "won't improve performance. Fixing broken strategy and optimizing the marketing budget will."[2] CVA® is not *just* an important measure. It provides managers with structure and *forward control* for improving marketing strategic decisions and marketing tactical decisions.

Marketing strategy decisions concern target marketing, positioning, and branding. This chapter shows how CVA® can be employed to improve those decisions. The following chapter shows how CVA® can be utilized to improve tactical decisions.

TIAA-CREF: Focusing on Customers

TIAA-CREF was established in 1918 as a financial services provider for those who work in the academic field. Ninety years later, we manage $420 billion* in assets and help 3.2 million people in the academic, medical, cultural, and research fields plan for and live in retirement. Despite our size and success of paying $10 billion annually in retirement income to 500,000 TIAA-CREF participants, we discovered in 2004, when we began our intensified brand building work, that unaided brand awareness was relatively low among our own participants. As larger, for-profit competitors began targeting our core audience, it became imperative that we not only increase brand awareness, but also deepen brand affinity.

Through our "Brand Stages"°° research, which began in 2004, we are able to correlate brand affinity with assets held at TIAA-CREF. The stronger the affinity with the brand, the greater the assets held at the company. We have categorized our participants into five brand segments: "unengaged," "convertible," "vulnerable," "committed," and "entrenched." As one might expect, "unengaged" has the lowest amount of assets with us while "entrenched" has the highest. Our goal is to improve brand affinity and, thus, increase asset acquisition opportunities. As such, we focus marketing programs against the "convertible" and "vulnerable" targets as they are more likely to move up the brand stages scale than is the "unengaged" target. We also focus programs against the "committed" and "entrenched" audiences to maintain their strong commitment to the brand, retain their current assets, and further seek the consolidation of their assets with TIAA-CREF.

The five participant brand segments differ in market importance, brand behavior, brand development, and brand perceptions. We can link brand affinity with assets and more precisely target our marketing efforts.

—Jamie DePeau, Senior Vice President, Marketing, TIAA-CREF

° Assets as of 6/30/08.

°°"Brand Stages" is an internal designation. This analysis is formally known as ABLe.

Reprinted with permission

Targeting

In general, targeting consists of focusing on a certain group of customers. For maximum effect, these customers should be similar with respect to their needs for a product or service and how they perceive the value provided by various brands of that product or service.

Such groups of customers, of course, are known as *market segments*, as discussed in Chapter 6, "Managing CVA®."

Identifying market segments is not a process of dividing markets. Identifying market segments starts with individual customers and is a process of grouping similar individual customers to form market segments. The comparison between *dividing* and *grouping* is not merely a semantic distinction—it is a distinction between two kinds of processes.

Market segmentation is a process of grouping customers.

Targeting Market Segments the Wrong Way

There are three major mistakes commonly made by organizations when they attempt to segment markets: failure to think of market segments as customers, failure to consider needs or benefit sought by customers, and failure to develop strategies on a segment basis.

Failure to Think of Market Segments as Customers

In numerous marketing plans, market segments are defined only in product terms such as the "hot cereal market" and the "cold cereal market" or the "large copier market" and the "small copier market." Market segments consist of *customers*, not products or services. Defining market segments as particular products or services neatly avoids one of the most complicated and most important procedures in marketing—trying to identify distinct market segments. Market segments defined by products or services generally provide no information for managing CVA®, which, in turn, means that they do not provide information for managing revenue and contribution.

Failure to Consider Needs or Benefits Sought

To segment a market properly one needs two types of information: the benefits sought by the customers, which define the segment, and the characteristics of the customers, which allow one to find them with marketing tactics such as communications and promotion. Many times organizations focus primarily—or exclusively—on the characteristics, such as demographics or psychographics for business-to-consumer markets or industry membership or company size measures for business-to-business markets. Information on customer characteristics is needed in order to focus marketing efforts, but such information is useful only if the characteristics used are associated with benefits sought by the customers. Benefits sought are associated with perceived value, and consequently, behavior and market segments are defined to capture potential behavioral differences among customers.

A colleague was working with a company that sells potatoes to various organizations. His contacts told him they used five segments: fast food restaurants, fancy restaurants, universities-hospitals-prisons, corporations, and the US government. When he asked them why they segmented the market in that particular way, they replied that they had always done it that way; their sales force was organized that way; their competitors did it that way; and that is how the data were available. None of those reasons included any mention of customer needs as a basis for their segmentation scheme. In fact, one of the reasons was especially worrisome—using the same segments as their competitors. Copying the market segmentation scheme of one's competitor can be dangerous—if competitors know what they are doing and are segmenting the market in such a way that they can win the market segments that they target.

Failure to Develop Strategy on a Market Segment Basis

Suppose an organization has successfully developed a market segmentation scheme. Then each market segment should have its own market strategy. The whole purpose of identifying market segments is to provide a foundation for developing marketing strategies that are more precisely targeted for certain customers.

After the author gave a presentation on market segmentation at one company, one of the managers came over during the coffee break and said, "I agree totally with what you said about finding distinct segments. We used to have 14 segments, but we found many were the same; so we consolidated them into 6 segments." The author replied,

"Great. How many marketing strategies do you use?" The manager answered, "Oh, just one. We treat everyone the same."

Treating everyone the same can be a grave mistake—especially if one has gone to the trouble of identifying market segments consisting of customers who can be expected to differ in their behavior.

CVA® and perceived value can be used to provide a foundation for identifying and selecting market segments.

CVA® and Market Segmentation

It is difficult to find laws in the social sciences. When one is considering human behavior, variety flourishes—thankfully. However, there is, perhaps, one certain law in marketing and in economics.

Sexton's Law of Micro-Targeting

The more one can target one's offerings to smaller and smaller groups of customers, the more revenue one will achieve.

Note that the law is about maximizing *revenue*, not about maximizing contribution or profits. Revenue will always increase the more market segments are targeted, but contribution or profits may increase or decrease. To determine how to maximize contribution or profits, costs must also be considered. As smaller and smaller groups of customers are targeted, costs may increase and offset any revenue increases.[3]

Corollary to Sexton's Law of Micro-Targeting

If one can target individual customers, then revenue is maximized.

Please note that in many situations, charging different prices to different customers may be illegal—so check with an attorney before proceeding.

Basis for the Law of Micro-Targeting

Sexton's Law of Micro-Targeting can be explained intuitively—by appealing to selling experience—and by economics.

Selling

For anyone who has ever sold anything, when a customer says "Yes" and makes the purchase, there is always a nagging feeling that perhaps something has been left "on the table." Perhaps the sales person might have quoted a higher price that the customer would have accepted.

Experienced sales people watch and listen to customers carefully to try to price as close to the maximum as possible. Of course, the difficulty is that if the price is set too high, then the customer may be lost. However, the closer the price is to the customer's perceived value, without surpassing that ceiling, the more revenue is obtained. Effective sales people are able to extract significant revenue from a market.

Economics

As discussed in prior chapters, a demand curve shows the relationship of the number of units sold in a given time period to the price charged per unit. For example, in Exhibit 8.1, at a price of $15, exactly 210 units are sold, producing revenue of $3,150. A price of $15 in this example happens to be the price that maximizes revenue for the market described by this demand curve if just one price must be quoted for all customers in this market. With micro-targeting, higher revenue can be achieved from the same market.

Quoting one price for the entire market produces revenue that is less than the maximum possible. In the market described by the demand curve in Exhibit 8.1, there were some customers who would have paid more than $15 per unit, but they were not given the chance because there was just the one price for the market. The lost revenue that those customers represent is the area of the triangle to the left of 210 units and above the price of $15, or *$1,575*.

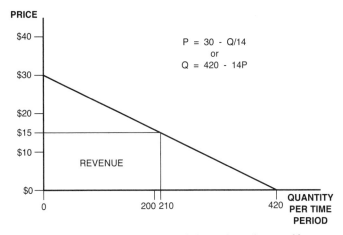

PRICE

$40 —

P = 30 - Q/14
or
Q = 420 - 14P

$30 —

$20 —

$15 —

$10 —

REVENUE

$0 —

0   200 210   420

QUANTITY
PER TIME
PERIOD

Reprinted with permission from "How Private Label Brands Work," Donald E. Sexton, New York, NY, 2008.

Exhibit 8.1   Market demand curve—maximum revenue

There were also customers who did not want to pay at least $15 per unit, but would have paid something. They also represent lost revenue equal to the area of the triangle to the right of 210 units, or *$1,575.*

If a separate price is charged each customer (and, again, keep in mind that there are often laws preventing such practices), then the total revenue obtained would be the area in the entire triangle defined by the demand curve, or *$6,300* (Exhibit 8.1). With micro-targeting carried to its extreme—where every customer is a separate market segment—then every customer in the market is secured and revenue is maximized. That is what effective sales people do when they are free to quote price.

Exhibit 8.2   Maximum Revenue and Maximum Contribution with Single Price

Price	Variable Cost per Unit	Units	Maximum Revenue
$15.00	$3	210	$3,150.00
			Maximum Contribution
$16.50	$3	189	$2,551.50

Reprinted with permission from "How Private Label Brands Work," Donald E. Sexton, New York, NY, 2008.

A similar argument can be made for increasing contribution—up to a point.

If only one price is charged and the variable cost per unit is $3, then the price that maximizes contribution for the demand curve in Exhibit 8.2 is *$16.50*—189 units are sold and contribution is $2,551.50 (Exhibits 8.2 and 8.3). However, there were potential customers who would have paid more than $16.50 but were not allowed to do so. In addition, there were potential customers willing to pay more than the variable cost of $3 per unit but were also not allowed to do so. Those two situations each represent an additional contribution of *$1,275.75* or, in total, another *$2,551.50*.

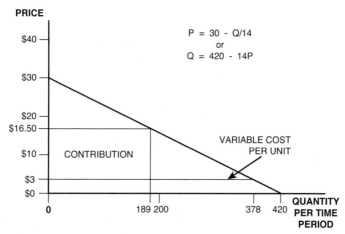

Reprinted with permission from "How Private Label Brands Work," Donald E. Sexton, New York, NY, 2008.

Exhibit 8.3   Market demand curve—maximum contribution

If a separate price is charged to each customer and the variable cost per unit is the same for all units sold, then contribution would be doubled with micro-targeting.

However, there is a limit to the number of offerings one should bring to a market even if there are numerous identifiable segments.[4] That is the cost of attempting to serve smaller and smaller groups of customers. The variable cost per unit will likely vary by segment and may increase as the needs of customers in the segment are met. Fixed costs may also increase as more segments are targeted. At some point, the costs (operations, logistics, customer service, communications, and so on) may eradicate any additional revenue that would be associated with targeting a product or service to ever fewer customers.

> *There are limits to the number of offerings one should bring to market—both due to costs and customers.*

Even if the costs would allow additional micro-targeting, it still may not be a good idea to pursue all the micro-market segments one might identify because, at some point, the customers may become confused with all the different offers available. There is a limit as to how many product or service offerings—at different price points—a customer is able to process. For example, proliferation of entries in the beverage industry—Diet Cherry, Diet Coke with Lemon, Vanilla Coke, Caffeine-free Classic, Diet Cherry—eventually can erode the brand position even of a Coca-Cola.[5] Bayer introduced a line of products called Bayer Select—different products for different pains such as headaches, sinus discomfort, and minor arthritis pain. The product failed because Bayer Aspirin already handled all those types of pain. Bayer Select just added another kind of pain—the headache of trying to find out which form of Bayer Select to use—when all they needed to use was Bayer Aspirin.[6]

> *The Law of Micro-targeting maximizes revenue but may not maximize contribution.*

Using CVA® to Target Market Segments

Targeting marketing segments with CVA® involves the following steps:

1. Identify possible segments.
2. Estimate the demand curve for each segment.
3. Determine the optimal pricing for each segment.
4. Repeat steps 1, 2, and 3 to find the optimal segments to target.

Market segmentation schemes can be developed with a variety of approaches such as those discussed in Chapter 6. The approaches include judgment and the application of statistical tools such as cluster analysis. The main drivers of the segmentation are the components of perceived value for the product or service. The results consist of a set of possible market segments composed of customers with similar perceived value for the product or service. Each segment is defined by benefits sought and identified by various classification variables such as demographics or company characteristics.

The demand curve for each segment needs to be estimated with one of the techniques mentioned in Chapter 4, "Perceived Value." Because the segments are developed utilizing the components of perceived value, customers in a given segment can be expected to behave according to a similar demand curve. That has two positive aspects: The estimated demand curve for any given segment will be more likely to be statistically significant, and, consequently, prediction of behavior based on the demand curve will be more likely to have higher accuracy.[7]

Suppose three market segments are identified and their demand curves are estimated (Exhibit 8.4). Customers in Segment A are relatively price-insensitive, those in Segment C relatively price-sensitive, and those in Segment B in the middle. Notice that the three market segment demand curves sum to the demand curve for the entire market.

Market Demand Curve

$$P = 30 - Q/14 \quad \text{or} \quad Q = 420 - 14P$$

Market Segment A Demand Curve

$$P = 40 - Q/2 \quad \text{or} \quad Q = 80 - 2P$$

Market Segment B Demand Curve

$$P = 35 - Q/4 \quad \text{or} \quad Q = 140 - 4P$$

Market Segment C Demand Curve

$$P = 25 - Q/8 \quad \text{or} \quad Q = 200 - 8P$$

Reprinted with permission from "How Private Label Brands Work," Donald E. Sexton, New York, NY, 2008.

Exhibit 8.4   Market and market segment demand curves

The prices that maximize revenue can be determined for each segment (Exhibit 8.5). Total maximum revenue from the three segments totals $3,275 (Exhibit 8.6), which is higher than the maximum revenue from the one-price situation, $3,150—although lower than the maximum revenue if a different price is charged each customer.

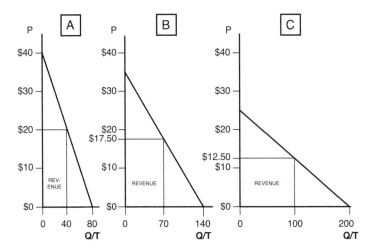

Reprinted with permission from "How Private Label Brands Work," Donald E. Sexton, New York, NY, 2008.

Exhibit 8.5   Market segment demand curves—maximum revenue

Exhibit 8.6   Maximum Revenue for Segments

Market Segment	Price	Units	Maximum Revenue
A	$20.00	40	$ 800.00
B	$17.50	70	$1,225.00
C	$12.50	100	$1,250.00
Total		210	$3,275.00

Reprinted with permission from "How Private Label Brands Work," Donald E. Sexton, New York, NY, 2008.

Of more importance is the impact on contribution from pursuing the three market segments. Assuming, for illustration, different variable costs per unit: $5 for Segment A, $3 for Segment B, and $2 for Segment C, the contribution-maximizing prices can be determined

(Exhibit 8.7). Given the assumed costs, total maximum contribution from the three segments is $3,275, which is substantially higher than the maximum contribution from the one-price situation, $2,551.50—although lower than the maximum contribution if a different price is charged each customer (and the variable cost per unit is $3).

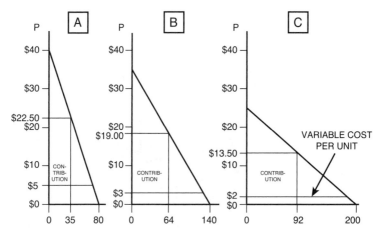

Reprinted with permission from "How Private Label Brands Work," Donald E. Sexton, New York, NY, 2008.

Exhibit 8.7   Market segment demand curves—maximum contribution

If segments are formed so that customers in each segment are associated with distinct demand curves, then more segments will always increase revenue. Whether contribution also increases depends on the behavior of the relevant costs (Exhibit 8.8).

Exhibit 8.8   Maximum Contribution for Segments

Market Segment	Price	Variable Cost per Unit	Units	Revenue	Maximum Contribution
A	$22.50	$5.00	35	$ 787.50	$ 612.50
B	$19.00	$3.00	64	$1,216.00	$1,024.00
C	$13.50	$2.00	92	$1,242.00	$1,058.00
Total			191	$3,245,50	$3,275.00

Reprinted with permission from "How Private Label Brands Work," Donald E. Sexton, New York, NY, 2008.

Positioning

The positioning of a product or service is defined by four questions (Exhibit 8.9).

| Target Customer? |
| Target Competitor? |
| Benefit Advantage? |
| Competitive Advantage? |

Exhibit 8.9   The components of positioning

1. Who is the individual customer being targeted?
2. What is (are) the competitor(s) being targeted?
3. What are the key benefit advantages for the target customer?
4. What are the key competitive advantages?

The individual customer may be the sole decision-maker for the purchase, or he or she may be a specific member of a decision-making unit—all those involved in making the purchase decision. Whoever the target customer is, their needs must be met by the benefit advantages.

The target competitors consist of one or more competitors whose products or services are under consideration or can be expected to be under consideration by the target customer.

The benefit advantages, as explained in Chapter 6, consist of one or more benefits that the customer wants that the organization provides at a higher level than do the target competitors. The competitive advantages are the capabilities of the organization that allow them to provide the benefit advantages. Benefit advantages affect perceived value; competitive advantages affect costs.

© Ashleigh Brilliant, 2008. Used with permission.

Determining Positioning the Wrong Way

Mistakes in positioning include: Ignoring the customer, ignoring the competitors, selecting ineffective benefits, and misevaluating the capabilities of the organization.

Ignoring the Customer

The largest disasters in the history of marketing, such as the Tigershark fighter aircraft, Premier cigarettes, Polavision instant movie film, and the RCA Videodisc, all had one thing in common—a lack of attention to the needs of customers.[8] For example, the Tigershark was developed without appreciable input from the US Air Force and US Navy—the prime customers. When the US Air Force and US Navy both declined to purchase the aircraft, no other country would buy it because they believed they could not be assured of spare parts. In contrast, Charles Schwab employs traditional marketing research but also has recruited several hundred interested clients who provide them with ongoing insights regarding their investing habits.[9]

Ignoring Competitors

Organizations may ignore current competitors but even more of a concern is the potential of ignoring new competitors—from other geographies or with other technologies. During the 1970s, Harley-Davidson ignored Honda, Kawasaki, Yamaha, and Suzuki because they produced small motorcycles. Consequently, Harley nearly went bankrupt in the 1980s. Kodak, the photographic film market share leader in many countries, was slow to respond to the threat of digital cameras from companies such as Canon.

Ignoring the Environment

Changes in the environment such as social trends, economic trends, and demographic trends may decrease the effectiveness of a positioning. The Hummer was a popular vehicle among certain market segments in the United States when gasoline was relatively inexpensive. When US gasoline prices increased, Hummer sales declined due to its relative fuel inefficiency.[10]

Selecting Ineffective Benefits

Organizations may select benefits of low interest to the target customers. Airlines that tout their food are not focusing on a benefit of high importance to most passengers. Scott Paper Company failed memorably by trying to launch Scott Towels Junior. The product was designed for customers who wanted a high-performing paper towel but at a lower price so the towels were only 8.2 inches wide instead of the usual 11 inches. Just one of the problems with the product was the lack of paper towel holders to fit this new size. It was a product built without thinking through the impact on CVA® for the target customers. In contrast, Procter & Gamble introduced Bounty Select-A-Size—towels with the perforation at shorter intervals than usual so the customer could use less towel if he or she wished—a benefit that was desired.[11]

Having Too Many Features

Too many features can confuse the customer. Include those features that provide the main benefits that maximize CVA®. Do not add features that increase cost without increasing CVA® at least as much as the cost changes.[12]

Misevaluating Capabilities

A benefit advantage must be both important to the target customer and a benefit that the organization can provide at a higher level of performance than others. Banks that boast of their friendly customer service lose their positioning when customers encounter rude employees.

CVA® and Positioning

Positioning must be managed to maximize CVA®. That is done by designing with *value engineering*—examining the value provided the target customer for various levels of costs. Note that effective positioning can lead to either higher or lower costs per unit. What is crucial is the difference between perceived value and unit costs. Given appropriate design, positioning must be effectively communicated to the target customer to ensure the value of the product or service is perceived.

Using CVA® to Determine Positioning

Following are the steps to determine positioning by maximizing CVA®:

1. Select the target segment.
2. Estimate the impact of benefits on perceived value.
3. Estimate the cost impact of altering benefits.
4. Determine the benefits and levels of performance for the target segment.

The initial selection of target segment is typically a tentative choice. Until one knows the positioning appropriate for that segment, it is difficult to decide whether or not to target a segment.

For customers in the target segment, one employs one of the approaches described in Chapter 4, such as conjoint analysis, to examine the monetary value to the customer of different benefits and different levels of benefit performance. The costs of providing new benefits or changing the performance level of existing benefits (either to a higher or lower level) need to be estimated—both variable and fixed.

The perceived value to be created and the likely per unit costs are compared by calculating CVA®. Keep in mind that before the benefit changes affect CVA®, the target customers must understand them; if they don't understand the benefits, the benefit changes will not affect perceived value and CVA®. Design alone does not change perceived value. Benefits must be communicated to the target customer before they have an impact on perceived value.

The optimal positioning is determined by examining the values of CVA® associated with various bundles of benefits provided at various performance levels.

Using CVA® to Evaluate Multiple Positions

Coordinating positions across markets can be a problem wherever a market is sufficiently large to consist of several segments. Coordinating positions across countries is a frequent problem in international marketing. Should managers in market or country be allowed to determine their own product or service position? Should there be one (global) position in all markets?[13]

Determining what to do in such situations is complex. Usually there are many sound arguments both for using just one position for all markets (standardization) and for tailoring a position to a specific market (localization).[14] The solution is often a combination of global and local positions. For example, L'Oreal develops global brands with attention to what local customers value, adjusting the amount of moisturizer in their lipsticks and stressing their French origins (or not) according to the needs of customers in specific country markets.[15] 3M uses input from European country managers as they develop their global strategy.[16] MTV has had a policy of 70 percent local content for their programming in their different country markets.[17] CVA® can be used in a systematic way to determine how to coordinate a product or service across markets.[18] The approach has been used in practice and appears to be a very efficient process.

The more one can standardize components of a product or service position, the lower costs due to efficiencies. However, the more one can localize components of a product or service—tailor them to the priorities of customers in specific markets—then the higher the potential perceived value for customers in those markets. Note that no positioning is likely to be fully standardized or fully localized. There always are some elements of positioning that are specific to a market and other elements that are common across all markets.

Standardization lowers costs, localization raises value—
both can increase CVA®.

CVA® can guide the trade-off between standardization and localization by exploring how possible changes in perceived value and cost per unit might affect revenue and contribution (Exhibit 8.10).

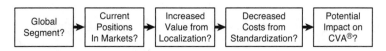

Reprinted with permission from "Should Your Brand Be Global?" *Chazen Web Journal of International Business*, March, 2004, pp. 1-13.

Exhibit 8.10   Coordinating positions across markets

First, one should check the segmentation structure being used, especially if the product or service is marketed in several countries. The most powerful way to coordinate positioning is to identify global segments—customers in different markets who are seeking similar benefits.

For example, Coca-Cola focuses much of its marketing attention on 18 to 25 year olds throughout the world. Despite being from different countries, many in this age group have similar preferences for music, clothing, and soft drinks, and they form a global segment. One of Procter & Gamble's first "Euro-brands" was Vizir, a heavy-duty, liquid detergent targeted to those who wash at low temperatures. Honda globalized the motorcycle industry by initially focusing on young riders.[19]

Note that there is nothing in the definition of a market segment that specifically mentions a country. A market segment is a group of customers or potential customers who are seeking the same benefits. As regards consumer products, young people or seniors in one country may have more in common with their counterparts in other countries than with fellow citizens in different demographic groups. Global segments may be even more likely to occur with business-to-business markets—large shoe manufacturers or small furniture companies, for example, may have more in common with organizations like theirs in other countries than with organizations in other industries or of different size in their own country.

If the target segment is a global segment, then it is more likely that a standardized positioning strategy should be utilized. Dove's "one quarter cleansing cream" offer seems to appeal to skin-conscious women everywhere. MasterCard uses their "Priceless" campaign for credit-card users throughout the world, touching emotions that seem to be part of experiences common to people in all countries.

Even though there may not be a global segment, there may be certain benefits that are of high priority for customers in several segments. Local managers can identify the relative importance of various benefits to customers in their markets. That information can be unified in a chart similar to the Segment Identification Chart introduced in Chapter 6.

Each segment under consideration needs to be evaluated as to its importance to the organization—both in terms of attractiveness (for example, size, growth rate, price insensitivity) and the organization's relative ability to succeed in the segment (as suggested in Chapter 6). Those market segments that are more important to the organization should have more impact on the standardization/localization tradeoff.

By looking horizontally across the segments in the Segment Identification Chart, it is possible to find those attributes that are desired by customers in the more important market segments. Those attributes that have high priorities in the more important markets are attributes that might be considered for standardization across markets. To decide which attributes should be standardized requires estimating the likely changes in revenue and costs, and consequently contribution, if the current positioning in any market is changed.

For their Accord model, Honda was one of the first automobile companies to develop a versatile global platform that allowed them to meet local needs without incurring the high costs of completely tailoring the car to each country market. They developed a chassis for the Accord that could be made both longer or shorter and wider or narrower. That allowed them to make larger Accords for the US market and smaller Accords for the Japanese and European markets, all with the same chassis, the most expensive part of the automobile.[20] They maximized CVA® with their ability to build cars that met the disparate needs of different country markets while controlling production costs.

Heineken pursues a long run global strategy with its country brand positions. Heineken has a global brand position involving friendliness, pride, and tradition, among other attributes. However, the brand offer can vary somewhat by country according to the development stage of the beer market. Over time, as the beer market globalizes, Heineken consciously and systematically evolves its local brand positions so that they take on the global brand position as each country beer market becomes mature.[21]

Revenue depends on the perceived value to the customers in the target segments in each country. Knowing the relative contributions to perceived value of the various product or service benefits permits one to estimate the impact of any benefit changes on the financial performance of the product or service. One can also estimate the costs involved in changing position, which will include both design costs and communications costs.

The key metric is the CVA® for each market. The value of CVA® depends on the changes in the perceived value and the costs per unit. CVA® allows an evaluation of the potential contribution for any moves to either standardize or localize the position of the product or service across markets. Changes in fixed costs should also be considered, so changes in profit can be evaluated as well.

Pfizer: Global Learning

Brand relevancy plays a critical role in sustaining brand value and in contributing to cash flow and shareholder value. When faced with dynamic changes in a market environment, marketers need to be creative in exploring ways to extend brands beyond their traditional equities or they risk having the brand become less relevant to customers resulting in at minimum a slow decline in sales and profits and at maximum, the potential for a brand to become antiquated.

Over a decade ago, Pfizer faced this situation with Visine® eye drops. Visine was known as the brand that "gets the red out" and despite holding the majority of the eye drop market (defined as redness relievers), was experiencing a steady erosion of unit share. Analyses of the broader eye drop market showed that products focused on dry eyes like artificial tears that did not reduce redness were growing rapidly. Unless Visine found a way to extend its equity into this and other segments of the market its long term viability was threatened. Despite this evidence, there were concerns about taking a brand that stood for "gets the red out" could extend itself to segments that did not include this benefit.

In order to move forward, a newly formed global team surveyed other markets where Visine was marketed and found that colleagues in Canada had already introduced a product to compete in the artificial tears market with no detrimental affect to the brand. There remained the question as to whether the Canadian experience could be extrapolated to the US so qualitative and quantitative market research was performed that entry into this and other segments was viable. Based on this evidence, a product strategy was established to sequentially introduce line extensions of Visine into the artificial tears segment (Visine Tears), allergy segment (Visine-A which replaced the brand Occuhist) and contact lens relief (Visine for Contacts). US sales and profits of Visine increased substantially over this period.

Pfizer has subsequently sold its Consumer Health Care business to Johnson & Johnson for over $16 billion dollars and while much of this value was supported by larger products like Listerine® mouth-wash , a stronger Visine franchise most certainly contributed to the value that J&J was willing to pay Pfizer.

—Michael P. Bentivegna, Senior Director/Group Leader,
WW Atherosclerosis and Thrombosis, Pfizer Inc.

Reprinted with permission

In general, if one is going to standardize components of the product or service, then one would want to standardize those that have the most financial impact in various market segments in various countries. These components, then, become the attributes that are globally coordinated. Local country managers can then manage the other product or service components as they see fit.

CVA® and "Grey Markets"

An important aspect of coordinating positioning concerns *grey markets*—when products are shipped from one market to another outside of the intended distribution channels. Grey markets occur because perceived value, and therefore CVA®, can sometimes vary across markets. That means potentially higher prices in some markets. If there are sufficient discrepancies among prices, importers will move products through grey market channels, shipping product from low-price markets to high-price markets. Importers are arbitraging the product.

Grey markets are accompanied by product availability at lower prices than those intended. Grey markets usually displace high-margin business with low-margin business and, therefore, are a concern to both the producing organization and its resellers.

Grey markets are simply the effect of globalization as prices across borders become visible. In the long run, grey markets disappear as the world becomes a truly global market and CVA® is leveled. However, in the short run, grey markets can be managed by considering CVA®.

There are three main options for managing grey markets: legal approaches, pricing, and positioning.

Legal approaches, such as contracts with resellers not to sell outside of their geographical area, are attempts to put a cap on the pressure to transship. The pressure and the incentive still exist, so legal measures are not always effective.

Changing prices in various markets to remove the incentives for transshipping can work, but requires substantial information regarding not only existing prices in all markets, but also information about the shipping costs among all markets in which products may be transshipped. In addition, when exchange rates change, the prices that remove grey market incentives need to be recalculated.

Positioning—and thereby controlling CVA®—is likely the most effective way to take control of grey markets. By considering what aspects of the positioning of the product or service should be standardized, what aspects should be localized, and when those choices should be made, the incentives for grey markets can be managed.

Generally, over time one would expect positioning to become more standardized, as global segments emerge. The more positioning is standardized and the more perceived value, cost per unit, and CVA® become similar across markets, the less incentive there is for grey markets.

Branding

Branding consists of embedding the benefit advantages in the target customer's perceived value for the product or service.[22]

Brand-related attributes may comprise substantial portions of perceived value for many products and services (Recall Exhibit 3.7).

As discussed in Chapter 4, the three main components of a brand are: identifiers, attributes, and associations (Exhibit 8.11). The *identifiers* are the cues that lead customers to associate attributes with a brand and include the brand name and logo. *Attributes* should consist of needs or benefits, but are anything that the customer associates with the brand. *Associations* refer to the clarity with which a customer links an attribute to a brand.

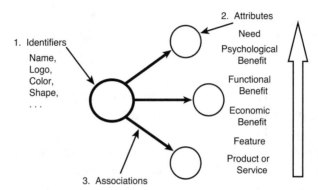

Reprinted with permission from "Building Global Brands," Donald E. Sexton, New York, NY, 2008.

Exhibit 8.11   Components of a brand

Building a Brand the Wrong Way

There are at least two common mistakes in building brands: preoccupation with brand awareness and selecting ineffective benefits for the brand positioning.

Preoccupation with Awareness

Many managers appear to attempt to develop brands by building awareness rather than perceived value. For approximately 80 percent of organizations, brand awareness is their key measure of brand health.[23]

The problem with brand awareness alone as a brand-building objective is that it is nondirectional. High brand awareness may be associated with either positive or negative feelings toward a brand. As recounted in Chapter 7, "Managing CVA® over Time", several studies seem to agree that awareness alone does not constitute a foundation for a brand. In the customer's mind, *value* must be linked to the brand so that perceived value is affected. Many dot-com companies failed because they focused on brand awareness to the exclusion of value.

> *Brand awareness alone is not an effective measure*
> *of a brand's strength.*

Selecting Ineffective Benefits for the Brand Positioning

This failing is the same as was mentioned for positioning in general. If a benefit is unimportant to the target customer, then the brand should not be built on that benefit. Pets.com, an Internet provider of pet supplies, overestimated the appeal to pet-owners of the convenience of ordering on the Internet.[24]

CVA® and Building a Brand

Branding affects CVA® through perceived value. A strong brand can raise perceived value beyond the value provided directly by the benefits experienced by the customers. The brand impact on perceived value can be increased through design, communications, and association with other brands.

Effective design improves actual value, while effective communications ensures that customers perceive the improvements in actual value. Association with other brands, such as use of a corporate brand or co-branding, can transfer other positive attributes to a brand and add to perceived value.

Using CVA® to Build a Brand

To build a brand, one must focus on CVA®. Here are the steps:

1. Select the target segment.
2. Evaluate the current brand position.
3. Consider alternative brand positions.
4. Determine the desired brand position.
5. Communicate the desired brand position consistently over time.

All marketing and branding efforts begin with selection of a target segment.

The current brand position is evaluated by examining perceived value and its benefit components with some of the methods discussed in Chapter 4.

If the current brand position is not satisfactory, then alternative brand positions are examined by evaluating their likely perceived values. The desired brand position would be one of the positions that likely increases CVA®.

The new brand position is constructed with consistent brand communications over time. Communications at all points of contact with the customer should support the desired band position.

The Mountain Dew example in the previous chapter is a striking example of repositioning a brand. Even more dramatic was the repositioning of Marlboro cigarettes. Initially, Marlboro was targeted toward women. The desired brand position was changed 180 degrees to focus on men—very masculine men. The first campaign featured men with tattoos. One of the tattooed men was a cowboy—and that ad worked so well that the Marlboro cowboy was born and served as the basis for Marlboro's branding campaign for many years.[25]

The Conference Board: The Impact of "Community"

We are about to enter a new era of marketing, driven by the growth of the Internet and the communities that it continues to spawn.

The growth of the Internet is old news, of course. Nevertheless, we are at the beginning of the new era, not in the middle as some might claim. It is only as recently as 18 months ago that business could assume, reasonably, that its customers had access to the Internet, and the company could tailor its offerings or service model accordingly. More importantly, consumers in very large numbers are only now beginning to become comfortable participating in online communities, learning the behaviors necessary to extract value from these communities while understanding the safeguards necessary to protect them.

The existence of a population that is comfortable leveraging the wisdom of a large, anonymous crowd has enormous implications. What happens when physical access to "the market" is no longer a constraint to provide service to that market? For example— schools will no longer be the only place for people to learn. Magazines, newspapers, televisions, and theaters will no longer be the only place people can go for news and entertainment. Nearby doctors and hospitals will no longer be the only place to go for knowledgeable medical advice.

I can't see the future clearly—but I'd like to put forward one idea that may become important: *in the new world, the voice of the customer* (or of the community, if you prefer) *will matter more than the voice of the provider.* Marketing will need to change profoundly to adapt to this new reality. Positioning products will become less important; understanding customers' experiences, and ensuring these are fully articulated, will become much more important. Brands as the conveyors of "trust" will become less important; the sum of customers' actual experiences, as conveyed by the anonymous community, will supplant brands as the "trusted source."

In my own organization (The Conference Board) we are working on ways to leverage the power of our community—comprised of more than ten thousand senior executives around the world with extraordinary insights on today's (and tomorrow's) crucial business issues. How well we achieve this will go a long way toward determining our relevance, our impact, and our success.

—Jonathan Spector, Chief Executive Officer,
The Conference Board

Reprinted with permission

CVA® and Brand Architecture

Brand architecture refers to the relationship of the corporate brand and all the other brands the organization may employ. In some organizations, such as General Electric and IBM, the corporate brands represent a substantial amount of brand equity relative to the sub-brands. In other organizations, such as Procter & Gamble and Unilever, the sub-brands represent the more substantial share of brand equity.

Whether or not to utilize corporate brands in connection with sub-brands is a question that can be answered through use of the concept of CVA®. Pharmaceutical firms, in particular, face the issue of how to use their corporate brands. Many pharmaceutical brands try to associate their corporate brands with "life" but usually that is far too broad an association to be helpful to the CVA® of their product brands.

Some corporate brands can have a negative effect on perceived value for a specific market. Some organizations employ what are called *hidden brands*. For example, Gallo did not actively employ their corporate brand for marketing their Bartles & Jaymes wine coolers, and Marriott does not prominently use their corporate brand for their Ritz-Carlton hotels.

The effect of a corporate brand can be examined by evaluating its impact on CVA® and, therefore, contribution (Exhibit 8.12). The impact on CVA® is due primarily to the impact on perceived value, although there may be some cost changes.

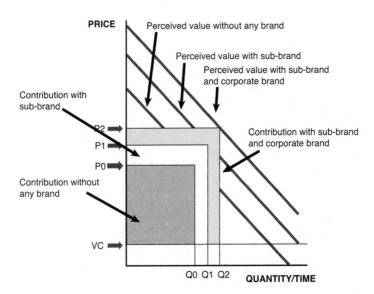

Reprinted with permission from "How Marketing Affects Shareholder Value," The Arrow Group, Ltd.®, New York, NY, 2008.

Exhibit 8.12   Impact of corporate brand on contribution

If CVA® increases as a result of the addition of the corporate brand, then use of the corporate brand name should be considered. If CVA® declines as a result, then perhaps the corporate brand name should not be utilized.

Evaluating the Corporate Brand Layne Acutech* Case

Acutech is a small company that produces a device, the MX-1, used for monitoring certain electronic processes. Customers include companies in the computing and aerospace industries.

Recently Acutech was acquired by a larger corporation, Layne Industries, which manufactures instruments used in a wide variety of fields. Over the years Layne has carefully built their brand so that it is widely regarded as standing for accuracy and reliability. Their policy is to add their brand name to that of any acquisition.

Layne has a Market Analysis Department which develops estimates of demand for all their products and services. Exhibit 8.13 shows their estimate for the demand curve for the MX-1. The Market Analysis Department has also estimated the MX-1 demand curve if the product is known as the Layne Acutech MX-1. Because of the generally high regard for Layne Instruments, it is expected that the demand curve would shift to the right with the addition of the Layne brand name. In particular, the maximum perceived value per unit—the y-intercept—would increase from $500 to $600. Variable cost per unit is assumed to remain constant at $160.

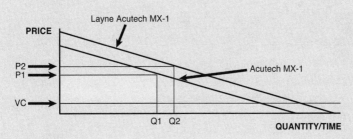

Demand Curves

Acutech MX-1

P = 500 - .01 Q   or   Q = 25,000 - 50P

Layne Acutech MX-1

P = 600 - .01 Q   or   Q = 30,000 - 50P

Variable Cost Per Unit = $160

Reprinted with permission from "Layne Acutech Case," The Arrow Group, Ltd.®, New York, NY, 2008.

Exhibit 8.13   Demand curve for MX-1—Layne Acutech case

Their communications agency has estimated that for the first year it will cost $460,000 to rename the product the Layne Acutech MX-1 and $200,000 per year thereafter for maintenance.

The optimal price for the MX-1 before the addition of the Layne brand name is given by the sum of the maximum perceived value per unit and the variable cost per unit divided by two or $330 which yields sales of 8,500 units and a contribution of $1,445,000 (Exhibit 8.14). After the addition of the Layne brand name, the optimal price is $380 with sales of 11,000 units and contribution of $2,420,000. Annual contribution change would be $975,000.

Acutech MX-1

P1 = $330   Q1 = 8,500 units

Contibution = ($330 - $160) (8,500) = $1,445,000

Layne Acutech MX-1

P2 = $380   Q2 = 11,000 units

Contribution = ($380 - $160) (11,000) = $2,420,000

Return on Brand Investment

Year	Discount Factor*	Contri-bution Change	PV of Contrib Change	Brand Invest-ment	PV of Brand Investment
1	.87	$975,000	$848,250	$460,000	$400,200
2	.76	$975,000	$741,000	$200,000	$152,000
3	.66	$975,000	$643,500	$200,000	$132,000
4	.57	$975,000	$555,750	$200,000	$114,000
5	.50	$975,000	$487,500	$200,000	$100,000
Total			$3,276,000		$898,200

Return on Brand Investment = ($3,276,000) / ($898,200) = 3.65
* Interest rate = .15.

Reprinted with permission from "Layne Acutech Case," The Arrow Group, Ltd.®, New York, NY, 2008.

Exhibit 8.14   Return on investment for corporate brand—Layne Acutech case

For simplicity, assume that the annual contribution change is constant (in reality, it would likely increase each year). If one uses an annual interest rate of 15% for determining present values, over five years, the present value of the annual contribution change is $3,276,000 and the present value of the communications investment is $898,200 producing a return on communications investment of 365%.

* All names are fictitious—any resemblance to real names is coincidental.

Source: "Layne Acatech," The Arrow Group, Ltd.®, New York, NY, 2008. Used with permission.

CVA® and Brand Extensions

Brand extensions are situations in which an existing brand is used on a product or service new to the organization. Brand extensions are sometimes viewed opportunistically. They represent strategic choices and should be evaluated carefully. Brand extensions have two types of effect on CVA®: impact on the CVA® of the new product or service and impact on the CVA® of the brand itself.

Successful brand extensions are usually built on attributes that customers already associate with the brand (Exhibit 8.15). For example, the Disney brand is universally known to stand for wholesome entertainment. That has allowed the brand to be extended to several other family-oriented products such as cruises, television shows, and Broadway shows. One would not expect the Disney brand to be extended to adult-themed movies because the Disney brand would not be expected to provide lift to such products and, perhaps of greater concern, such a brand extension would negatively affect the brand itself.

Possible brand extensions can be evaluated by considering the effect of the extension on the perceived value (and CVA®) of the new product or service and the perceived values (and CVA®s) of the products and services for which the brand is already being used.[26] Not only should the brand extension make sense in terms of associations, it should also make sense because the product or service performs at the same level as other products or services under the brand umbrella.[27]

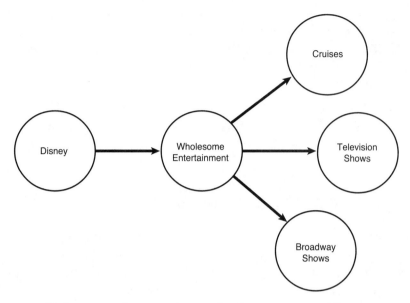

Reprinted with permission from "Extending Brands," The Arrow Group, Ltd.®, New York, NY, 2008.

Exhibit 8.15 Brand extensions

There have been many brand extensions that failed famously: Frito-Lay Lemonade, Ben Gay Aspirin, Cracker Jack Cereal, Smucker's Premium Ketchup, and Louis Sherry No Sugar Added Gorgonzola Cheese Dressing. All these extensions departed from the brand position of the mother brand and therefore lowered CVA®.[28]

Sometimes organizations are tempted to extend their brand in too many directions, especially through licensing. Licenses often represent quick money but too many licensees can dilute the master brand and consequently affect the CVA® of all products and services that share the mother brand. For example, the YSL brand had been licensed to 167 different firms, considerably diluting its strength. During the year 2000, management cut back the number of licensees to just 62 to attempt to refocus the YSL brand. A similar pattern of events occurred with Gucci.[29] Virgin has had brand successes but also failures such as Virgin Vodka and Virgin Cola in the US while expanding their brand to 150 companies.[30]

CVA® and Co-Branding

Co-branding consists of a sharing of the attributes of two (or more) separate brands. Co-branding includes complementary branding, ingredient branding, and endorsement branding. While initially a co-branding opportunity—exploiting someone else's brand equity—may appear attractive—there are possible problems. The foremost concern with a co-branding relates to whether or not the associations of the partner brands can blend to achieve the desired market performance.[31]

Just as brand extensions, co-branding arrangements should be viewed strategically and evaluated carefully. A co-brand has the potential to increase contribution through higher CVA®, which leads to higher price and unit demand for the co-branded product or service.

The attributes of each partner brand combine to create the co-brand (Exhibit 8.16). The attributes of the partner brands should be complements. Christy's, a UK manufacturer of towels, partnered with the World Wide Fund for Nature to produce a co-brand associated with style and environmental friendliness (going "green").[32] The baked goods section of supermarkets includes many effective co-brands. For example, Hershey's provides taste and Betty Crocker supplies the baking know-how for their brownie co-brand.

Tata-BP Lubricants in India combined the local trust associated with Tata with the lubricant knowledge associated with BP Amoco. Teflon from DuPont attaches non-stickiness to many branded products.

Co-branding arrangements can be evaluated in advance by examining the attributes associated with each of the prospective co-brand partners and their mutual impact on the CVA® of the co-branded product or service. Each co-brand partner should provide one or more attributes that will increase the perceived value of the product or service.

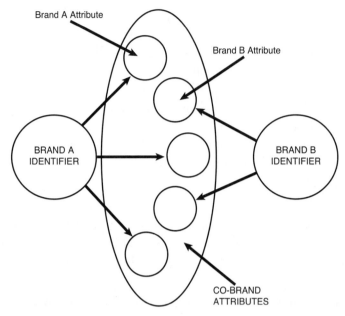

Reprinted with permission from "Establishing a Successful Co-Brand," Donald E. Sexton, New York, NY, 2008.

Exhibit 8.16   Components of a co-brand

General Mills is known for its expertise in producing breakfast cereals. Curves is the name of an international network of popular weight-loss facilities targeted towards women. Their co-brand is a low-calorie cereal that succeeds because the attributes are complementary. Each boosts the perceived value and the CVA® of the product.[33]

Due diligence applies when evaluating the associations of a potential co-branding partner. One organization uses the following criteria to screen possible co-brand alliances. It will not use its master brand if:

- The potential partner's reputation is not consistent with the organization's reputation.
- The co-brand alliance will not enhance the organization's position as a global leader.
- Failure of the venture would likely damage the organization's master brand.

- The potential partner's position on human rights and the environment is not consistent with the organization's.

Successful co-branding efforts increase CVA®.

NASCAR: Sponsors Make Fans the Stars

NASCAR fans turned around Kasey Kahne's season.

In 2008, the driver had been having little luck until the NASCAR Sprint All-Star race at Lowe's Motor Speedway. After Kahne failed to qualify for the $1-million winner-take-all event, fans voted him in as part of a special Sprint promotion. Kahne made the most of the opportunity and won the May race. Eight days later in Charlotte, Dodge's top driver won his first points race of the season, the Coca-Cola 600. Two weeks later, he took the checkered flag at Pocono. A few weeks later, he finished second in Michigan.

"The fans gave momentum to us in the all-star race when they gave us that boost," Kahne said. "It's done a tremendous amount for our confidence in the last month."

NASCAR fans are famously loyal to the sport and its sponsors. Research shows fans vote with their wallets and consciously purchase the products of the businesses spending millions of dollars to be involved with the #2-rated regular season sport on TV. Sprint's promotion shows how a fan-first mentality among NASCAR and its partners creates a virtuous circle of continued loyalty among fans—a highly passionate and thoroughly engaged customer base.

Other sponsors have creatively made fans the stars. Best Western and Hellmann's have put fans' faces on the race car. Little 3-year old Benjamin Tedeschi was on David Reutimann's Best Western Toyota as part of an April Fool's promotion, and 67 year-old grandfather Ron Bernheim was on Kasey Kahne's Dodge as Hellmann's Fan of the Year.

Office Depot and Harlequin got together for a promotion to put a fan's Marriage Proposal on Carl Edwards' Ford at the All-Star race Kahne won with a little help from the fans.

Crown Royal and Richmond International Raceway even teamed up to name a Sprint Cup Series race after a fan. "The Crown Royal Presents the Dan Lowry 400" race made Mr. Lowry of New Waterford, Ohio, forever famous in NASCAR circles.

One sponsor found a way to create hundreds of stars in one fell swoop. Nicorette, an official NASCAR partner, made 300 fans who had quit smoking using their product Grand Marshal of the Nicorette 300 at Atlanta Motor Speedway. They received exclusive behind-the-velvet-rope access and gave the infamous, "Gentlemen, Start Your Engines" command. It was a pretty loud statement from a sport that understands how to put its true customers first.

—Andrew Giangola, Director of Business Communications, NASCAR

Reprinted with permission

Conclusions

CVA® concepts can be used to guide decisions in the key strategic areas of targeting, positioning, and branding. In brief, strategic decisions need to be made with the impact on CVA®—both short-term and long-term—firmly in mind.

For targeting, that means identifying and selecting segments that have the potential of high CVA®. For positioning, that means, choosing benefits, then designing and communicating to deliver high CVA®. For branding, that means building brands on value and evaluating all branding opportunities with regard to their possible effects on CVA®.

CVA® concepts can also be employed to guide decisions in the key tactical areas of communications, pricing, and distribution—the contents of the next chapter.

9

Utilizing CVA® for Marketing Program Decisions

Marketing programs are sometimes referred to as "tactics." Marketing program decisions include decisions regarding advertising, personal selling, promotion, public relations, pricing, and distribution (Exhibit 9.1). The concept of CVA® can help guide many choices in these areas. This chapter explores how CVA® can be used to improve decision-making for programs in the entire marketing system.[1]

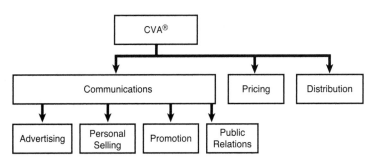

Reprinted with permission from "How Marketing Affects Shareholder Value," The Arrow Group, Ltd.®, New York, NY, 2008.

Exhibit 9.1   CVA® and marketing programs

MasterCard Worldwide: Marketing the Ecosystem

When I first joined MasterCard Worldwide, I was struck by the complexity of the business model and what that complexity suggested for our marketing mission.

Our actual customers are financial institutions, not consumers, and those institutions define many of the features most important to consumers. For example, by the time a credit card with the MasterCard logo ends up in your wallet, a financial institution has decided the terms on which it will extend credit to you and what kind of rewards you will enjoy. To actually use the card, consumers then need to interact with another entity: a merchant.

The above, in a nutshell, is the quintessential ecosystem: the financial institution, the merchant, the consumer, and MasterCard.

As marketers, our role is to add value to the overall ecosystem. Our economic interests merge with those of our customers and of our merchant partners when consumers (or businesses or government end users) actually use our products. As brand franchisors, we know that our customers depend on us to maintain a brand with strong consumer strength. Yet brand strength alone is not sufficient to differentiate us competitively among payment brands to our customers. Our marketing must also help our customer and merchant partners realize their business objectives. We have found ways, especially using digital channels, to create marketing "real estate" in order to deliver value to our entire ecosystem.

One illustrative case: In the US, our marketing plans had for years included brand sweepstakes promotions in the already-active fourth quarter holiday season to drive overall usage and brand salience. Mass media, including a large broadcast television presence, was the primary channel.

We have moved to a strategy far more reflective of consumer media consumption and technology advances (aka digital media) which, at the same time, created opportunities for both bank customers and merchant partners. We maintained our mass media presence to efficiently reach our mass target audience and used it to drive significant consumer volume to our priceless.com website, where we designed engaging experiences for consumers. This consumer traffic was then transformed into valuable opportunities for the ecosystem. For example, each of our participating banks sent their consumers a code to enter in priceless.com, which in turn generated a tailored cross-sell message from the bank, for any product in their arsenal. We also included on the site content from a merchant partner on selecting the perfect gift, which led to significant clicks to that merchant's own site.

Such ecosystem marketing has proven its power to drive consumer response and behavior, such as: usage of MasterCard cards; immediate response to the banks' cross-selling messages; and incremental visits to the merchants' web site—to deliver new value, beyond brand strength alone—to our ecosystem.

—Amy Fuller, Group Executive, Global Marketing, MasterCard Worldwide

© 2008 MasterCard. Reprinted with permission.

Communications

Communications, with design, are the major ways managers can influence perceived value. Yet many managers do not seem to understand how communications affect financial returns through perceived value. Often indirect measures such as awareness and knowledge are used to evaluate communications efforts.

Communications consist of all the ways an organization might be in touch with its target customers such as advertising, personal selling, and public relations, especially including the new digital media.[2] Designing communications strategies to increase perceived value usually increases CVA® unless the communications spending adds more to the per unit cost than it does to the per unit perceived value. In turn, increased CVA® leads to more effective outcomes from decisions concerning other tactics such as pricing and distribution.

Effective communications increase perceived value which increases CVA®.

CVA® can inform communications decisions, especially with respect to spending and to the development of the message to be conveyed to the target customer.

Determining Communications Spending the Wrong Way

Many practitioners and most marketing textbooks suggest three different ways to determine spending on communications: percentage of sales revenue, competitive parity, and objective and task. All three approaches have serious and well-known limitations.

Percentage of Sales Revenue

In the percentage of sales approach, the communications spending is set as a budgeted percentage of expected sales. The percentage of sales approach is much like cost-plus pricing (discussed later in the chapter)—it is simple and it is likely wrong.

The main problem with a percentage of sales approach is that it reverses the communications/sales relationship. Instead of making the assumption that communications leads to sales, use of a percentage of sales rule rests on the assumption that expected sales should determine what communications are affordable. With no underlying strategic rationale to support communications spending, the communications budget, then, becomes a justifiable target for cost-cutters.

The percentage of sales approach also takes what often should be thought of as a fixed cost and makes it look like a variable cost. Such a change can confound decisions (just as it does in full cost-plus pricing).

Competitive Parity

With the competitive parity approach, communications budgets are set in relation to competitors' spending. Such thinking can lead to advertising spending wars, which can be as destructive as price wars. There is some rationale for the competitive parity approach—which increases the chance it is applied. In many cases, it seems to be the relative share of spending on communications that affects market share, not the absolute level of spending. Such conditions would tempt organizations to try to out-spend their competitors.

The author documented such behavior in an article for the *Journal of Advertising Research*, "Overspending on Advertising." The article summarized a number of studies on the sales effects of advertising. In many mature markets, advertising was found to change only relative market share, not the absolute level of sales. In such conditions, increased advertising expenditures could actually result in negative returns—not only to the firms involved, but to society as a whole.[3]

Objective and Task

The objective and task approach has a rich history going back to Russell Colley's DAGMAR model.[4] Advertising objectives such as unit sales are defined, and then tasks, such as building awareness or preference, are determined that supposedly will achieve those goals. To many, the approach has strong face validity, but may result in large communications outlays. One high-placed executive in a leading advertising agency explained to members of one of the author's Columbia University classes that the agency's clients did not want to use the objective and task approach because it led to high spending. He observed that most of the clients employed a percentage of sales approach.

The objective and task approach can easily lead to high spending in that it often includes no explicit calculation of the value of the objectives and the costs of the tasks.

Objective and task communications budgeting can lead to overly high expenditures.

Another possible problem is that the tasks that lead to sales and their sequence may not be known. The objective and task approach is based on the hierarchy of effects model (Exhibit 9.2), and it is not at all clear that that model is relevant to many purchase decision situations.

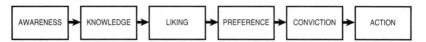

Exhibit 9.2   Hierarchy of effects model

The hierarchy of effects model has superficial validity and appears to be widely accepted by marketing managers and by marketing professors—one leading consulting company still touts the model to their clients. However, the empirical evidence for the hierarchy of effects model is not consistent. In a tour-de-force article published in the January, 1999, *Journal of Marketing*, Demetrios Vakratsas and Tim Ambler surveyed more than 250 articles on the effects of advertising and did not find any systematic evidence for the hierarchy of effects model typically used to support the objective and task approach.[5] What they found was support for more than one model of how advertising affects sales, suggesting that perhaps the objective and task approach might be more useful if coupled with a more comprehensive view of how advertising works.

One way to understand how to apply the hierarchy of effects model has been suggested by the advertising agency Foote, Cone, and Belding. They suggest that purchase situations can be classified by how much involvement the customer has in the decision—the significance of the purchase—and whether cognitive (functional) or affective (emotional) benefits are of higher priority (Exhibit 9.3). In low involvement situations, such as purchasing ballpoint pens or snacks, it is easier for the customer to act first and react second—hence these situations are known as "Do-Learn-Feel" or "Do-Feel-Learn." For high involvement situations, more thought will typically occur before purchase, so these situations are known as "Learn-Feel-Do" or "Feel-Learn-Do." (See Chapter 4, "Perceived Value," for more dicussion of buying situations.)

In particular, "Learn-Feel-Do" is probably typical of most business purchase situations and consumer purchase decisions involving large purchases where functional benefits have a high priority, such as purchases of snow-blowers or lawn mowers and cars used for basic transportation. This situation is the only one that corresponds to the traditional hierarchy of effects model. The other three situations require a different sequence of effects and a revised model (Exhibit 9.4).

	Cognitive	Affective
High Involvement	LEARN/FEEL/DO	FEEL/LEARN/DO
Low Involvement	DO/LEARN/FEEL	DO/FEEL/LEARN

Adapted from R. Vaughan, "How Advertising Works," *J. Advertising Research*, 26(1), pp. 57-66.

Exhibit 9.3   Purchase situations

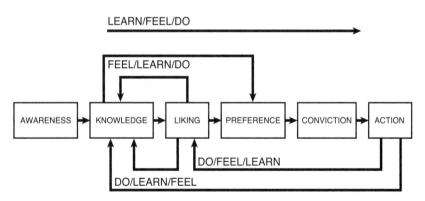

Reprinted with permission from "Managing Communications ROI," The Arrow Group, Ltd.®, New York, NY, 2008.

Exhibit 9.4   Hierarchy of effects model revised

American Management Association: Branding Makes the Invisible Visible

Marketing an intangible such as professional development services presents unique challenges. As we know from our experience at the AMA, a prospect cannot kick the tires or smell the coffee, so they need other cues to guide their decision-making. This is where branding has a unique purpose. Through branding we tell our story in a way that creates confidence and trust. In this way, branding helps the prospect see the value of the services that we offer.

Many times, before a prospect ever talks to us, they go online to do their homework and research what is available in the marketplace. They may start at our website, but will also search everything from blogs to social networks. They are hearing stories about us from many sources including other prospects, current and past customers. To get the AMA brand story out there, we use advertising, including online, direct mail, print, search engine, webcasts and podcasts. We build share of voice to reinforce share of mind.

Of course, others involved in management development will be telling their brand stories too. If the prospect cannot see a difference between our brand stories, then the prospect will look for the lowest price. In that situation, marketing becomes a price war with declining margins for everyone. We need to tell a better brand story than the others in our field so that the high quality of AMA's professional development services is clearly understood. We are in the age of competing brand stories.

To craft our brand story in a way that is compelling and relevant, we start by understanding our prospects. Through many years of experience and literally millions of participants taking our courses, we have discovered that our prospects, management professionals, see their careers as an ongoing journey. They are looking for a reliable expert who will help guide them at key moments when they want to find a new path or take on a new challenge. We use these insights to create new advertising that truly engages prospects and conveys the value of our educational experience.

As a rule of thumb, the more intangible the offering the more important is the branding and advertising to business performance. The company with the most engaging brand story will win.

—Edward T. Reilly, President and CEO, American Management Association

Reprinted with permission

CVA® and Communications

Whichever sequence behavior follows, there are a variety of actions on which communications may focus, and these generally vary throughout the competitive life cycle (Exhibit 9.5). Each action may require a somewhat different message to affect CVA®.

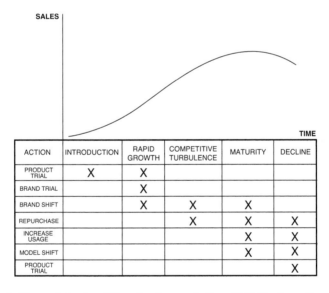

ACTION	INTRODUCTION	RAPID GROWTH	COMPETITIVE TURBULENCE	MATURITY	DECLINE
PRODUCT TRIAL	X	X			
BRAND TRIAL		X			
BRAND SHIFT		X	X	X	
REPURCHASE			X	X	X
INCREASE USAGE				X	X
MODEL SHIFT				X	X
PRODUCT TRIAL					X

Reprinted with permission from "Managing Communications ROI," The Arrow Group, Ltd.®, New York, NY, 2008.

Exhibit 9.5   Customer action objectives over time

During the Introduction stage, communications should be focused on gaining trial of the new product or the new service. Stimulating product trial requires an explanation of why the new product or service meets the needs of the target customer more effectively than do the existing products or services—thereby providing increased perceived value to the customer.

However, during the Rapid Growth stage, communications must have two objectives—one is to continue to encourage trial of the new product or service, the second is to encourage trial of the organization's brand of the product or service. Both campaigns may be operating simultaneously. The difference is that the product or service campaign emphasizes the benefit advantages of the new product or service, while the brand campaign stresses the specific benefit advantages of the organization's own brand of the new product or service, increasing the CVA® of the brand. Without the second campaign, the pioneer is vulnerable to a fast-follower that is more effective in extolling their brand (as was Nestles' Taster's Choice versus Kraft's Maxim in the illustration described in Chapter 7, "Managing CVA® over Time").

The key communications action objectives during the Competitive Turbulence stage are to persuade current customers to repurchase and to persuade customers of competitors' products or services to shift their purchases to the organization's brand. Both of these action objectives require managing CVA® by conveying the brand benefit advantages to the target customers to well-defined segments.

During the Maturity stage, communications action objectives continue to include brand repurchases and brand shifts; but, in addition, they may suggest increasing usage to customers. For example, a provider of home insurance may advise customers to increase the coverage on their home and possessions. Action objectives may also include model shifts—persuading customers to upgrade their purchases—perhaps a home entertainment system with more features and higher performance, or perhaps an alcoholic beverage with more taste or more status. Increasing usage requires communications focused on the perceived value obtained from using more, while persuading customers to shift models calls for explaining the higher perceived value from the new models.

During the Decline stage, some communications efforts might focus on repurchasing, increasing usage, and model shifting; but, of more importance, is to prepare the customer to purchase the product or service on the new life cycle that is emerging—if the organization has such a product or service. In this situation, communications focus on building the CVA® of the new product or service.

© Ashleigh Brilliant, 2008. Used with permission.

Using CVA® to Determine Communications Spending

The return on communications expenditures depends on the extent to which the communications have increased CVA®. In turn, that depends on the resulting changes in perceived value per unit and cost per unit due to the communications.

Following are the steps for using CVA® to determine the return on communications:

1. Estimate the value of perceived value and CVA® before the communications spending.
2. Estimate the value of perceived value and CVA® after the communications spending.
3. Predict the change in contribution due to the change in CVA®.

4. Compare the change in contribution to the communications investment.

Return on communications campaigns can be estimated by examining the value of CVA® before and after the campaign and the consequent impact on contribution. For the increase in contribution due to the change in CVA® to be positive, the increase in perceived value per unit must be greater than any related increases in costs per unit, and the contribution change must be greater than the fixed cost change. The change in contribution due to the campaign and the overall cost of the campaign are the return on the communications investment represented by the campaign.

Evaluating Communications Effects: Groupe Le Soleil* Case (continued)

Recall in Chapter 2, "How CVA® Affects Financial Performance," that the demand curve for mushrooms in thousands of units was initially given by:

$p = 5 - (1/10,000)Q$

or

$Q = 50,000 - 10,000p$

A price of 3.2 euros provided the maximum contribution of 32,400,000 euros.

GLS conducted an advertising campaign in France to build its brand position in the minds of French consumers. As a result, the demand curve for GLS mushrooms in France shifted to the right:

$P = 6 - (1/10,000)Q$

or

$Q = 60,000 - 10,000P$

At a price of 3.7 euros, GLS achieved the maximum contribution of 52,900,000 euros.

The relative change in maximum contribution was:

$52,900,000 / 32,400,000 = 163\%$

The change in maximum contribution was predicted with Sexton's Contribution Law. Relative change in CVA® was:

(6 - 1.4) / (5 – 1.4) = 4.6 / 3.6 = 128%

giving the change in maximum contribution as:

$128\%^2 = 163\%$

In this illustration, suppose that the advertising campaign cost 15,000,000 euros. Given that the change in perceived value and the corresponding change in CVA® suggested that contribution would increase by 63 percent, the immediate return on the investment in that campaign can be calculated as:

$$\text{Return on Communications Investment} = \frac{(52{,}900{,}000 - 32{,}400{,}000)}{15{,}000{,}000} = \frac{20{,}500{,}000}{15{,}000{,}000} = 137\%$$

°All names are fictitious—any resemblance to real names is coincidental.

Pricing

What is the most difficult component of the marketing mix to get right? In surveys, managers most often say it's pricing. Many managers believe they are pricing too low and "leaving something on the table." Other managers feel they are pricing too high and are losing sales.

The reason pricing can seem difficult to many managers is that they are not thinking about price the right way. They approach pricing from the standpoint of costs, not value perceived by the customer. Looking at pricing only from the cost vantage point makes it difficult to determine price—and difficult to manage price. Looking at pricing from the viewpoint of CVA® provides managers with approaches to determine price and ways to manage price.

The purpose of price is to capture the value provided to the customer and measured by CVA®—by achieving margin or volume or both.

Determining Pricing the Wrong Way

Many companies—likely the majority—use some form of cost-plus pricing. Cost-plus pricing is simple and, like percentage of sales budgeting for communications, most often leads to serious pricing mistakes.[6]

The most misleading method of cost-plus pricing is full-cost pricing, which consists of the following steps: First, unit sales is forecast. Next, average full cost per unit is calculated, where *full cost* includes overhead allocation. Finally, the price is computed by increasing average cost per unit by some percentage markup.

Example calculations for cost-plus pricing are shown in Exhibit 9.6. One can think of the illustration as pertaining to a book. Paper and other production costs are assumed to be $2 per book, while set-up and other fixed costs are assumed to be $10,000.

1. Estimate sales volume.

$$S = 1000 \text{ units}$$

2. Calculate average cost per unit.

$$\text{Average Cost} = \text{Variable Cost} + \frac{\text{Fixed Cost}}{\text{Sales Estimate}}$$

$$= \$2 + \$10,000/1000 = \$12$$

3. Set price equal to average cost plus mark-up.

$$\text{Price} = \text{Average Cost} + (\text{AC}) \text{ X \% (Mark-up)}$$

$$= \$12 + (\$12 \text{ X } 40\%) = \$16.80$$

Assumptions: Variable cost per unit is $2.
Fixed cost is $10,000.
Mark-up is 40%.

Reprinted with permission from "Managing Pricing ROI," The Arrow Group, Ltd.®, New York, NY, 2008.

Exhibit 9.6   Example of cost-plus pricing

This approach is simple and almost always results in the wrong price—a price that is either too low or too high.

The most basic problem with this approach is the construction of the sales estimate. Unit sales are forecast *before* price is set, so the implicit assumption is that price has no effect on unit sales. This may be true in certain situations such as some types of government contracts where unit volume is agreed in advance, but it is false in open markets.

An argument sometimes offered for cost-plus pricing is that the markup is a guaranteed profit margin per unit. Of course, that is simply not so because the percentage markup assumed would signify a specific profit percentage only if the sales forecast were accurate. If sales are lower than expected, then margin per unit is lower. If sales are higher than expected, then margin per unit is higher.

Finally, if the fixed costs include both direct costs and indirect costs, especially overhead, then the average cost per unit is dependent on the overhead allocation policy of the organization. In other words, price is being set implicitly by the organization's method of allocating overhead—which is unlikely to have been set up to optimize pricing.

The overall problem with cost-plus pricing is that it makes *costs* the center of the pricing process rather than *value*. Costs do have a role to play in pricing, but only in relationship to value as perceived by the customer. Cost-plus pricing remains a common approach to pricing because it is simple and does not require much thinking.

Accounting-based approaches to pricing such as cost-plus pricing lead to pricing strategies in which if they do maximize contribution, it is primarily through luck. Pricing begins with understanding value as perceived by the customer. Unfortunately many pricing managers do not seem to understand perceived value and are unaware of how it can be measured and used to develop sound pricing decisions. In addition, managers who develop prices with cost-based approaches may not consider communications as an efficient way to manage price. Communications content and budget can be utilized to increase perceived value and make pricing a much less puzzling and less difficult part of the marketing mix.

If cost-plus pricing maximizes contribution or profits,
it is most likely by luck.

CVA® and Pricing

As explained in Chapter 2, the lower the price, the higher the incentive per unit to the customer, and therefore, the more sales in units— with a lower variable margin per unit (Exhibit 9.7). The higher the price, the lower the incentive to the customer, and therefore the fewer sales in units, but with a higher variable margin per unit.

Many pricing problems can be diagnosed as communications problems—either a failure to communicate value to the target customer, a failure to put enough effort into communications, or both. Effective communications programs make it possible for companies to price more successfully to achieve increased contribution, cash flow, and return on investment.

In management seminars, the author often asks participants if they would like to have a new sales record set. Even with no idea of what a product or service does and the ways it is superior to those of competitors, one can always set a new sales record. To do so, one need make only one small request: "Give me permission to cut price."

The point should be clear. If one is allowed to cut price, one can sell almost anything. Good selling is not about cutting price. Good selling is selling the product or service at the price you want. To sell at that price you need to manage the value perceived by the customer, and most of the time that needs to be done with some form of communications.

Using CVA® to Determine Pricing

In CVA® pricing, the center of the pricing process is *perceived value*—not costs. As can be seen in Exhibit 9.7, pricing problems occur if perceived value is allowed to be too low. If price is near the incremental cost per unit, then there is very little maneuverability with regard to price. In microeconomics, such a situation describes a *commodity*—a product or service with no differentiation perceived by the customer—arguably one of the most unappealing words in marketing.[7]

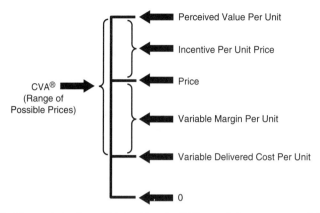

Reprinted with permission from "Pricing, Perceived Value, and Communications," Donald E. Sexton, New York, NY, 2008.

Exhibit 9.7   Customer Value Added and Price

There are certainly cases in which products and services are not differentiated, but there are also many cases in which an advertisement or a sales representative has not effectively made the argument that the product or service is different in ways that the customer should care about and be willing to pay for. It is those cases in which pricing problems are really communications problems.

CVA® pricing deals with the weaknesses of cost-plus pricing. It is not simpler to apply—it does require information about customers and competitors. However, it can be expected to lead to financial returns superior to those associated with the cost-plus approaches.

CVA® pricing consists of a sequence of six steps:

1. Estimate perceived value.
2. Determine variable delivered cost per unit.
3. Set objectives for overall contribution.
4. Specify tentative marketing strategy, including tentative price.
5. Forecast likely actions of competitors.
6. Evaluate financial consequences of price and select best price.

The ceiling on price is perceived value, the maximum the customer is willing to pay for the product or service, which can be estimated in monetary terms as explained in Chapter 4. Variable delivered cost per unit is the floor on price.

In most situations, one must set a price between perceived value and incremental cost per unit (CVA®). Companies with higher perceived value and lower unit costs have more pricing options and are rewarded with higher contributions either through high margins, high volumes, or both.

Steps 3, 4, 5, and 6. Given the prices available to a company, setting price depends on the objectives: margin, unit volume, or contribution. The difference between price and incremental cost per unit is the variable margin (or contribution) per unit. The difference between perceived value and price is the incentive to the customer to buy—and that determines number of units sold. Contribution is the product of variable margin (contribution) per unit and number of units sold (Exhibit 9.8).

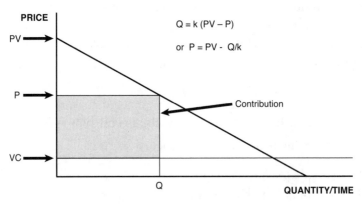

Reprinted with permission from "Managing Pricing ROI," The Arrow Group, Ltd.®, New York, NY, 2008.

Exhibit 9.8   Contribution

Determining price can be thought of as determining how much of the interval between perceived value and the incremental cost per unit is kept by the company as margin per unit and how much is given as an incentive to the customer to stimulate demand. In a penetration strategy, the price is set low, and the customer is provided a lot of incentive because the main objective is unit volume. In a skimming strategy, price is set high to provide high margin per unit, but unit volume is expected to be low (see Exhibit 7.7).

To determine the most desirable price, one considers scenarios involving different prices and different marketing strategies and projects the financial implications for each. One selects that price and marketing strategy that appears to be most effective to achieve the objectives.

Pricing in Multiple Markets

The key to pricing in multiple markets is the ability to charge different prices to take advantage of differences in perceived value and CVA®. Important: Before charging different prices in multiple markets, be sure to confer with an attorney. Laws governing pricing are common and vary by location.

Private label brands show the appeal of multiple prices for multiple markets. Private brands command sizable market shares and generate large revenues and cash flows in certain categories, especially consumer nondurables. They fill a gap in the market between the more widely known brands and products and services that are commodities.

Most well-known brands can be expected to command higher prices than private label brands, although some private label brands such as Tesco's Finest have at times retailed at higher prices than national label brands. On the other hand, products or services that are more like commodities—namely have little or no differentiation— might be expected to be sold at prices lower than the well-known brands, often just somewhat above their costs. Because the costs of commodity-like brands are likely much lower than those for well-known brands, their prices can be expected to be especially low as compared to the prices of the well-known brands.

The relatively high prices of many well-known brands and the relatively low prices of commodities can leave a substantial middle market for the private label brands. In Exhibit 9.8, this market would be that part of the demand curve corresponding to a middle range of prices. Private label brands can dominate this middle market. Studies by A.C. Nielsen have shown that, on average globally, private label prices are about a third below those of the national or global brands; and up to 85 percent of consumers in developed markets consider private labels a viable alternative to well-known brands.[8]

This middle market seems to be growing. A report from Packaged Facts found that five years ago 36 percent of United States shoppers described themselves as frequent buyers of retailer brands, but now 41 percent consider themselves in that group.[9]

Private labels often represent a single-brand strategy. However, some retailers offer different levels of private labels. For example, Coles, the giant Australian supermarket retailer, offered two private labels in their stores: "Savings," which was like a commodity and "Farmland," which was a value-added private label. They were therefore able to command a large part of the demand curve.

According to A.C. Nielsen, one-third of consumers in developed markets believe private labels offer higher quality than well-known brands. With that consumer foundation, and given the amount of market information now available to retailers and their supplier relationships, the differentiation provided by some private labels may be expected to increasingly rival those of national or global brands. Last November, for example, in the United Kingdom, Asda launched nylon mesh tea bags as a premium product under their Extra Special label. These tea bags are superior to most of those offered by well-known brands and place Asda at the top of the brand ladder.[10]

Similarly, in the United States, Giant Food introduced a Simply Enjoy line that includes premium products such as coffee and imported pastas, while Safeway sells crème brulee desserts and artisan breads under its Safeway Select label.[11]

Nowadays the perceived value of a private label may be higher than that of a well-known brand. For *Which? Magazine*, six professional tasters rated Sainsbury's champagne ahead of big-name brands, such as Moet & Chandon, and sales increased by 3000 percent.[12]

Even if the perceived value of a well-known brand is higher than that of a private label brand, the private label may still be more powerful in the market. The per unit costs of a private label brand are generally below those of a well-known brand (Exhibit 9.9) That can allow both the retailer more margin per unit and the consumer more incentive per unit—double jeopardy for the national or global brand producer.

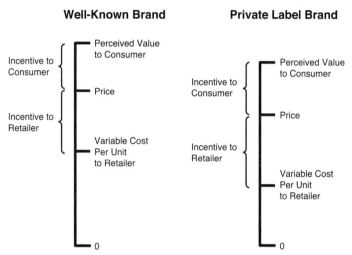

Reprinted with permission from "How Private Brands Work," Donald E. Sexton, New York, NY, 2008.

Exhibit 9.9   Brand pricing

Clearly, the response to private labels by the well-known brand is to either increase their perceived value to the consumer or decrease the per unit costs to the retailer—or a combination of both strategies. The problem is that increasing perceived value will likely raise per unit costs. The solution is to find initiatives that will increase perceived value much more than incremental costs.

Historically, large companies would utilize initiatives based on fixed costs such as research and development to compete with smaller players. For example, a large producer of laundry detergents might be expected to develop products with improved stain-removing benefits. Such a strategy might still work in some product categories, but with the emergence of giant, well-financed retailers that are well-connected with suppliers, it is more difficult for a fixed-cost based strategy to succeed.

General Motors: A Better Mousetrap Is Not Enough

Emerson wrote that if you 'build a better mousetrap, the world will beat a path to your door.' What Emerson failed to observe is that you first need to get the world's attention. And if you have a bad brand image, you won't get the world's attention and your better mousetrap could languish unused until it's reinvented by someone with a better brand image.

We see this phenomenon again and again at General Motors: Customers choosing between products that are virtually identical will never consider those products with a poor brand image.

Some of this brand preference reflects prudence. In a world where everyone can claim to have the better mousetrap (and where people's claims are time-consuming to evaluate), people rely on brands they can trust. As a result, only a few brands are seriously considered. (Some academicians report that many people consider only one brand in the automotive industry.) And if a brand has disappointed customers in the past, they may never consider any product from that brand again.

Some of this brand preference also reflects the image the customer wants to convey. We all know that you should go to the 'right schools,' vacation in the 'right places,' buy clothes from the 'right stores,' have the 'right opinions' and drive the 'right brand of cars.' You risk losing the approval of your peers if you buy the 'wrong brand.'

Sometimes the structure of the industry can also make brands important. In the automotive industry, vehicles are sold in dealerships which typically specialize in a broad range of vehicles made by the same brand. Hence the first serious commitment a customer makes is deciding which dealerships to visit (which determines which brands will be considered.)

Brand image might seem less important when customers trust third-party advisors to recommend products for them. But even third-party advisors are affected by a product's brand image.

So it's not as simple as having a better mousetrap...

—Dr. Robert F. Bordley, Technical Fellow, General Motors Labs

Reprinted with permission

CVA® and Distribution

Distribution concerns the path followed by the product or service from the producer to the end-user. CVA® can be calculated at each level of the distribution system. The overall CVA® for a product or service—perceived value per unit to the end-user minus unit cost of the producer—depends on the CVA® at each level of the distribution system. The higher the perceived value to the end-user, the more profit potential there is in the distribution chain.

Perceived value depends on the benefits and brand attributes of the product or service. It also depends on the value provided and communicated by the reseller at each level (Exhibit 9.10). Resellers add to perceived value with their services as well as provide convenience in both location and assortment of products and services.

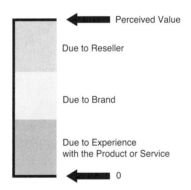

Exhibit 9.10   Components of perceived value

For simplicity, assume that there is just one reseller between the producer of a product or a service and the end-user. The CVA® structure of a distribution channel with more than two levels is similar to that of one with just two levels (Exhibit 9.11). The perceived value to the reseller depends on the value perceived by the end-user due to the efforts of the producer and the reseller. The higher the perceived value to the end-user, the higher the potential contribution to the reseller.

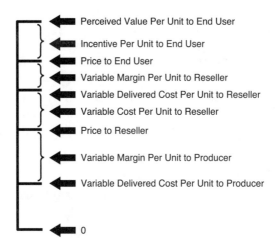

Perceived Value Per Unit to End User

Incentive Per Unit to End User

Price to End User

Variable Margin Per Unit to Reseller

Variable Delivered Cost Per Unit to Reseller

Variable Cost Per Unit to Reseller

Price to Reseller

Variable Margin Per Unit to Producer

Variable Delivered Cost Per Unit to Producer

0

Exhibit 9.11   Distribution levels

The distance between the perceived value per unit to the reseller and the variable delivered cost per unit of the producer is the Customer Value Added for the reseller. The producer's price likely falls somewhere in that interval. In that instance, the reseller's variable delivered cost per unit for the end-user will be the sum of the price the resellers pay and their variable costs per unit such as storage and selling. In turn, that determines the Customer Value Added to the end-user—the difference between the perceived value to the end-user and the variable delivered cost per unit of the reseller. If the product or service is sold through one or more levels of resellers, this essential structure still holds.

The distance between the perceived value per unit to the end-user and the variable cost per unit for the producer, CVA®, represents the maximum per unit contribution. A price must be set at each level of the distribution chain; but, the issue remains the same: How much of the total per unit contribution will be kept by the producer and how much will be kept by each reseller and how much of an incentive will be provided the end-user?

The difference between the perceived value per unit to the end-user and the variable cost per unit to the producer is the maximum per unit contribution for the product or service.

Successful producers, such as DuPont, understand how these CVA® dynamics work. For example, when it introduced Stainmaster fiber for carpets, DuPont conducted initial perceived value research with end-users—potential buyers of carpets—to determine how much the buyers would be willing to pay to be able to remove stains more easily from their carpets. DuPont used constrained choice models to make those estimates. Then the company went to the carpet manufacturers, explained the increase in perceived value that the Stainmaster technology would provide, and proposed a split of the resulting increase in contribution per unit.[13]

Similarly, Peter Ueberroth, former head of Major League Baseball, has pointed out that the value perceived by the baseball fan [the end-user] determines the economic outcomes for the sport: "…Who the heck is paying the bill? It's the fan. The owners or the union might say TV is paying the bill, and there are advertisers selling products via TV, but the fan is the ultimate payer. Unless you respond to the fan, your economic model is going to crumble."[14]

Understanding CVA® at each level of the distribution channel, as well as overall—from end-user to producer—allows sounder distribution decisions.

MetLife: Putting the Brand to Work in Distribution

Spinach is to kids what life insurance and retirement savings is to adults. They both need a push.

While spinach is generally believed to be good for growing children and insurance protection and retirement savings is good for young families and aging adults, both consumer segments share a common challenge. They need to be "sold" by parents and advisors acting in the best interests of their wards. It has been well documented that in many countries around the world, including in the United States, consumers are under-insured and retirement savings inadequate.

MetLife is the largest life insurance company in America with significant operations in many parts of the world. The company manufactures a wide range of products that protect individual consumers from the risks of mortality, morbidity and longevity. MetLife is also the largest underwriter of life insurance and retirement solutions for employers and counts among its customers 96 of the Fortune 100 companies.

Life insurance solutions protect family incomes from the risks of premature death or disability of a breadwinner. Annuities protect retirement incomes from the risks of erosion from inflation and outliving life savings. MetLife is one of the most recognized brands in America. Most consumers are familiar with a brand that represents financial strength, integrity and friendliness that is brought to life by its brand ambassador, Snoopy. These attributes help to position the company as providing products with intrinsic "value" rather than competing merely on "price."

But brand value is created at two levels, consumer and distributor. Many of the products offered by insurance companies are complex, "intangible" and do not have a sense of urgency in the buying decision process. Consumers typically need to be persuaded to buy these products by financial advisors who perform three critical functions. First, they assess the needs of their clients and evaluate risks. Second, they create a portfolio of financial solutions to match their clients' needs. Third, they persuade their clients to act in their own best interest by executing on the needs-based recommendations. Push.

The critical part of the supply chain is the financial advisor. So brand may be even more important here than with the end consumer. These professionals have a choice of insurance providers to select from when creating a portfolio of products to recommend to clients. It is here that MetLife creates additional value for the brand by investing heavily in value added services focused on distributors including ongoing education and training of financial advisors, technology-based solutions for client selection and relationship management, dedicated wholesaling teams and thought leadership studies that influence key opinion leaders.

The strength of MetLife's consumer brand is complemented by a disciplined and focused approach on building value for distributors. These advisor-centric initiatives help to insulate the company in markets around the world from competing primarily on price and eroding its margins. In a crowded market where providers are vying to create shelf space for their financial solutions, MetLife recognizes that advice is the product.

Now if parents only had similar help with spinach...

—Dr. Shailendra Ghorpade, Group Managing Director, MetLife Europe, Middle East, and India

Reprinted with permission

Conclusions

Marketing programs change throughout the competitive life cycle because action objectives of the marketing strategy change. Initially, communications, pricing, and distribution are focused on developing the number of users trying the product or service. Next, they build the brand to persuade target customers to try the brand, shift from other brands, and remain brand loyal. When products or services are mature, marketing programs maintain loyalty, increase usage, and stimulate model shifts. Finally, marketing programs ready the target customer for the next product or service that will meet their needs more effectively than the existing products and services. Throughout, the objective is to manage CVA® optimally.

Managing CVA® requires measuring CVA®—the subject of the next chapter.

10

Building the Marketing Accountability Scorecard

There is a wide choice of measures for evaluating the health of a product or service.

Many of these have been used for a long while and appear to be deeply entrenched in organizations. This chapter considers the question: Are these the correct measures, and are all of them necessary?

© Ashleigh Brilliant, 2008. Used with permission.

General Practice

The measures used by organizations to monitor marketing effectiveness are generally measures that have been employed for many years. For example, an Association of National Advertisers (ANA) study in 2007 found that the most commonly tracked measures were sales, market share, and customer satisfaction (Exhibit 10.1).

Exhibit 10.1   Effectiveness and Use of Measures

Measure of Brand Health	Most Effective (%)	Tracked (%)
Brand Preference	40	63
Customer Experience/Satisfaction	37	75
Market Share	32	79
Net Promoter Score	31	41
Price Premium Gap	29	40
Brand Image	25	68
Brand Recognition	24	76
Sales	20	85
Conversion Rate	15	43
Market Penetration	11	62
Purchase Intent	10	52
Customer Share of Wallet	10	33
Employee Satisfaction and Retention	7	47
Purchase Frequency	6	48
Extent of Discounts Offered	1	26
Traffic to Web Site	1	71

Source: Association of National Advertisers, "Brand Deterioration: How to Identify, Measure, and Respond." New York: April 2007.

In the survey, overall, there was little unanimity among the respondents regarding what measures were most effective. The measures considered most effective by the largest percentages of respondents were brand preference (40 percent) and customer experience/satisfaction (37 percent). There were also sizable gaps between those considering a measure most effective and those who tracked it. Only two of the top five measures considered most effective were among the top five measures that were tracked.

Notably, perceived value and CVA® were absent from this list of measures. Of the measures mentioned, perhaps price premium gap (cited by 29 percent as most effective) is closest to perceived value; but, as explained in Chapter 2, "How CVA® Affects Financial Performance," price premium gap can be used as a measure of marketing effectiveness *only if price approaches perceived value per unit*— which may be true in only some markets, such as those for luxury products, or possibly in certain mature products or services.

In another ANA study, brand awareness was found to be the measure tracked by the most organizations—81 percent (Exhibit 10.2). That is discouraging because, as explained in Chapter 7, "Managing CVA® over Time," brand awareness is typically a trailing indicator of marketing effectiveness, not a leading indicator. Still, widespread use of brand awareness to track brand health persists— perhaps due to the inertia of managers who may not welcome change in how they view the world. In both ANA surveys, market share was the number two measure. Seventy-nine percent reported that they tracked their share—which seems low. One would think most companies would track their market share.

Exhibit 10.2   Measures Currently Tracked

Measure	Tracked (%)
Brand Awareness	81
Market Share	79
Consumer Attitudes Toward Brand	73
Purchase Intention	59
Return on Objective	36
Lifetime Customer Value	23
Brand Equity	20

Source: Association of National Advertisers, "Fourth Annual ANA/MMA Marketing Accountability, Study." New York: July, 2007.

In these and many other similar surveys, perceived value and CVA® are missing from the list of measures the respondents use despite findings that perceived value or related measures have been found to be consistent, positive leading indicators of financial performance.

Perceived value is rarely mentioned in surveys of managers as a measure used to track marketing accountability despite evidence that it is a leading indicator of financial performance.

In short, general practice has consisted of repeated use of the same measures such as market share and brand awareness. It is no wonder progress in measuring marketing accountability has been made slowly—if at all.

IBM: Value, Values, and Valuation

In the brand game and world of intangibles, the words value, values and valuation are used every day. They form a constellation of interlocking concepts that help inform business decisions and allocate resources.

Value is understood as a fair exchange of money, or barter, for commodities, goods, services, experiences, or transformations.

Values are common ground for drawing economic actors together while creating trust for each other and the customers they serve.

Valuation is the translation of ongoing economic worth, with intangible valuation being a repository of future sales—the estimate of customers' future desire to do business with a company. It is also a bank of goodwill that allows businesses to keep operating through periods of economic distress. Economic valuation is what attracts and retains investors.

In unison: *Values* inform why economic actors are drawn together to deliver *value* to a particular set of customers, resulting in *valuation* that attracts and retains investors. This in turn reinforces the values that create and deliver customer value—forming a virtuous cycle of *value creation*.

Taken in reverse order, *valuation* gets most of the attention from investors and Wall Street. What is it worth? You choose the "it"—product, service, experience, or enterprise. Valuation is an expression of worth, good as far as it goes, yet limited in its numeric vocabulary.

Values tell you more. What a company has believed in the past and believes today will be more predictive in how it will behave and increase its valuation in the future. Values are more fundamental and express the long-term view of a sustainable enterprise. IBM is a good example of a values-driven company. IBM employees embrace:

- "Dedication to every client's success
- "Innovation that matters—for our company and for the world, and
- "Trust and personal responsibility in all relationships"

These are the foundational values that guide professional and over-all IBM company behavior.

In my book *Brandscendence*, from the chapter "In Crisis, Culture is Destiny": Values inform how employees will behave when left to use their own judgment in the context of the company culture, and also predict how the enterprise will behave in crisis.

Value: When you blend the core *values* of an organization and the *valuation* of what people are willing to pay for what they make or do, value is right in the middle of both concepts. Value encompasses both the tangible and intangible benefits that represent the total worth and frequency of transactions.

The dance of value, values and valuation represent both the art and science of brand management and customer experience strategy. Companies will pay close attention to all three when they embrace long-term customer relationships that are the foundation for sustained revenue and profit.

—Kevin Clark, Program Director, Brand and Values Experience, IBM Corporate Marketing & Communications and Founder and Managing Member of Content Evolution LLC.
Reprinted with permission.

Use of Specific Marketing ROI Measures

The Marketing Investment Research Working Group of the Conference Board conducted an in-depth study of measures used by organizations to monitor their businesses. Metrics examined included customer measures such as awareness and loyalty, tactic measures such as price premium and coupon redemption rates, and financial result measures such as channel margins and marketing spend. Respondents were asked to use 5-point scales (where 1 = low, 5 = high) to evaluate their use and the effectiveness of each measure. The general impression of these findings is that no single metric is considered particularly effective in monitoring marketing return on investment (ROI)—no measure averaged above 4 on the 5-point effectiveness scale.

Among the customer measures (Exhibit 10.3), loyalty/satisfaction and retention were reported as the most used measures—an encouraging result because these are important components of lifetime customer value. Surprisingly, however, lifetime customer value was one of the least used measures. Many organizations are aware of lifetime customer value, but apparently few actually have calculated the lifetime value of their customers. That seems especially unfortunate because in a regression analysis of the relationship of each of these customer measures with success in evaluating marketing ROI conducted by the author, loyalty and customer acquisition cost (another important component of lifetime customer value) were the only measures that were highly correlated with success in evaluating marketing ROI.

Exhibit 10.3　Evaluation of Customer Measures

Measure	Usage	Effectiveness
Awareness	3.5	3.1
Penetration	3.6	3.3
Market Share	4.0	3.2
Usage	3.2	3.2
Loyalty/Satisfaction	4.4	3.9
Netpromoter Score	2.3	2.9
Recency	3.0	3.0
Retention	4.2	3.3
Customer Profit	3.0	3.2
Customer Lifetime Value	2.9	3.3
Customer Acquisition Costs	3.0	3.2

Evaluation calculated on a scale of 1=Low and 5=High.
Source: Karen V. Beaman, Gregory R. Guy, and Donald E. Sexton, *Measuring Return on Marketing Investment*. The Conference Board: New York, 2008.

With respect to the effectiveness of these customer measures, on the average, none was evaluated at a rating of 4 or higher, and a highly publicized measure, the Netpromoter Score, was rated below 3.[1]

Among the marketing tactic measures (Exhibit 10.4), only Web site visits averaged 4 or more for usage, and none averaged 4 or more for effectiveness. The effectiveness of one of the relatively more widely used measures—the sales funnel— was evaluated as just 3.4, perhaps not surprising given that the applicability of the sales funnel varies considerably with the type of product or service (see Chapter 9, "Utilizing CVA® for Marketing Program Decisions"). Price premium, suggested by several branding experts, received usage and effectiveness measures below 3. As explained earlier, price premium is a limited measure as it captures only one aspect of increased CVA®, a lift in price, but does not capture the lift in quantity sold.

Exhibit 10.4   Evaluation of Marketing Tactic Measures

Measure	Usage	Effectiveness
Sales Funnel	3.7	3.4
Sales Force Effectiveness	3.4	3.1
Sales Forecast	3.8	3.2
Product Profits/Volume	3.9	3.4
Inventories/Markdowns	2.0	2.0
Price Premium	2.9	2.8
Promotion Lift	3.6	3.4
Coupon Redemption Rates	2.3	2.1
Average Deal Depth	1.8	20
Pass Through Price	1.8	2.2
Web Site Visits	4.1	3.1
Cost per Click	3.3	2.9

Evaluation calculated on a scale of 1 = Low and 5 = High.
Source: Karen V. Beaman, Gregory R. Guy, and Donald E. Sexton, *Measuring Return on Marketing Investment*. The Conference Board: New York, 2008.

When all the marketing tactic measures were examined with respect to their association with success in evaluating marketing ROI, the only measure that was highly correlated with success was coupon redemption rates—possibly because it may be a leading indicator of the success of a marketing program. In contrast, somewhat correlated with success— but negatively—was a measure concerned with inventories and markdowns. This may not be surprising because inventories/markdowns would be a backward-looking measure.

Several of the financial result measures were used frequently, receiving a score of 4 or more (Exhibit 10.5). Those measures were marketing spend, target volume, net profit, and return on investment. However, none of them was rated 4 or more with respect to effectiveness, suggesting that perhaps they did not provide sufficient diagnostic information to be helpful to the managers. These financial result measures are all *ex post* measures—they provide information on what has happened, but do not necessarily provide managers with steering control—information that helps managers make decisions that affect future performance. Consequently when all the financial result measures were examined in a regression analysis in which success in evaluating marketing ROI was the dependent variable, *not one* of the financial result variables was highly associated with success in evaluating marketing ROI.

Exhibit 10.5   Evaluation of Financial Result Measures

Measure	Usage	Effectiveness
Channel Margins	3.9	3.5
Contribution per Unit	3.2	3.1
Marketing Spend	4.5	3.4
Target Volume	4.4	3.5
Net Profit	4.1	3.8
Return on Sales	2.9	3.3
Return on Investment	4.0	3.5
Return on Marketing Investment	3.3	3.4
EVA (Economic Value Added)	2.4	2.7
Payback	2.6	2.7
Net Present Value	3.1	3.3
Internal Rate of Return	2.9	3.1

Evaluation calculated on a scale of 1 = Low and 5 = High.
Source: Karen V. Beaman, Gregory R. Guy, and Donald E. Sexton, *Measuring Return on Marketing Investment*. The Conference Board: New York, 2008.

In a Conference Board study, the variable with the
highest association with success in evaluating marketing
ROI was not measures or skills or data, but the amount
of time spent trying to do it.[2]

Westpac: Value Exchange

Value exchange is what we offer in a relationship to the other party. Everyone in society exchanges value among themselves. While this is not quantified in our personal relationships (e.g., being trustworthy in friendship), in commercial relationships it is somewhat quantified through a market mechanism (i.e., price).

However, price does not always reflect the true value exchange. If customers decide not to buy a product/service for a given price then we can conclude that the price is above the benefit that they expect to get from the product/service. On the other hand, if customers decide to purchase, we can only conclude that the price matches at least the expected benefit of the product/service.

The critical term in the above statement is "at least," as in many instances companies do not know what the maximum amount that customers are willing to pay for the goods and services that company offers is (i.e., perceived value).

Understanding and managing the perceived value or willingness to pay is a crucial factor that determines the company's success. Hence, companies should clearly articulate what benefits of service/product they provide from a customer perspective before they set any price.

Customer/market research is a fundamental tool to understand what trade-offs customers are ready to make at what price. Research should target specific segments and clearly focus on the decision makers, so the company has a clear understanding of what benefits the customers seek, price they are willing to pay, etc. This understanding then should drive the company's communication strategy. In 1980s, IBM was a good example of the above practice. They identified reliability of PCs in the corporate world was a more important factor than other factors such as speed, capacity, etc. They developed a communication strategy based on this theme and commanded a significant price premium relative to other brands.

Customer preferences or the benefits that they seek are constantly changing; therefore companies need to establish a framework that measures customer pulse continuously. The car industry is a very good example with customers preferences changing from power to economy to safety to low emission over time.

—Dr. Serdar Avsar, Head of Research, Customer Experience, Westpac

Reprinted with permission.

Searching for a Marketing Accountability Scorecard

The author facilitated the efforts of the Conference Board's Council on Corporate Brand Management to develop a scorecard for monitoring brands.[3] At the time, Council member firms included companies such as FedEx, Lockheed Martin, 3-M, John Deere, CIGNA, eBay, Eli Lilly, Wal-Mart, and Nissan.

Initially, over one hundred possible measures were identified that might be useful for monitoring the performance of a product or a service (Exhibit 10.6). These measures were measures that had been suggested by consulting firms such as Interbrand, advertising agencies such as Young & Rubicam, organizations such as the American Productivity and Quality Center, and various academics and journalists as well as members of the Council on Corporate Brand Management.

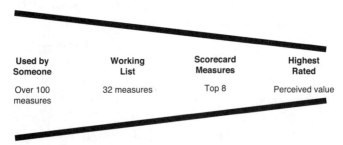

Used by Someone	Working List	Scorecard Measures	Highest Rated
Over 100 measures	32 measures	Top 8	Perceived value

Reprinted with permission from "Building the Brand Scorecard," Don Sexton, *The Advertiser*, February 2005, pp. 54-58.

Exhibit 10.6   Brand scorecard measures

After removing measures that seemed to focus on similar dimensions, there were 32 measures left for consideration (Exhibit 10.7).

Exhibit 10.7   Possible Scorecard Measures

Name Recall	Credibility
Logo Recall	Esteem
Tag Line Recall	Leadership
Ad Recall	Trust
Economic Benefits	Considered Set
Functional Benefits	Brand Preference
Emotional Benefits	Price Premium
Differentiation	Purchase Intent
Ad Message	Inquiry
Brand Understanding	Brand Trial
Familiarity	Repurchase
Salience	Increase Usage
Importance	Customer Satisfaction
Relevance	Complaints
Favorability	Recommend Intent
Perceived Value	Recommend

Reprinted with permission from "Building the Brand Scorecard," Don Sexton, *The Advertiser*, February, 2005, pp. 54-58.

Candidate measures for the scorecard were evaluated based on the following criteria:

- Actionable: Useful as a guide for decisions.
- Measurable: There must be a straightforward, hopefully economical, way to find the value for the measure.
- Make common sense: Understandable and easy to explain.
- Make theoretical sense: Be justified with marketing, economics, and finance concepts.
- Effective: Has worked in practice.

Next, it was necessary to develop a framework to organize all these measures. Many companies were using several measures, but few reported using any overall model to tie all the measures together. Lack of an overall model can easily lead to a plethora of brand measures, where more than one measure may be used to monitor the same brand phenomena—increasing information costs without necessarily increasing insight.

One dimension of the framework was chosen to be the components of a brand. While there are several brand models available, one that is both powerful and parsimonious stems from the work of Peter Farquhar and others. In this model, explained in Chapter 4, "Perceived Value," the key components of a brand are:

- Identifiers—name, logo, color—anything that cues the brand attributes in the customer's mind.
- Attributes—benefits, needs, features—any characteristic that a customer associates with the brand.
- Association—the relation between the identifier and the brand attribute.

The various measures proposed to monitor a product or service generally focus on one of these brand components. At a minimum, a useful scorecard should inform managers as to how their product or service is performing on these three brand components.

The second dimension of the framework was the purchase cycle, including after-purchase behavior (Exhibit 10.8). The purchase cycle allows one to add the time dimension to evaluating marketing accountability. For new products or services, one might utilize measures from early in the purchase cycle such as trial. For more mature products or services, one might employ measures more concerned with repeat purchases such as satisfaction or loyalty.

Considerable research has focused on the purchase cycle model, and it appears that the purchase cycle may not be as straightforward as shown in Exhibit 10.8. In particular, as discussed in Chapters 4 and 9, the order of the stages of the cycle may vary depending on the type of product or service. For example, for important consumer purchases such as automobiles or most business-to-business purchases such as production machinery, there may be substantial information-gathering before purchase. However, for relatively less important purchases, including many consumer purchases such as a razor or a magazine, customers may simply make the purchase on a trial basis and do their information-gathering after the purchase.

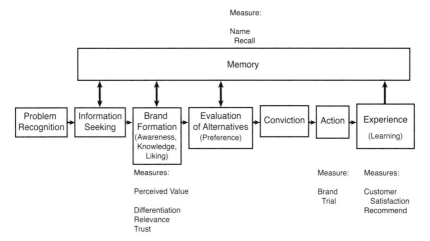

Reprinted with permission from "Building the Brand Scorecard," The Arrow Group, Ltd.®, New York, NY, 2008.

Exhibit 10.8   The purchase cycle

The purchase cycle model must be tailored to the target customers and to the product or service and that, in turn, may have an impact on the measures included in the scorecard for a particular brand.

When the measures under consideration were organized on these two dimensions, there appeared to be multiple measures available for each aspect of the product or service (Exhibit 10.9).

The final step in developing the performance scorecard was to ask members of the Council on Corporate Brand Management which measures they considered to be the "most important" measures to use in the scorecard and which measures they considered "absolutely essential" to use in the scorecard.

The survey was opportunistic rather than scientific. The respondents in the sample were not randomly chosen; therefore, one cannot extrapolate the results as reflecting the opinions of all managers. Nonetheless the opinions of these 20 managers are valuable, given that they manage some very well-known and valuable products and services.

Purchase Cycle

Brand Dimension	Awareness	Knowledge	Liking	Preference	Conviction	Action	Experience	Learning
Identifiers (eg, name, logo)	Aided/unaided Name Recall Logo Recall Tag Line Recall Ad Recall							
Attributes (eg, feature, benefit)		Benefits Economic Functional Emotional Differentiation	Importance Relevance Evaluation of Benefit Favorability Perceived Value	Considered Set Brand Preference Price Premium Perceived Value				Benefits Economic Functional Emotional Differentiation
Associations (eg, message, familiarity)		Ad Message Brand Understanding Familiarity Salience	Credibility Esteem Leadership Trust	Credibility Esteem Leadership Trust				Brand Understanding Familiarity Salience
Behavior (eg, trial, repeat purchase)					Purchase Intent	Active Search / Increase Usage; Product Trial / Share of Spend; Brand Trial / Value of Customer; Repurchase	Customer Satisfaction Complaints Recommend Intent to Recommend	
Business Outcomes						Market Share / Sales; Margin / Profits; Cash flow / Brand Value; Shareholder Stock Price / Value		

Reprinted with permission from "Building the Brand Scorecard," The Arrow Group, Ltd.®, New York, NY, 2008.

Exhibit 10.9   Measure framework

The measure considered the most important to include in the scorecard was perceived value (Exhibit 10.10). The opinions of these managers are quite consistent with the message of this book, namely, that CVA®—especially its major component perceived value—is an important leading indicator of revenue, contribution, and profits. If one must choose just one measure to monitor a brand, choose perceived value.

Exhibit 10.10   Measures Used to Determine Brand Performance

Measure	"Most Important"°	"Absolutely Essential"°	Measure	"Most Important"°	"Absolutely Essential"°
Name Recall	.40	.35	Esteem	.10	.10
Logo Recall	.10	.05	Leadership	.30	.20
Tag Line Recall	.10	.05	Trust	.45	.45
Ad Recall	.05	.00	Considered Set	.15	.10
Economic Benefits	.05	.00	Brand Preference	.35	.25

Measure	"Most Important"°	"Absolutely Essential"°	Measure	"Most Important"°	"Absolutely Essential"°
Functional Benefits	.30	.25	Price Premium	.30	.15
Emotional Benefits	.30	.20	Purchase Intent	.30	.15
Differentiation	.50	.50	Inquiry	.05	.05
Ad Message	.25	.00	Brand Trial	.40	.35
Brand	.30	.05	Repurchase	.15	.30
Understanding	.15	.25	Increase	.15	.00
Familiarity			Usage		
Salience	.25	.10	Customer Satisfaction	.50	.35
Importance	.20	.10	Complaints	.10	.10
Relevance	.50	.35	Recommend Intent	.20	.30
Favorability	.15	.10	Recommend	.45	.50
Perceived Value	.70	.55			
Credibility	.40	.30			

° Percentage of mentions
Reprinted with permission from "Building the Brand Scorecard," Don Sexton, *The Advertiser*, February 2005, pp. 54-58.

There were seven other measures that the Council members considered useful to include in the scorecard:

- Name recall
- Differentiation
- Relevance
- Trust
- Brand trial
- Customer satisfaction
- Recommend

The first four measures focus on the components of a brand. Name recall concerns the identifier; differentiation and relevance refer to the attributes; and trust relates to the association.

The other three measures correspond to the different stages in the purchase cycle. *Brand trial* is the initial purchase. *Customer satisfaction* corresponds to the in-use performance of the product or service. *Recommend* provides a measure of the willingness of the customer to suggest the product or service to someone else.

Bacardi: Perceived Value Metrics

Over the past years, the major brand owners in the global Spirits industry have shifted from a product and volume orientation toward a brand and value approach. Some players in the alcoholic drinks business had historically followed a luxury goods model, and other players still retain a volume orientation, today. But, the sweet spot is now generally recognized to be value.

Spirits consumers are willing to pay significantly more for higher perceived value, and to some degree these consumers perceive price as a signal of brand value. For brand owners, premium and super premium brands are attractive propositions for generating shareholder value.

Many of the marketing metrics developed for FMCG (fast moving consumer goods) are applicable to measuring perceived value for Spirits brands. Choice-based models can be applied strategically to measure price elasticity and to optimize pricing for value creation in a retail purchase decision context; retail scanner data can be analyzed to look at price sensitivity in the "real world" of promotion and discounting in a competitive context. However, there are many dimensions of Spirit brands that go far beyond the retail shelf.

Standardized Brand Equity models offered by the major international market research agencies tend to fall short for Spirits brands. These standardized models typically measure the behavioral, rational, and emotional dimensions of the consumer-brand relationship, but measuring Spirits brands requires more emphasis on the emotional and social dimensions. An implicit marketing mindset of driving awareness/trial/repeat might tend to undermine the special feeling that consumers seek in premium Spirits drinking occasions and experiences.

While there is a rich complexity of value drivers that can be mined in ad hoc consumer studies, senior management requires the simplicity of a few key consumer tracking metrics. By focusing on a combination of the most important rational and emotional metrics, an effective senior management scorecard can be created that tracks consumer perceived value in a competitive context with trends over time and geography.

—Evan Oster, Director Planning & Research Americas, Bacardi Global Brands

Reprinted with permission.

Conclusions

A scorecard should provide steering control.[4] While that means some measures of current performance may be included, especially valuable measures are those that are *leading* indicators of performance. CVA® and perceived value, in particular, are leading indicators of financial performance and provide steering control. Most organizations do not appear to track either CVA® or perceived value.

Why organizations do not employ perceived value as a key measure is discussed in the final chapter.

11

Organizing to Manage CVA®

There has been a long-held and enduring interest in improving measures of marketing accountability and, at the same time, a singular lack of progress—according to the studies cited in Chapter 1, "Marketing and Financial Performance." There is great desire to improve the measurement of marketing return; but, satisfactory results are achieved by only a few such as Cisco, Sony, and other organizations represented in this book.

How can that happen?

For any action to take place, many factors must be in alignment such as objectives, effort, and capabilities. Over the past ten years, there have been numerous surveys of managers conducted by several organizations such as the Association of National Advertisers (ANA), the Conference Board (TCB), and the American Productivity and Quality Center (APQC). Remarkably, these diverse studies all reach similar conclusions: Most of these factors have been and continue to be out of alignment in many companies. It is no surprise that little progress has been made in improving measures of marketing accountability—and measures of marketing return in particular. This chapter examines those forces and considers what may be the underlying issues preventing or slowing progress in improving measures of marketing return.

Cisco: Managing Marketing for Financial Return

For Fortune 100 companies such as Cisco, the role of marketing is broad and complex. Marketing must not only help generate demand for the company's products and services, but build brand and customer equity and ultimately help shape the market in which the company competes. By using a model based on generating demand, establishing preference and accelerating market transitions, Cisco marketers have built a robust framework for strategy development and planning, and have clarified expectations for what marketing does relative to other business functions.

Different marketing activities serve different purposes, e.g., demand generation programs don't accomplish thought leadership objectives and awareness-focused, brand-building programs don't necessarily accomplish immediate sales objectives. Attaining an appropriate mix of activities is imperative for the success of the marketing function. Whether it's field marketing, corporate marketing, or public relations, different disciplines perform some form of communications function intended to benefit the company's business. Managers in each area demonstrate their organization's value in terms of leads generated or favorable impressions, for example, but ultimately, senior leadership is keenly interested in how their function drives results in terms of financial benefits such as sales revenue and shareholder value.

One approach Cisco took to help further uncover how various communications activities drive value was to look at the company's overall efficiency across the paid and non-paid media landscape. On one dimension, we explored the efficiency of advertising spend relative to sales revenue for Cisco and a set of other companies in the IT sector. On another dimension we explored efficiency of news release output relative to media uptake and prominence, again for Cisco and its IT peers. Correlating the two efficiency measures, we could better understand the effectiveness of our paid and non-paid media activities in a competitive context. We could also demonstrate how Cisco compared to certain competitors in terms of weighted media focus and the ultimate communications impact each company was making. This kind of analysis helped us advocate for modulating our approach and optimizing resources for greater impact.

—Cheryl Sawyer, Director, Brand Strategy and Management, Cisco

Reprinted with permission

How Individuals and Organizations Behave

Between *desiring a result* and *achieving a result* are several steps, any of which can interfere with progress if not managed appropriately (Exhibit 11.1).[1]

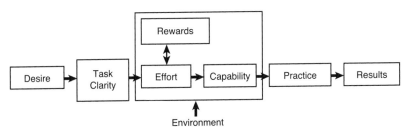

Reprinted with permission from "Marketing Accountability," The Arrow Group, Ltd.®, New York, NY, 2008.

Exhibit 11.1   From desire to results

Behavior begins with knowing where one is going. That is called *task clarity*— the extent to which objectives are understood. If objectives are not clear, neither is the direction of one's efforts, as in the Chinese proverb, "If you don't know where you're going, any road will take you there."

To achieve objectives, clearly one must invest *effort*—the amount of time and other resources devoted to an activity. To call forth effort usually requires some kind of *reward*— what motivates people and how it is linked to the task so that effort will be made. Rewards include money, recognition, or internal satisfaction.

A great deal of effort can be invested with no effect unless there is *capability*—skills and resources that allow one to achieve the task. Motivating people without providing them the capabilities to succeed creates frustration.

Effort and capability are present in an *environment*—which may be supportive or nonsupportive of achieving the objectives. Organizational culture, sense of mission, prioritization of goals—all combine to define the environment of an organization. If the environment is not supportive of activities, they will not happen despite effort and capability.

Finally, success in learning and doing requires *practice*—doing something not just thinking about it—learning from failures and successes.

In sum, for people to accomplish a task, they must be able to answer "Yes" to *each* of the following questions:

- Do I know what I am supposed to do?
- Do I have the capability to perform?
- If I put in the effort, can I perform?
- If I perform, will I be rewarded?
- Will my environment help me perform?
- Will I be able to learn how to perform better?

Generally, with respect to marketing accountability, either this entire system or important components are not working in many organizations—some or all of the questions are being answered "No." Given those conditions, it is no surprise that progress on measuring marketing effectiveness and marketing ROI in particular has been inconsistent at best.

> *In many organizations, there appears neither the will nor the way to assess the return on marketing efforts.*

© Ashleigh Brilliant, 2008. Used with permission.

Task Clarity

Lack of clarity regarding marketing ROI is a major barrier. Without knowing what one is looking for, it is difficult to find it.

Many managers believe that it is important to agree on a definition of marketing ROI—57 percent of managers surveyed by the ANA considered it "important or very important" to agree on a marketing ROI definition (Exhibit 11.2). Yet, in 2007, the ANA found that only 12 percent of respondents were "satisfied or very satisfied" with agreement on a marketing ROI definition in their organization, and only 22 percent thought that their senior management had communicated a clear definition of marketing accountability.

> Is it important or very important to agree on a definition of marketing ROI?   57%
>
> Are you satisfied or very satisfied with agreement on a definition of marketing ROI?
> | | | |
> |---|---|---|
> | 2005 | (ANA) | 22% |
> | 2006 | (ANA) | 36% |
> | 2007 | (ANA) | 12% |
>
> Senior management has communicated a clear definition of marketing accountability   22%
> 2007 (ANA)

Source: "Fourth Annual ANA/MMA Marketing Accountability, Study." New York: Association of National Advertisers, July 2007.

Exhibit 11.2   Defining marketing ROI

As discussed in Chapter 10, "Building the Marketing Accountability Scorecard," numerous measures to evaluate the effectiveness of marketing efforts have been employed. Many measures were mentioned by respondents to a 2004 ANA study (Exhibit 11.3), but none of the measures compared a financial return such as contribution or profit to a marketing outlay. Especially concerning, the second most common definition of marketing ROI mentioned by the respondents was changes in brand awareness (57 percent)—which is likely a trailing indicator of financial performance (see Chapter 7, "Managing CVA® over Time").

Exhibit 11.3   Definition of Marketing ROI

Which is closest to your company's current definition of marketing ROI?

Definition	Percent
Incremental sales from marketing	66%
Changes in brand awareness	57
Total sales from marketing	55
Purchase intent	55
Attitudinal changes	51
Market share	49
Number of leads	40
Ratio of ad cost to revenue	34
Cost per lead	34
Reach/frequency	30
GRPs delivered	25
Cost per sale	23
Media post-buy analysis	21
Financial value of brand equity	19
Customer lifetime value	17

Source: Association of National Advertisers, "ANA Marketing Accountability Study,"
New York: June 2004.

Marketing ROI is not a difficult concept. It is the return measured in monetary units for an effort measured in monetary units.

$$\text{Marketing ROI} = \frac{\text{Return}}{\text{Marketing Investment}}$$

There are different ways to calculate return (such as contribution, profit, or cash flow) and different ways to calculate investment. However, measures such as brand awareness and market share clearly do not fit the definition of ROI.

This lack of clarity regarding a definition of marketing ROI may reflect a lack of understanding of financial concepts among some marketing managers, or it may reflect a lack of data or analytical capabilities.

Effort

In a recent Conference Board study, time spent working on marketing ROI was clearly and overwhelmingly the most important single indicator of success in measuring marketing ROI (Exhibit 11.4).[2] Yet when the CMO Council was polled in 2007, "introduced a formal marketing performance measurement system" ranked number 11 (with 15.2 percent mentions) among last year's "top three accomplishments." (Number 1 with 45.7 percent mentions was "restructured marketing to better support sales" and Number 2 with 29.2 percent mentions was "overhauled brand image.")[3]

Exhibit 11.4 Time versus Success in Measuring Marketing ROI

Time spent on ROI	No progress	Some progress	Good progress
<6 months	63%	10%	0%
6–<12 months	6	19	9
1–<2 years	6	29	0
2–<3 years	19	33	18
>3 years	6	10	73

Source: Karen Beaman, Gregory R. Guy, and Donald E. Sexton, *Managing and Measuring Return on Marketing Investment*, Research Report 1435-08-RR. New York: The Conference Board, 2008.

Time spent working means exactly that. In the 2008 Conference Board study, number of meetings and number of communications about marketing ROI were not significantly associated with progress in measuring marketing ROI—but personal days per month were significantly associated.

One can speculate that managers and others simply do not assign a high priority to measuring marketing ROI. In one telecommunications company, an interview with various marketing research managers indicated that they were quite satisfied with what they were already doing to evaluate marketing—despite not knowing the ROI of their marketing efforts and not even using lifetime customer value. They simply had no time and, therefore, no interest in improving their understanding of marketing ROI.

Rewards

Lack of effort in measuring marketing ROI may stem from lack of motivation provided.

The APQC found that almost 60 percent of firms they surveyed in 2003 made no use of marketing ROI in determining compensation (21 percent made "moderate use" of marketing ROI in compensation).[4]

However, rewards do not need to be financial. They need to be something that people value. In the study recently concluded by the Conference Board's Marketing ROI study group, including marketing ROI in performance reviews and recognition programs was highly associated with progress in measuring marketing ROI, while including marketing ROI in compensation plans was not significantly associated with progress (Exhibit 11.5).[5]

Success in measuring marketing ROI

Versus

MROI part of corporate scoreboard
MROI included in performance reviews .05 level
MROI included in compensation plans
MRPI recognition programs in place   .05 level
$R^2 = .37$

2008 (TCB)

Source: Karen Beaman, Gregory R. Guy, and Donald E. Sexton, *Managing and Measuring Return on Marketing Investment*, Research Report 1435-08-RR. New York: The Conference Board, 2008.

Exhibit 11.5   Rewarding work on marketing ROI

For people to be motivated, they have to believe they will receive a reward for their actions *and* the reward must be something they value. If the consequence of their actions is simply to be assigned more work, that is not a situation that motivates. More likely it is a situation that de-motivates.

In some organizations, it is clear that there is no reason to improve understanding of marketing return because there is no reward for doing so and no penalty for not doing so. In a meeting at one well-known consumer packaged goods company, the head of marketing research showed no interest in finding improved approaches to marketing return. She was satisfied with what she was doing and felt no need to change.

Hubris plays a role as well. In a conference with members of the business research department at a major industrial producer, one of the largest exporters for the US, the managers explained that they had had no success in improving their marketing ROI methodology and so, therefore, saw no reason to try a different approach! Their arrogance was obvious—if they were unable to develop marketing ROI measures, then no one else could.

Capabilities

Even if organizations have the will to improve their marketing ROI methodology, they may not have the way. A 2007 survey concluded that approximately 40 percent of organizations believe that they do not have the time, capacity, or internal capabilities to improve their evaluation of marketing ROI.[6] The 2008 Lenskold Group survey found only 17 percent of those responding considered that their marketing ROI measurement abilities were as "good as they needed to be or a real source of leadership" while 43 percent thought their marketing ROI measurement capabilities were "a long way" from what they needed.[7]

The Conference Board's 2008 study found that all the skills that respondents considered important for marketing ROI were consistently rated lower with respect to their availability (Exhibit 11.6). Overall, the majority of Conference Board study respondents agreed that, "lack of technology and appropriate infrastructure have affected significantly, or a lot, the ability to measure marketing ROI."[8]

Capabilities include skills, such as analytical skills and data management skills, and resources, such as data and time. A 2007 study by the Prophet brand consultancy found that about 40 percent of companies believed that they did not have the right models or analytic tools and did not have the necessary market data.

Those findings were confirmed by the 2008 Conference Board study that indicated companies felt data, metrics, and methodology were the most important resources for assessing marketing ROI, but rated their analytical capabilities relatively low across the board (Exhibit 11.7).

Exhibit 11.6   Skills

Skills	Importance	Evaluation
Strategic decision-making	4.7	3.8
Analytical thinking	4.5	3.8
Financial acumen	4.1	3.7
General business knowledge	4.2	4.0
Sales and marketing knowledge	4.4	3.9
Collaboration	4.3	3.5
Mobilizing resources	4.0	3.4
Openness to change	4.5	3.3
Goal orientation	4.4	3.7
Process orientation	3.9	3.5

Source: Karen Beaman, Gregory R. Guy, and Donald E. Sexton, *Managing and Measuring Return on Marketing Investment*, Research Report 1435-08-RR. New York: The Conference Board, 2008.

Exhibit 11.7   Resources

Resource	Importance	Evaluation
Data integrity	4.7	3.1
Predefined metrics	4.4	3.1
Data availability	4.6	3.0
Master data management	4.1	2.9
Reporting/dashboards	4.2	2.9
Single platform	3.3	2.8
Common ROI methodology	4.4	3.1

Source: Karen Beaman, Gregory R. Guy, and Donald E. Sexton, *Managing and Measuring Return on Marketing Investment*, Research Report 1435-08-RR. New York: The Conference Board, 2008.

In particular, the availability of data appropriate to study market-ing ROI continues to be a problem for many organizations. Fewer than 20 percent of companies surveyed by the ANA in 2007 were "satisfied or very satisfied" with the quality of their information. None were satisfied with the timeliness of their information even though the 2008 Lenskold study reported that 49 percent of responding firms had access to detailed sales data at the individual customer level. A 2008 study of 450 marketing executives by the CMO Council found that less than 7 percent of the respondents believed that they had excellent knowledge of their customers with regard to demographic, behavioral, psychographic, and transactional information.[9]

The 2007 ANA study also hinted at what might be a major barrier—sharing of data within the organization. In many companies, managers seem to "own" data and do not necessarily share with others. In the ANA survey, only 24 percent were "satisfied or very satisfied" with their access to internal data, and only 12 percent (!) were "satisfied or very satisfied" that data were aligned and that everyone was working from the same data or information. In the CMO Council survey, only 15 percent of the respondents said that their companies were doing an extremely good or effective job of integrating disparate customer data sources.

At one telecommunications company, efforts to develop new ways to measure marketing return were blocked by managers who "owned" data and were not willing to allow others access.

Companies overall are not optimistic about being able to improve their data for evaluating marketing ROI. Depending on the data category, the ANA found that anywhere from 36 percent to 79 percent of the respondents believed it would be "somewhat or very difficult" to improve their information (Exhibit 11.8). In a more recent study, the ANA concluded that fewer than 20 percent of respondents were "satisfied or very satisfied" that they had abilities to improve their data (Exhibit 11.9). Nonetheless, the 2008 Lenskold Group study did find some cause for optimism—for example, asked where they had improved over the past year, 36 percent mentioned measurements of marketing's impact on sales, 34 percent internal data systems, 29 percent profitability measurements, and 26 percent modeling analytics.

Money is being spent on marketing accountability by around 40 percent to 50 percent of organizations according to the ANA; but, for the majority, less than 1 percent of the working marketing budget is spent on marketing accountability. The 2008 Conference Board survey showed a positive relationship between spending on marketing ROI efforts and progress. Money alone does not bring success but it helps.

Exhibit 11.8   Ability to Improve—I

It will be somewhat or very difficult to improve:

Information type	Percent
Comprehensiveness of sales data	79%
Reporting systems	64
Timeliness of sales data	63
Accuracy of sales data	69
Granularity of sales data	46
Granularity of marketing data	39
Comprehensiveness of spending data	36

Source: Association of National Advertisers, "ANA Marketing Accountability Study," New York: June 2004.

Exhibit 11.9   Ability to Improve—II

Are you satisfied or very satisfied with your ability to improve:

Data quality	Percent
Timeliness of data	18%
Accuracy of data	16
Effectiveness of planning process	15
Marketing technology support	13

Source: Association of National Advertisers, "Fourth Annual ANA/MMA Marketing Accountability, Study." New York: July 2007.

What does bring success is the obvious—assigning people to work on marketing ROI issues (and, as mentioned earlier, allowing them time to work on marketing ROI issues). In the Conference Board 2008 study, half the organizations reporting no progress on marketing ROI had no people working on marketing ROI (Exhibit 11.10)!

Marketing people alone cannot develop marketing ROI methodologies. They need to be working with others, especially those from finance and accounting.[10]

Exhibit 11.10   People Assigned to Marketing ROI

Head count working on MROI	No progress	Some progress	Good progress
None	50%	25%	0%
1–2	44	45	70
3–4	6	20	30
>4	0	10	0

Source: Karen Beaman, Gregory R. Guy, and Donald E. Sexton, *Managing and Measuring Return on Marketing Investment*, Research Report 1435-08-RR. New York: The Conference Board, 2008.

However, for a long period of time, cooperation between marketing, finance, and accounting has seemed to be the exception rather than the rule. For example, in 1998, in a study conducted by the APQC, only 17 percent of respondents stated that "brand management and accounting cooperate to determine marketing ROI" (Exhibit 11.11).[11] In 2008, the ANA found that 33 percent of companies reported "full cooperation between marketing and finance," but only 22 percent had cross-functional teams working on marketing ROI (Exhibit 11.12).

Exhibit 11.11   Cooperation Between Marketing and Finance

Type of cooperation	Percent	Reference
Brand management and accounting cooperate to determine MROI	17%	1998 (APQC)
Full cooperation between marketing and finance	25%	2006 (ANA)
	22%	2007 (ANA)
Marketing and finance share common metrics	25%	2007 (ANA)

Exhibit 11.12   Use of Cross-Functional Teams

How many have cross-functional teams working on MROI?

Reference	Percentage
2006 (ANA)	45%
2007 (ANA)	20%
2008 (ANA)	22%

Marketing managers need to be working with managers from other functions to develop marketing ROI methodologies.

Perhaps in a competitive environment where pressure is intense and managerial time is scarce, participating in a collaborative marketing ROI effort that is not well-defined, not well-rewarded, and not well-supported is a luxury that few managers—marketing or finance—can afford.

Sony: Customer Valuation

Taking your brand's health for granted is perilous. At Sony, we enjoy a leadership position in our industry because we offer products that are reliable, intuitive and enable people to enjoy entertainment and to be creative. Even across consumer categories, Sony has been ranked at the top of favorite brand lists for decades. We must continue to build on this position or risk everything. New companies have succeeded in capturing the consumer's attention in ways we could not have anticipated even five years ago. Consumers also have changed the way they engage in brands.

Earlier than for almost any consumer product or service, people have used the web for shopping for electronics. People typically seek various sources of information to understand category and brand differences, and the web obviously adds new dimensions to this process. Understanding this, Sony has sought many different ways to tell consumers about our products in a variety of ways, from creating a site designed for learning as well as for buying, traditional advertising, and engaging with consumers in forums they create. As a result of facilitating the shopping experience, our online strategy has generated increased sales. But does it help consumers connect with our brand story?

To answer this question, we set out to measure the brand impact of our online initiatives. Working with selected sites ranging from technology focused web portals to subject-specific sites—such as those visited by sports fans—we measured the brand impact of our online campaigns much in the same way we have measured the brand impact of television and print advertising. We know the campaigns drive traffic using conventional click-through analysis, so we needed to see if the same consumers who were clicking were also paying attention to our brand story. We interviewed visitors to the selected sites as well as a control group to determine if our online campaign helped tell a brand story.

As with many marketing activities, the results are mostly positive but we have room to improve. Our interviews indicate consumers pay attention to the message of the campaign and want to learn more about the products as a result. Ultimately, this leads to a better conversation between Sony and our customers. However, few of the respondents who visited sites with our online ads had a substantially better view of key brand health metrics than the control group. On the one hand, this is expected because they had a favorable impression of Sony before they saw the online campaign. On the other hand, we need to find more engaging ways to tell our brand story online so that the brand keeps getting better.

As we have moved from a Web 1.0 approach (we talk, consumers listen) to a Web 2.0 approach (we engage with our customers in a two-way dialogue), we have found we can have a greater impact on the brand. We will continue to leverage the web for more than sales, and we will continue to do-test-learn-adapt as we go.

—Chris Gaebler, Vice President, Corporate Marketing, Sony Electronics

Reprinted with permission

Environment

While often discussed, it is not clear that cultural resistance is the main barrier to progress on marketing ROI. In an analysis of cultural resistance and marketing ROI progress using the responses from the 2008 Conference Board study, there was very little association. When respondents were asked to describe specific barriers, about 30 percent to 45 percent named lack of clarity and lack of resources, themes that appeared in many other studies and which are less due to the cultural values of an organization and more due to managerial decisions.

Not surprisingly, the majority (63 percent) of respondents in the 2008 Conference Board study believed that "leadership commitment" was the most important driver of marketing ROI success—but that would be true of almost any endeavor in any organization (Exhibit 11.13). Unfortunately, "leadership commitment" is an actionable variable only for senior managers such as the CEO, CMO, and CFO.

Exhibit 11.13   Drivers of Measuring Marketing ROI

Driver	Percentage
Leadership commitment	63%
Data availability/integrity	43%
Executive sponsorship	37%
Strategic alignment	37%
Budget pressures	25%

Source: Karen Beaman, Gregory R. Guy, and Donald E. Sexton, *Managing and Measuring Return on Marketing Investment*, Research Report 1435-08-RR. New York: The Conference Board, 2008.

The driver with the second most support (43 percent) in the Conference Board study was "data availability/integrity" and that is consistent with the findings discussed earlier under "Capabilities." Data availability/integrity was also considered to be the Number 1 barrier (Exhibit 11.14). However, lack of other capabilities such as technology and methodology also ranked high among barriers.

Exhibit 11.14   Barriers to Measuring Marketing ROI

Barrier	Percentage
Data availability/integrity	47%
Technology/infrastructure	41%
Resource dedication	39%
Methodology/know-how	22%
Individual capabilities	20%

Source: Karen Beaman, Gregory R. Guy, and Donald E. Sexton, *Managing and Measuring Return on Marketing Investment*, Research Report 1435-08-RR. New York: The Conference Board, 2008.

In short, the barriers to marketing ROI are not necessarily due to an overall organization culture that is inimical to marketing ROI measurement. The barriers generally fall in areas under the control of management—such as task clarity, effort and rewards, and capabilities—and can be remedied if marketing or marketing research managers wish to make the effort.

Results

Suppose the system is aligned with task clarity, effort, rewards, capabilities, environment, and practice all moving to encourage progress in measuring marketing ROI. Are organizations ready to use that information?

No—according to a study by the ANA in 2005. Only 16 percent of respondents considered themselves "satisfied or very satisfied" with their ability to respond quickly to marketing ROI information, and only 20 percent were "satisfied or very satisfied" with their ability to eliminate unprofitable marketing programs (Exhibit 11.15).

Exhibit 11.15   Ability to Use Marketing ROI Information

Ability	Important or very important	Satisfied or very satisfied
Change established marketing strategies and budgets	63%	27%
Respond quickly to marketing ROI information	55%	16%
Eliminate unprofitable marketing programs	61%	20%

Source: Association of National Advertisers, "Second Annual ANA/MMA Marketing Accountability Study." New York: June, 2005.

Even if organizations succeed at establishing methodologies to evaluate marketing ROI, it is not clear that they can or will use that information for decision-making!

Conclusions

In sum, many managers are:

- Not clear what to measure.
- Not putting in the time.
- Not motivating people to put in the time.
- Not providing the skills and resources.
- Not working with finance and accounting.
- Not using new measures.

Otherwise, everything is going fine.

In addition, there are basic data issues, such as use of the appropriate cost data, and basic analytical issues such as establishing causality. However, for many organizations, they do not seem to be at a stage where they are confronting those thorny issues.

Success in assessing marketing effectiveness is a bit like making a shot in pool—everything needs to be lined up. If just one of the factors discussed is out of alignment, the marketing ROI efforts may not succeed.

The good news is that all these problems are solvable. What it takes is some managerial attention and some openness to change.[12]

Here are some specific suggestions:

1. Use perceived value and CVA® as key metrics to manage and monitor marketing and branding strategy.
2. Make sure everyone knows what marketing return and marketing ROI mean.
3. Recognize efforts people make to improve understanding of the financial effects of marketing.
4. Acquire the data or analytical skills needed to conduct the appropriate analyses of marketing and branding activities.
5. Get started—the data and skills will improve.

The ideas and approaches in this book are intended to help structure and guide these efforts. May all your efforts result in satisfying returns. For current information on CVA®, please log onto www.cva.us.com.

Endnotes

Chapter 1

1. See Kate McArthur, "CMO's, You Have 23 Months to Live," *Advertising Age* (June 19, 2006): 1, 25; David Court, "The Evolving Role of the CMO," *The McKinsey Quarterly*, no. 3 (2007): 28–39; Mercedes M. Cardona, "CMO's Under Fire," *Advertising Age* (May 3, 2004): 1, 81; Martha Rogers, "ROC [return on customer]: The CFO Is Not the Enemy," *1-to-1 Weekly* (April 30, 2007): 2–3; and John Quelch, "The Rise and Fall of the CMO," (Harvard Business School Paper presented at the Columbia Club, New York City, November, 2005).

2. "Fifth Annual ANA/MMA Marketing Accountability Study." New York: Association of National Advertisers, June, 2008; "Fourth Annual ANA/MMA Marketing Accountability Study." New York: Association of National Advertisers, July, 2007; "Third Annual ANA/MMA Marketing Accountability Study." New York: Association of National Advertisers, July, 2006; "Second Annual ANA/MMA Marketing Accountability Study." New York: Association of National Advertisers, June, 2005; and "ANA Marketing Accountability Study," New York: Association of National Advertisers, June, 2004.

3. Jeffrey Marshall, "Finance: Friend or Foe?—The CFO Perspective," (Paper presented at the 2008 ANA Marketing Accountability Conference, July 14, 2008).

4. Interbrand/ANA, "Survey of Senior Marketers," September, 2008.

5. For related academic research, see Suleyman Cem Bahadir and Kapil R. Tuli, "Measuring Marketing Productivitiy: Linking Marketing to Financial Returns," Marketing Science Institute, Report No. 02-119, 2002 and Thomas S. Gruca and Loo L. Rego, "Customer Satisfaction, Cash Flow, and Shareholder Value," Marketing Science Institute, Working Paper No. 03-002, 2003. For a survey of the field, see Donald R. Lehmann and David J. Reibstein, *Marketing Metrics and Financial Performance*, Cambridge, MA: Marketing Science Institute, 2006; and for several studies, see Christine Moorman and Donald R. Lehmann, eds., *Assessing Marketing Strategy Performance*, Cambridge, MA: Marketing Science Institute, 2004.

6. CMO Council, "Marketing Outlook," Palo Alto, CA, 2007.

7. Christine Hess and Donald E. Sexton, "Marketing Conference Survey of CMO Issues and Challenges," Unpublished report, The Conference Board, March 27, 2007).

8. Karen Beaman, Gregory R. Guy, and Donald E. Sexton, "Managing and Measuring Return on Marketing Investment," Research Report 1435-08-RR, New York: The Conference Board, 2008.

9. MarketingNPV®, "Marketing Professionals Survey," Princeton, New Jersey, 2007.

10. Lenskold Group, "Lenskold Group/Kneebone 2008 Marketing ROI and Measurement Study," Manasquan, New Jersey, 2008.

11. Prophet, "Prophet's View on the World of Marketing Effectiveness," Presentation at Senior Marketing Executive Roundtable, New York, April 18, 2007.

12. See also Joe Mullich, "The 10 Commandments of Total Accountability," *The Advertiser* (June, 2007): pp. 19–22.

13. Tim Ambler and John Roberts, "Beware the Silver Metric," *Marketing Science Institute*, Report No. 06-113, 2006.

14. Nanette Byrnes, "The Unraveling of AIG," *Business Week* (September 16, 2008): p. 15.

15. See Tom Copland, Tim Koller, and Jack Murrin, *Valuation: Measuring and Managing the Value of Companies*, New York: Wiley, 2000; Jeremy Quittner, "Determine Your Company's Worth," *Business Week* (April 1, 2008): p. 42; and Timothy A. Luehrman, "What's It Worth? A General Manager's Guide to Valuation," *Harvard Business Review*, (May-June, 1997): pp. 133–142,

16. Baruch Lev, "Sharpening the Intangibles Edge," Harvard Business Review (June, 2004): pp. 1–9.

17. John Davis, *Measuring Marketing*, New York: Wiley, 2007.

18. Clayton M. Christensen, Stephen P. Kaufman, and Willy C. Shih, "Innovation Killers," *Harvard Business Review* (January, 2008): pp. 1–8.

19. Michael E. Porter, *Competitive Strategy*, New York: Free Press, 1980; Michael Treacy and Fred Wiersama, *The Discipline of Market Leaders*, New York: Addison-Wesley, 1995; and Jack Trout, *Differentiate or Die*, New York: Wiley, 2000.

20. David A. Aaker and Robert Jacobson, "The Value Relevance of Brand Attitudes in High Technology Markets," *Journal of Marketing Research* (November 2001) pp. 485-93; Stuart Agres, "Evaluating Brands" talk at Columbia University, 1998; Robert D. Buzzell and Bradley T. Gale, *The PIMS® Principles*, New York: Free Press, 1987; David A. Aaker and Robert Jacobson, "The Financial Information Content of Perceived Quality," *Journal of Marketing Research* (May 1994) pp. 191-201; and James R. Gregory, *Driving Brand Equity*, New York: ANA, 2005.

21. "Lessons from Virgin's U.S. Brand Builder," *Business Week* (July 9, 2008): p. 22.

22. Ginger Conlon, "Electronic Arts Innovates Around the Customer," *1to1 Weekly* (October 22, 2007): pp.2–3.

23. Donald E. Sexton, "Old Brands, New Lives," *The Advertiser* (February, 2007): p. 33.

24. See Leonard M. Lodish and Carl F. Mela, "If Brands Are Built Over Years, Why Are They Managed Over Quarters?" *Harvard Business Review* (July-August, 2007): pp. 104–113 and "Winners and Losers: The US Motorcycle Industry," published later in this chapter.

25. Alan S. Cleland and Albert V. Bruno, "Building Customer and Shareholder Value," *Strategy and Leadership* (May-June, 1997): pp. 23–28.

26. Joann Muller, Jeff Green, and David Welch, "An Incentive to Halt Incentives: Carmakers Sabotage Profits as They Grab for Market Share," *Business Week* (November 20, 2000): p. 50.

27. Gordon Bethune, *From Worst to First*, New York: Wiley, 1998.

28. William K. Hall, "Survival Strategies in a Hostile Environment," *Harvard Business Review* (September, 1980): pp. 74–85.

29. Andrew Server, "Southwest Airlines: The Hottest Thing in the Sky," *Fortune* (March 8, 2004): pp. 86–90 and Len Lewis, *The Trader Joe's Adventure*, Chicago: Dearborn, 2005.

30. See Lauren Sherman, "World's Most Powerful Luxury Brands," *Forbes* (May 8, 2008)., and Joshua Levine, "Time Is Money," *Forbes* (September 18, 2000): pp. 178–185.

31. See James R. Gregory, *Driving Brand Equity*, New York: ANA, 2005; James R. Gregory, *The Best of Branding*, New York: McGraw-Hill, 2003; James R. Gregory and Jack Wiechmann, *Leveraging the Corporate Brand*, New York: McGraw-Hill, 1997; Kevin Keller, *Branding and Brand Equity*, Cambridge: Marketing Science Institute, 2002; Robert D. Buzzell and Bradley T. Gale, *The PIMS° Principles*, New York: Free Press, 1987; Mary E. Barth, Michael B. Clement, and Ron Kaznik, "Brand Value and Capital Market Valuation," *Journal of Accounting Studies* (March, 1998): pp. 41–68; David A. Aaker and Robert Jacobson, "The Value Relevance of Brand Attitudes in High-Technology Markets," *Journal of Marketing Research* (November, 2001): pp. 485–93; David A. Aaker and Robert Jacobson, "The Financial Information Content of Perceived Quality," *Journal of Marketing Research* (May, 1994): pp. 191–201; Shuba Srinivasan and Dominique M. Hanssens, "Marketing and Firm Value," (Working paper, January 12, 2007); Amit Joshi and Dominique Hanssens, "Advertising Spending and Market Capitalization," Marketing Science Institute, Report 04-110, 2004; Shruba Srinivasan, Koen Pauvels, Jorge Silva-Ross, and Dominique M. Hanssens, Marketing Science Institute, Report 06-002, 2006; Natalie Mizik and Robert Jacobson, "The Financial Value Impact of Perceptual Brand Attributes, *Journal of Marketing Research*, February, 2008, pp. 15–32; and Lerzan

Aksoy, *et al*, "The Long-Term Stock Market Valuation of Customer Satisfaction," *Journal of Marketing* (July, 2008): pp. 105–122.

32. E. C. Hoffman , III, and Helen Walters, "Building Better Brands," *Business Week* (May 25, 2007): p, 8.

33. David Kiley, "Xerox Gets a Brand Makeover," *Business Week* (January 7, 2008): p. 15 and Wendy Zellner, "Lessons from a Faded Levi Strauss," *Business Week* (December 15, 2003): p. 44.

34. Donald E. Sexton, "The Keys to Strategic Success," *Effective Executive* (January, 2007): pp. 32–34.

35. Peter Morton, "Reborn in the USA," *The Financial Post* (June 27, 1998): p. 8; Oliver Bertin, "Analysts Say Harley-Davidson's Success Has Been to Drive Into Buyers' Hearts," *Canadian Business and Current Affairs* (July 14, 2003): p. 17; and Joseph Weber, "Harley Just Keeps on Cruisin'," *Business Week* (November 6, 2006): pp. 71–72.

36. Donald E. Sexton, "China's Branding Challenge," *Effective Executive* (December, 2007): pp. 39–46.

37. "Best Global Brands," *Business Week* (September 18, 2008).

38. Vivian Yeo, "Lenovo Goes Global with Servers, *Business Week* (September 17, 2008): p. 90.

39. Ron Schramm, "Capital Efficiency in the US and China," unpublished paper, Columbia University, 2008.

40. Jean-Claude Usunier andCjislaine Gestre, "Product Ethnicity: Revisiting the Match Between Products and Countries," *Journal of International Marketing*, 15:2, .

41. Brad Stone, "Samsung in Bloom," *Newsweek* (July 15, 2002): p. 34; Jay Solomon, "Seoul Survivors," *The Wall Street Journal* (June 13, 2002): p. A1; Warren Brown, "Hyundai's Mission Possible: Beat the Luxury Brands," *The Washington Post* (April 1, 2007): p. G02; and "Hyundai Ads to Tout Brand Quality," *AMA Marketing Power* (September 10, 2007).

Chapter 2

1. See Kusum L. Ailawadi, Donald R. Lehmann, and Scott A. Neslin, "Revenue Premium as an Outcome Measure of Brand Equity," *Journal of Marketing* (October, 2003): pp. 1–17.

2. For further discussion, see any book on microeconomics such as Robert Pindyck and Daniel Rubinfeld, *Microeconomics*, Englewood Cliffs, N.J.: Prentice-Hall, 2008; Paul A. Samuelson and William D. Nordhaus, *Economics*, New York: McGraw-Hill, 2004; and Roger A. Arnold, *Microeconomics*, Cincinnati: South-Western College Publishing, 2007.

3. See Donald E. Sexton, "Estimation of Marketing Policy Effects on Sales," *Journal of Marketing Research* (August, 1970): pp. 338–47, and, more recently, Amit Joshi and Dominique Hanssens, "Advertising Spending and Market Capitalization," *Marketing Science Institute*, Report No. 04-110, 2004.

4. Donald E. Sexton, "A Microeconomic Model of the Effects of Advertising," *Journal of Business* (January, 1972): pp. 29–41.

5. For discussions of cash flow, see Charles T. Horngren and Walter T. Harrison, *Accounting*, Englewood Cliffs, N.J.: Prentice-Hall, 2006; Robert N. Anthony and Leslie K. Breitner, *Essentials of Accounting*, Englewood Cliffs, N.J.: Prentice-Hall, 2006; and Erich A. Hilfert, *Techniques of Financial Analysis*, Homewood, IL: Irwin, 1987.

6. For a thorough discussion of life time customer value, see Sunil Gupta and Donald R. Lehmann, *Managing Customers as Investments*, Philadelphia: Wharton School Publishing, 2005. Also see Roland Rust, Katherine Lemon, and Valerie Zeithaml, "Return on Marketing: Using Customer Equity to Focus Marketing Strategy," *Journal of Marketing* (January, 2004): pp. 109–127; Roland T. Rust, Valarie A. Zeithaml, and Katherine N. Lemon, *Driving Customer Equity*, New York: Free Press, 2000; Robert C. Blattberg, Gary Getz, and Jacquelyn S. Thomas, *Customer Equity*, Cambridge: Harvard Business School Press, 2001; and Don Peppers and Martha Rogers, *Return on Customer*, New York: Doubleday, 2005.

7. Donald E. Sexton, "Managing Communications ROI," *The Advertiser* (October, 2003): pp. 30, 32, and 34.

Chapter 3

1. Ricardo Roberts, "In a Flash, Polaroid Could Be Bankrupt," *Merger and Acquisitions Report*, September 10, 2001; and "Polaroid Firm Goes Bankrupt," *The Mirror*, October 13, 2001, p. 15.

2. For a discussion of overall strategies, see J.C. Larreche, *The Momentum Effect*, Upper Saddle River, N.J.: Wharton School Publishing, 2008.

3. Nariman K. Dhalla and Sonia Yuspeh, "Forget the Product Life Cycle Concept!" *Harvard Business Review* (January-February, 1976): pp. 102–111 and Youngme Moon, "Break Free from the Product Life Cycle," *Harvard Business Review* (May, 2005): pp. 2–10.

4. This simplification is also made in the classic life cycle article, Theodore Levitt, "Exploit the Product Life Cycle," *Harvard Business Review* (November-December, 1965): pp. 2–15.

5. Robert D. Buzzell and Bradley T. Gale, *The PIMS° Principles*, New York: Free Press, 1987.

6. Donald E. Sexton, "Why Your Branding Efforts May Be Your Most Important Investment," *Ideas at Work* (February 27, 2007): p. 13.

7. For surveys of brand equity definitions and brand valuation methods, see Kevin Keller, *Strategic Brand Management*, Englewood Cliffs, N.J.: Prentice-Hall, 1998 and Jonathan Knowles, "Varying Perspectives on Brand Equity," *Marketing Management* (August, 2008): pp. 20–26. See also Peter H. Farquhar, "Managing Brand Equity," *Marketing Research* (September, 1989): pp. 24–33 and David A. Aaker, *Managing Brand Equity*, New York: Free Press, 1991.

8. See also Donald E. Sexton and James Gregory, "Hidden Wealth in B2B Brands," *Harvard Business Review* (March, 2007), and John Gasper, "Companies Feel Benefit of Intangibles," *Financial Times* (April 23, 2007): p. 1.

9. Stratford P. Sherman, "How Philip Morris Diversified Right," *Fortune* (October 23, 1989): p. 72.

10. Cristina Binkley and Neal Templin, "Hilton Agrees to Pay $4 Billion for Promus," *Wall Street Journal* (September 8, 1999): p. A4; Mark Scott, "InBev: Lukewarm Results Show Need for Bud," *Business Week* (August 14, 2008): p. 19; and Tim Ferguson, "Google Now Britain's Top Tech Brand," *Business Week* (February 25, 2008): p. 14.

11. David Kiley, "Jaguar: Finally Ready to Roar?" *Business Week* (March 26, 2008): p. 32 and Timothy Dunne, "A Growth Model for China Automakers," *Business Week* (September 3, 2008): p. 21.

12. Jim Henry, "Which Auto Brands Should Go?" *Business Week* (May 5, 2008): p. 14.

13. Donald E. Sexton, "Valuing Brand Equity," *The Advertiser* (March, 2000): pp. 18–26.

14. The Conference Board, "Managing the Corporate Brand," New York: 1998; and American Productivity and Quality Center, Houston: 1999.

Chapter 4

1. Derek R. Allen and Morris Wilburn. *Linking Customer and Employee Satisfaction to the Bottom Line*. Milwaukee: ASQ Quality Press, 2002.

2. Elizabeth Glagowski, "Wynn, Home Depot Talk Trust, Employees, and Enablement," *1 to 1 Weekly*, April 2, 2007, p. 3.

3. Elizabeth Glagowski, *1 to1 Weekly*, May 14, 2007, pp. 2-3.

4. Warren Brown, "Hyundai's Mission Possible: Beat the Luxury Brands," *Washington Post*, April 1, 2007, p. G 02 and David Kiley, "Hyundai Still Gets No Respect." *Business Week*, May 21, 2007, pp. 68–72.

5. Peter Carlso, "The Flop Heard 'Round the World," *Washington Post*, September 4, 2007, p. C01 and Richard Truett, "The Past Ain't What It Used to Be," *Automotive News*, June 15, 2003, p. 170.

6. For a classic survey article, see Valerie Zeithaml, "Consumer Perceptions of Price, Quality, and Value," *Journal of Marketing*, July, 1988, pp. 2–22. For another view of the relationship of customers to products and services, see Rob Walker, "Buying In: The Secret Dialogue Between What We Buy and Who We Are," New York: Random House, 2008.

7. For a discussion of the role of identifiers, see Alex Simonson and Bernd H. Schmitt, *Marketing Aesthetics*, New York: Free Press, 1997.

8. Todd Wilkinson, "Adding Value to Priceless," *The Advertiser*, April, 2007, pp. 20–24.

9. Chris Warren, "Building a Brand," *The Advertiser*, December, 2006, pp. 55, 56, 59.

10. For a path-breaking discussion of providing experiences to customers, see Bernd H. Schmitt, *Experiential Marketing*, New York: Free Press, 1999.

11. A seminal work is by John Howard and Jagdish Sheth, *The Theory of Buyer Behavior*, New York: Wiley, 1969. Also, James R. Bettman, *An Information Processing Theory of Consumer Choice*, Reading, MA: Addison-Wesley, 1979. For overviews of the field of consumer behavior, see Michael R. Solomon, *Consumer Behavior*, Upper Saddle River, NJ: Pearson, 2009; Delbert I. Hawkins, David L. Mothersbugh, and Roger J. Best, *Consumer Behavior: Building Marketing Strategy*, New York: McGraw-Hill, 2008; and Roger D. Blackwell, Paul W. Miniard, and James F. Engel, *Consumer Behavior*, Cincinnati: South-Western College Publishers, 2005.

12. For a more elaborate model of buyer behavior, see Donald E. Sexton, "Microsimulating Consumer Behavior," in *Models of Buyer Behavior: Conceptual, Quantitative, and Empirical*, Jagdish N. Sheth, ed., New York: Harper & Row, 1974, pp. 88–107, and Donald E. Sexton, "Market Simulation: A Few Notes," *Computer Operations*, January, 1968, pp. 12, 13, 17. For empirical estimation of a buyer behavior model, see John U. Farley, John A. Howard, and Donald R. Lehmann, "A 'Working' System Model of Car Buyer Behavior," *Management Science*, November, 1976, pp. 235–247, and John U. Farley and Donald E. Sexton, "A Process Model of the Family Planning, Decision," *Management Science*, special issue on Marketing Planning, 1980.

13. See Gordon C. Bruner, III, and Richard J. Pomazal, "Problem Recognition: The Crucial First Step of the Consumer Decision Process," *Journal of Consumer Research*, v. 5 (1988), pp. 53–63.

14. For a discussion of how buyer behavior changes throughout the competitive life cycle, see John A. Howard, *Buyer Behavior in Marketing Strategy*, Englewood Cliffs, NJ: Prentice-Hall, 1994.

15. See Peter H. Block, Daniel L. Sherrell, and Nancy M. Ridgway, "Consumer Search: An Extended Framework," *Journal of Consumer Research*, June, 1986, pp. 119–126. See also the classic article, George J. Stigler, "The Economics of Information," *Journal of Political Economy*, June, 1961, pp. 213–225.

16. These two approaches to information processing are summarized in the "elaboration likelihood model of persuasion," where high-involvement purchase situations warrant more processing by the customer and low-involvement situations less. See Richard F. Petty, John T. Cacioppo, and David Schumann, "Central and Peripheral Routes to Advertising Effectiveness: The Moderating Role of Involvement," *Journal of Consumer Research*, v. 10, n. 2 (1983), pp. 135–146.

17. For studies of how messages affect customers' perceptions of quality, see J. Gottlieb and D. Sorel, "The Influence of Type of Advertisement, Price, and Source Credibility on Perceived Quality," *Journal of Academy of Marketing Science*, Summer, 1992, pp. 253–260, and S. B. Castlebury and A. V. A. Resurreccion, "Communicating Quality to Consumers," *Journal of Consumer Marketing*, Summer, 1989, pp. 21–28.

18. Robert Lavidge and Gary Steiner, "A Model for Predictive Measurements of Advertising Effectiveness," *Journal of Marketing*, October, 1961, pp. 59–62.

19. For discussions of cognitive and affective effects, see J. B. Cohen and K. Basu, "Alternative Models of Categorization," *Journal of Consumer Research*, March, 1987, pp. 455–472, and D. A. Aaker, D. M. Stayman, and R. Vezina, "Identifying Feelings Elicited by Advertising," *Psychology and Marketing*, Spring, 1988, pp. 1–16.

20. See Kevin Lane Keller, "Conceptualizing, Measuring, and Managing Customer-Based Brand Equity," *Journal of Marketing*, January, 1993, pp. 1–22.

21. Stuart Elliott, "A Brand Tries to Invite Thought," *New York Times Online*, September 7, 2007.

22. For discussions of the specific impact of price on evaluations, see Chr. Hjorth-Andersen, "Price as a Risk Indicator," *Journal of Consumer Policy*, v. 10 (1987), pp. 267–281, David M. Gardner, "Is There a Generalized Price-Quality Relationship?" *Journal of Marketing Research*, May, 1971, pp. 241–243, Kent B. Monroe, "Buyers' Subjective Perceptions of Price," *Journal of Marketing Research*, October, 1973, pp. 70–80, Donald R. Lichtenstein and Scott Burton, ""The Relationship Between Perceived and Objective Price-Quality," *Journal of Marketing Research*, November, 1989, pp. 429–443, and Akshay R. Rao and Kent B. Monroe, "The Effect of Price, Brand Name and Store Name on Buyer's Perceptions of Product Quality: An Integrative Review," *Journal of Marketing Research*, August, 1989, pp. 351-357.

23. For more discussion of multiattribute models, see Martin Fishbein, "An Investigation of the Relationship Between Beliefs About an Object and the Attitude Toward That Object," *Human Relations*, v. 16 (1963), pp. 233–240; Michael J. Ryan and Edward H. Bonfield, "The Fishbein Extended Model and Consumer Behavior," *Journal of Consumer Research*, v. 2 (1975), pp. 118–136; Morris B. Holbrook, "Comparing Multiattribute Models by Optimal Scaling," *Journal of Consumer Research*, December, 1977, pp. 165–171; William L. Wilkie and

Edgar A. Pessemier, "Issues in Marketing's Use of Multiattribute Models," *Journal of Marketing Research*, November, 1983, pp. 428–441; and Morris B. Holbrook and William I. Havlena, "Assessing the Real-to-Artificial Generalizability of Multi-Attribute Models in Tests of New Product Designs," *Journal of Marketing Research*, February, 1988, pp.25–35.

24. See James R. Bettman, "Memory Factors in Consumer Choice: A Review," *Journal of Marketing*, Spring, 1979, pp. 37–53.

25. See Leander Kahney, *Cult of iPod*, San Francisco: No Starch Press, 2005; Rob Pegoraro, "Apple Gets It Right With Sleek, Smart IPod Music Player," *Washington Post*, November 2, 2001, p. E01; Ian Cuthbertson, "It's All a Matter of Taste – How iPod Hits the Sweet Spot," *The Australian*, November 23, 2004, p. T07; and "The Meaning of iPod," *The Economist*, June 12, 2004.

26. Carolyn Cummins, "Kellogg's Wants to Be Even Bigger at Brekkie," *Sydney Morning Herald*, March 19, 1998, p. 28.

27. Katie Zezima, "Cranberries Go Abroad, A Tonic for an Ailing Industry," *The New York Times*, November 27, 2008, p. 26.

28. Richard C. Morais, "The Color of Beauty," *Forbes*, November 27, 2000, pp. 170-176.

29. Pat Wechsler, "A Curiously Strong Campaign," *Business Week*, April 21, 1997, p. 134.

30. See Kevin Clancy and Jack Trout, "Brand Confusion," *Harvard Business Review*, March, 2000, pp. 1–2.

31. For comments on Miller Lite advertising over time, see Ira Teinowitz, "Miller Lite: 'Ex-Jocks' Ad Prove to Be Losers in Long Run," *Advertising Age*, October 3, 1994, p. 56; "Miller Lite Ads Debated," *Advertising Age*, December 14, 1998, p. 24; and Melanie Wells, "Tastes great—Ho Hum Miller Lite Ad Campaign Comes Up Flat," *USA Today*, April 26, 1999, p. 4B.

32. Stuart Elliott, "With Its Fourth Miller Lite Campaign in Three Years, An Agency Hopes Consumers Are Thirsting for Change," *The New York Times*, November 3, 1994, p. D23.

33. Randall Rothenberg, "Burger King Ads: Which Way Now?" *The New York Times*, December 21, 1988, p. D1.

34. Mark Gleason and Laura Petrecca, "MasterCard in Play," *Advertising Age*, March 3, 1997, p. 1; James B. Arndorfer and Mercedes M. Carona, "MasterCard Taps McCann to Reignite Ad Efforts," *Advertising Age*, September, 8, 1997, p. 4; Mercedes M. Cardona, "New MasterCard Ads Show What the Card Can't Buy," *Advertising Age*, October 27, 1997, p. 22; Ong Bi Hui, "MasterCards Marketing Ads Were…Well, Priceless," *The Straight Times*, March 25, 2008.

35. "Now Levi's Puts its Brand on Shoes," *Business Week*, November 10, 1975, p. 124 and Chris Reidy, "Stride Rite Halts Sales of Levi Strauss Shoes," *The Boston Globe*, October 10, 1998, p. F2.

36. Brian Quinton, "Jump!", *Promo*, November 1, 2007, p. 8.

37. James Hamilton and John Tylee, "Ten Ads That Changed Advertising," *Campaign*, May 18, 2007, p. 20.

38. Julie Schmit, " 'Back from the Dead,' Continental Now Plans to Expand," *USA Today*, April 28, 1993, p. 18.

39. Jeff Green, "Jaguar May Find It's a Jungle Out There," *Business Week*, March 26, 2001, p. 62 and Kathleen Kerwin, "Ford Learns the Lesson of Luxury," *Business Week*, March 1, 2004, pp. 116–117.

40. Al Haas, "The Makers of Range Rover Make an Important Discovery," *The Philadelphia Inquirer*, April 29, 1994, p. F13 and Jennifer Comiteau with Jean Halliday, "Discovery Gets Out," *Adweek*, January 9, 1995.

41. Michael Arndt, "McDonald's 24/7," *Business Week*, February 5, 2007, pp. 64+.

42. Andrew Gaffney, Ebay, Neiman Marcus Stress Personalized Experiences," *1to1 Weekly*, September 10, 2007, pp. 2–3.

43. Martin Donovan, "Customer Care Vital with Online Firms," *South China Morning Post*, April 28, 2007, p. 30.

44. Robert M. McMath and Thom Forbes, *What Were They Thinking?*, NY: Random House, 1998, pp. 32–34.

45. Lori Rotenberk, "Leo Burnett's Lonely Maytag Campaign Still Washes," *Adweek*, January 17, 1985, p. 1A and Stuart Elliott, "Soon, Maybe He'll Have Even Less to Do," *The New York Times*, May 29, 2006, p. 6.

46. Elizabeth Glagowski, *1to1 Weekly*, May 14, 2007, pp. 2–3.

47. Valerie A. Zeithaml, Leonard L. Berry, and A. Parasuraman, *Delivering Quality Service*, The Free Press: New York, 1990.

48. Derek R. Allen and Morris Wilburn, *Linking Customer and Employee Satisfaction to the Bottom Line*, Milwaukee: ASQ Quality Press, 2002.

49. Jeremy Cato, "It's All About Building the Brand at Mini," *The Globel and Mail*, June 23, 2007, p. G14.

50. Mila D'Antonio, "How Do Sony, HP Align Customer Strategy and Brand?"*1to1 Weekly*, May 7, 2007, p. 3.

51. For further discussion of these and other methods and their use, see Donald R. Lehmann, *Market Research and Analysis*, Homewood, IL: Irwin, 1979 and Gary L. Lilien and Arvind Rangaswamy, *Marketing Engineering*, Victoria, B.C., 2004. For discussion of specific constrained choice methods, see, Bryan K. Orme, "Getting Started with Conjoint Analysis." Madison, WI: Research Publishers LLC, 2006; Paul E. Green and Yoram Wind, "New Way to Measure Consumers' Judgments," *Harvard Business Review*, July-August, 1975,

pp. 2–11;. Raghurian Iyengar, Kamel Jedidi, and Rajeev Kohli, "A Conjoint Approach to Multipart Pricing," *Journal of Marketing Research*, April, 2008, pp. 195–210; Rebecca W. Hamilton and Joydeep Srivastava, "When 2 + 2 Is Not the Same as 1 + 3," *Journal of Marketing Research*, August, 2008, pp. 450–461.

52. Interbrand, talk on brand valuation, ANA Masters of Marketing Conference, Orlando, October 18, 2008.

53. For discussions of the use of econometrics in estimation, see Jeffrey Woolridge, *Introductory Econometrics*, Cincinnati, OH: South-Western College Publishing, 2005 and Peter Kennedy, *A Guide to Econometrics*, Hoboken, NJ: Wiley-Blackwell, 2008.

54. For a discussion of experiments, see Thomas P. Ryan, *Modern Experimental Design*, Hoboken, NJ: Wiley, 2007.

Chapter 5

1. For comprehensive discussions of cost accounting, see Charles T. Horngren and Walter T. Harrison, *Accounting*, Englewood Cliffs, N.J.: Prentice-Hall, 2006; Robert N. Anthony and Leslie K. Breitner, *Essentials of Accounting*, Englewood Cliffs, N.J.: Prentice-Hall, 2006; and Erich A. Hilfert, *Techniques of Financial Analysis*, Homewood, IL: Irwin, 1987.

2. See Robert S. Kaplan and Robin Cooper, *Activity Based Costing: Introduction*, Cambridge, MA: Harvard Business School Press, 2008; Michael C. O'Guin, *The Complete Guide to Activity Based Costing*, Englewood Cliffs, N.J.: Pearson, 1991; and John K. Shank and Vijay Govindarajan, *Strategic Cost Management*, New York: Free Press, 1993.

Chapter 6

1. Donald E. Sexton, "Marketing Strategy and Marketing Tactics," *Effective Executive* (February, 2008): pp. 10–12 and Donald E. Sexton, "Making Marketing Work Together: Integrated Marketing," *The Advertiser* (April, 2008).

2. ANA, "Balancing Short-Term Profits and Long-Term Brand Equity," New York: 2008.

3. Christopher Power, "Flops," *Business Week* (August 16, 1993): pp. 76–82.

4. Christine Comaford, "The Power of Positioning," *Business Week* (June 2, 2008): p. 72.

5. For a more complete discussion of marketing strategy and additional examples, see Donald E. Sexton, *Marketing 101*, Hoboken, N.J.: Wiley, 2006.

6. Elizabeth Glagowski, "Wynn, Home Depot Talk Trust, Employees, and Enablement," *1to1 Weekly* (April 2, 2007): p. 3.

7. Nick Passmore, "Tequila Grows Up, and Gets More Expensive," *Business Week* (April 29, 2008): p. 48.

8. Robert M. McMath and Thom Forbes, *What Were They Thinking?*, New York: Random House, 1998, pp. 13–14.

9. Ian C. MacMillan and Rita Gunther McGrath, "Discovering New Points of Differentiation," *Harvard Business Review* (July-August, 1997): pp. 3–11.

10. Philip Seikman, "Becton Dickinson Takes a Plunge with Safer Needles," *Fortune* (October 1, 2007): p. 157.

11. Jim Webb and Chas Gile, "Reversing the Value Chain," *Journal of Business Strategy* (March-April, 2001): pp. 13–17; Leyland F. Pitt, Michael T. Ewing, and Pierre Bourthon, "Turning Competitive Advantage Into Customer Equity," *Business Horizons* (September-October, 2000): pp. 11–18; and Marco Vriens and Frenkel Ter Hofsteded, "Linking Attributes, Benefits, and Customer Value," *Marketing Research* (Fall, 2000): pp. 5–10.

12. C. K. Prahalad and Gary Hamel, "The Core Competency of the Corporation," *Harvard Business Review* (May-June, 1990): pp. 79–91.

13. Edward W. Desmond, "Can Canon Keep Clicking?" *Fortune* (February 2, 1998): pp. 98+.

14. Donald E. Sexton, "Selecting Successful Ventures," *Effective Executive* (April, 2007): pp. 34–38.

15. Moon Ihlwan, "Why Korea's SK Telecom Wants Sprint," *Business Week* (July 16, 2008): p. 43 and Matt Vella, "Why GE Is Getting Out of the Kitchen," *Business Week* (May 16, 2008): p. 21.

16. "Burger King Rebounds on Marketing," WJLA-TV (Television broadcast, June 16, 2007).

Chapter 7

1. Anthony Bianco and Pamela L. Moore, "Downfall X," *Business Week* (March 5, 2001): pp. 82–92 and David Kiley, "Xerox Gets a Brand Makeover," *Business Week* (January 7, 2008): p. 15.

2. See James R. Gregory, *Driving Brand Equity*, New York: ANA, 2005; James R. Gregory, *The Best of Branding*, New York: McGraw-Hill, 2003; James R. Gregory and Jack Wiechmann, *Leveraging the Corporate Brand*, New York: McGraw-Hill, 1997; Kevin Keller, *Branding and Brand Equity*, Cambridge: Marketing Science Institute, 2002; Robert D. Buzzell and Bradley T. Gale, *The PIMS® Principles*, New York: Free Press, 1987; Mary E. Barth, Michael B. Clement, and Ron Kaznik, "Brand Value and Capital Market Valuation," *Journal of Accounting Studies* (March, 1998): pp. 41–68; David A. Aaker and Robert Jacobson, "The Value Relevance of Brand Attitudes in High-Technology Markets," *Journal of Marketing Research* (November, 2001): pp. 485–93; David A.

323

Aaker and Robert Jacobson, "The Financial Information Content of Perceived Quality," *Journal of Marketing Research* (May, 1994): pp. 191–201; Shuba Srinivasan and Dominique M. Hanssens, "Marketing and Firm Value," (Working paper, January 12, 2007); Amit Joshi and Dominique Hanssens, "Advertising Spending and Market Capitalization," Marketing Science Institute, Report 04-110, 2004; Shruba Srinivasan, Koen Pauvels, Jorge Silva-Ross, and Dominique M. Hanssens, Marketing Science Institute, Report 06-002, 2006; Natalie Mizik and Robert Jacobson, "The Financial Value Impact of Perceptual Brand Attributes, *Journal of Marketing Research*, February, 2008, pp. 15–32; and Lerzan Aksoy, *et al*, "The Long-Term Stock Market Valuation of Customer Satisfaction," *Journal of Marketing* (July, 2008): pp. 105–122.

3. For more discussion of BAV, see Kevin Keller, *Strategic Brand Management*, Englewood Cliffs, N.J.: Prentice-Hall, 1998.

4. Eryn Brown, "Dot-Coms: What Have We Learned." *Fortune* (October 30, 2000): pp. 62–104.

5. L. Kahney, *The Cult of iPod*, San Francisco: No Starch Press, 2005.

6. For a theoretical discussion of the advantages of the pioneer, see Richard Schmalensee, "Product Differentiation Advantages of Pioneering Brands," *American Economic Review* (June, 1982): pp. 349–363. For managerial discussions, see Donald E. Sexton, "Managing Brand Equity Over Time," *Quarterly Review of Canada China Business Council* (Summer, 2004): pp. 9–11; W. Chan Kim and Renee Mauborgne, *Blue Ocean Strategy*, Cambridge: Harvard Business School, 2005; Gerard J. Tellis and Peter N. Golder, "First to Market, First to Fail," *Sloan Management Review* (Winter, 1996): pp. 65–75; and Ian C. MacMillan and Larry Selden, "The Incumbent's Advantage" *Harvard Business Review* (October, 2008): pp. 111–121.

7. Paul W. Farris, "Stainmaster," Charlottesville, VA: Darden School, June, 2001, UVA-M-0357.

8. Christopher Power, "Flops," *Business Week* (August 16, 1993): pp. 76–82.

9. "A Conversation with KISS' Gene Simmons," *Business Week* (September 5, 2008): p. 98.

10. Gary Loveman, "Diamonds in the Data Mine," *Harvard Business Review* (May, 2003): pp. 2–6.

11. Dina Boss, "Microsoft's iPod Challenge Strategy May Be Out of Tune," *National Post's Financial Post* and *FT Investing* (November 4, 2006): p. FP 116.

12. Nirmalya Kumar, "Strategies to Fight Low-Cost Rivals," *Harvard Business Review* (December, 2006): pp. 2–10.

13. David Field, "Fliers Give Continental Sky-High Marks," *USA Today* (May 10, 2000): p. 3B.

14. Paul W. Farris *Phillip E. Pfeifer, and Alan Zimmerman*, "Progressive Insurance," Charlottesville, VA: Darden School, April, 2008, UVA-M-0758.

15. For an excellent survey discussion of why companies do not divest failing businesses, see Kathryn Rudie Harrigan, "Deterrents to Divestiture," *Academy of Management Journal* (June, 1981): pp.306–323.

16. Bruce Upton, "Digital Dreams," *BRW* (September 1, 2001). Bruce Upton, "Kodak's Digital Moment," *Forbes* (August 1, 2000): pp. 106–112; Ravi Chandirami, "Can Kodak Thrive Amid the Digital Revolution?" Marketing (July 3, 2003): p. 13; David Henry, "A Tense Kodak Moment," *Business Week* (October 17, 2005): pp. 84–85; David Gianastasio, "Is Polaroid Ready for Its Close-Up?" *Adweek* (July 2, 2003): p. 6; and Faith Arner and Ira Sager, "Fuzzy Focus on Polaroid's Auction," *Business Week* (September 18, 2003): p. 8.

Chapter 8

1. Donald E. Sexton, *Marketing 101*, Hoboken, N.J.: Wiley, 2006.

2. Kevin J. Clancy and Randy L. Stone, "Don't Believe the Metrics," *Harvard Business Review* (June, 2005): p. 1.

3. For examples, see Jacquelyn S. Thomas, Werner Reinartz, and V. Kumar, "Getting the Most Out of All Your Customers," *Harvard Business Review* (July, 2004).

4. Chris Anderson, *The Long Tail*, New York: Hyperion, 2008.

5. Mark Pendergast, "Manager's Journal: Is Coke's Image Too … Vanilla?," *The Wall Street Journal* (May 28, 2002): p. B2.

6. Robert M. McMath and Thom Forbes, *What Were They Thinking?*, New York: Random House, 1998, pp. 186–187.

7. For application information, see Donald E. Sexton, "A Cluster Analytic Approach to Market Response Functions," *Journal of Marketing Research* (February, 1974): pp. 109–114.

8. Christopher Power, "Flops," *Business Week* (August 16, 1993): pp. 76–82 and Robert M. McMath and Thom Forbes, *What Were They Thinking?*, New York: Random House, 1998, pp. 103–106.

9. Don Peppers, "Schwab, Avaya Rediscover Customer Loyalty," *Inside 1to1* (March 6, 2008): pp. 3–4.

10. Tara Wingarten, Patrick Crowley, and Mary Chapman, "Love to Hate the Hummer," *Newsweek* (August 4, 2008) p. 36.

11. Robert M. McMath and Thom Forbes, *What Were They Thinking?*, New York: Random House, 1998, pp. 161–164.

12. Roland T. Rust, Debora Viana Thompson, and Rebecca W. Hamilton, "Defeating Feature Fatigue," *Harvard Business Review* (February, 2006): pp. 39–48.

13. See Donald E. Sexton, "Coordinating Brands Globally," *Global CEO* (July, 2007): pp. 9–13; Donald E. Sexton, "Should Your Brand Be Global?" *Chazen Web Journal of International Business* (March, 2004): pp. 1–13; and Donald E. Sexton, "Global Marketing: Balancing Global Thoughts and Local Actions," *The Advertiser* (January, 1999): pp. 12–18.

14. John A. Quelch and Edward J. Hoff, "Customizing Global Marketing," *Harvard Business Review* (May-June, 1986): pp. 2–12.

15. Richard Tomlinson, "L'Oreal's Global Makeover," *Fortune* (September 30, 2002): pp. 141–148 and Richard C. Norais, "The Color of Beauty," *Forbes* (November 27, 2000): 170–176.

16. Georg Tacke, "Business Europe: Unlocking 3M's Potential," *Wall Street Journal Europe* (January 29, 2001): p. 11.

17. Kerry Capell, "MTV's World," *Business Week* (February 18, 2002): pp. 81–84.

18. For a number of examples, see John A. Quelch and Edward J. Hoff, "Customizing Global Marketing," *Harvard Business Review* (May-June, 1986): pp. 59–68; Regina Fazio Maruca, "The Right Way to Go Global, *Harvard Business Review* (March-April, 1994): pp. 134–143; John A. Byrne, "The Horizontal Corporation," *Business Week* (December 20, 1993): pp. 76–81; and Shi Zhang and Bernd H. Schmitt, "Creating Local Brands in Multilingual International Markets," *Journal of Marketing Research* (August, 2001): pp. 313–325.

19. Donald E. Sexton, "Global Marketing: Balancing Global Thoughts and Local Actions," *The Advertiser* (January, 1999): pp. 12–18.

20. Keith Naughton and Emily Thornton, "Can Honda Build a World Car?," *Business Week* (September 8, 1997): pp. 100–108.

21. John A. Quelch, "Heineken Global Branding and Advertising," Cambridge, MA: Harvard Business School, October, 1995, HBS 596015.

22. For a more complete discussion of branding, see Donald E. Sexton, *Branding 101*, Hoboken, N.J.: Wiley, 2008. Also see Donald E. Sexton, "Branding—Get Your Basics Right," *OER* (August, 2005): pp. 38–39; Donald E. Sexton, "Building Global Brands," *The Advertiser* (June, 1997): pp. 40, 42, and 44; Donald E. Sexton, "Principles of Building Strong Brands," *Effective Executive* (August, 2006): pp. 12–15; and Donald E. Sexton, "Old Brands, New Lives," *The Advertiser* (February, 2007): p. 33.

23. Association of National Advertisers, "Fourth Annual ANA/MMA Marketing Accountability Study," New York: July, 2007.

24. Clayton M. Chistensen, Scott Cook, and Taddy Hall, "Marketing Malpractice," *Harvard Business Review* (December, 2005): pp. 4–15.

25. "75 Years of Ideas," *Advertising Age*, January 31, 2005, p. 13.

26. See Rohini Ahluwalia, "How Far Can a Brand Stretch?," *Journal of Marketing Research* (June, 2008): pp. 337–350.

27. Anne Tergesen, "Sure, It's from AARP. But Is It a Good Deal?," *Business Week* (February 14, 2008): p. 40.

28. Robert M. McMath and Thom Forbes, *What Were They Thinking?* NY: Random House, 1998, pp. 23–24.

29. Joshua Levine and Matthew Surbel, "To Protect the Gucci Brand, Domenico De Sole Lops Off Retailers," *Forbes* (May 28, 2001): p. 72.

30. Melanie Wells, "Red Baron," *Forbes* (July 3, 2000): pp. 151–160.

31. Donald E. Sexton, "Establishing Effective Co-Brands," *Effective Executive* (March, 2008): pp. 61-64.

32. For several examples of co-branding, see Tom Blackett and Bob Boad, eds., *Co-Branding*, London: Macmillan, 1999.

33. "Survey Reveals Best, Worst Brand Extensions," *Progressive Grocer* (January 8, 2008).

Chapter 9

1. For discussions and examples of marketing mix modeling, see Roger Kerin and Rob O'Regan, *Marketing Mix Decisions: New Perspectives and Practices*, Chicago: American Marketing Association, 2008, and Dominique Hanssens, Daniel Thorpe, and Carl Finkbeiner, "Marketing When Customer Equity Matters," *Harvard Business Review* (May, 2008): pp. 1–9. For a general discussion of optimization models, see Donald E. Sexton and William A. Clark, *Marketing and Management Science*. Homewood, IL: Irwin, 1970.

2. Rachael King, "How Companies Use Twitter to Bolster Their Brands," *Business Week* (September 6, 2008): p. 32. Tracy L. Tuten, *Advertising 2.0*, Westport, CT: Praeger, 2008; Larry Weber, *Marketing to the Social Web*, Hoboken, NJ: Wiley, 2007; and Steve Weber, *Plug Your Business*, Falls Church, VA: Weber Books, 2007.

3. Donald E. Sexton, "Overspending on Advertising," *Journal of Advertising Research* (December, 1971): pp. 19–25.

4. Russell Colley, *Defining Advertising Goals for Measured Advertising Results*, New York: Association of National Advertisers, 1961.

5. Demetrios Vakratsas and Tim Ambler, "Advertising Effects," *Journal of Marketing* (January, 1999): pp. 26–43. Also see William A. Weilbacher, "Does Advertising Cause a Hierarchy of Effects?" *Journal of AdvertisingResearch* (December, 2001): pp. 17–26.

6. Robert J. Dolan, "How Do You Know When the Price Is Right?" *Harvard Business Review* (September-October, 1995): pp. 4–11.

7. Donald E. Sexton, "Pricing, Perceived Value, and Communications," *The Advertiser* (April, 2006): pp. 56–58.

8. "SA's Consumers Give No-Name Brands the Cold Shoulder," *Africa News* (October 5, 2006).

9. "Private Label Sales to Top $56 Billion by 2011," *Progressive Grocer* (February 2, 2007)..

10. Mark Ritson, "Mark Ritson on Branding," *Haymarket Publishing* (November 28, 2007): p. 23.

11. Jen Haberkorn, "Grocers; Private Labels Gain Market Share," *The Washington Times* (November 30, 2006): p. C-8.

12. "Own-Labels Have All Guns Blazing in Bubbly Wars," *Off License News* (March 23, 2007): p. 25.

13. Paul W. Farris , "Stainmaster," Charlotesville, VA: Darden, June, 2001, UVA-M-0357.

14. Richard M. Smith, "A Baseball Champion," *Newsweek* (October 20, 2008): p. E20.

Chapter 10

1. For a discussion of the reservations associated with the Netpromoter Score, see Gina Pingitore, "The Single-Question Trap," *Marketing Research* (Summer, 2007): pp. 8–13.

2. Karen V. Beaman, Gregory R. Guy, and Donald E. Sexton, "Measuring Return on Marketing Investments," New York: The Conference Board, 2008.

3. Donald E. Sexton, "Building the Brand Scorecard," *The Advertiser*, February 2005, pp. 54-58.

4. For general discussions of measures and scorecards, see Thomas H. Davenport and Jeanne G. Harris, *Competing on Analytics*, Cambridge: Harvard Business School Press, 2007; Robert S. Kaplan and David P. Norton, *The Balanced Scorecard*, Cambridge, MA: Harvard Business School Press, 1996; and Michael Kravis, "Marketing Dashboards Drive Better Decisions," *Marketing News* (October 1, 2001): p. 7.

Chapter 11

1. Donald E. Sexton, "Managing the Performance of Individuals," *Effective Executive* (August, 2007): pp. 34–39.

2. Karen Beaman, Gregory R. Guy, and Donald E. Sexton, "Managing and Measuring Return on Marketing Investment," Research Report 1435-08-RR, New York: The Conference Board, 2008.

3. CMO Council, "Marketing Outlook," Palo Alto, CA, 2007.

4. APQC, "Managing Marketing Assets for Sustained Returns," Houston: 2003.

5. Karen Beaman, Gregory R. Guy, and Donald E. Sexton, "Managing and Measuring Return on Marketing Investment," Research Report 1435-08-RR, New York: The Conference Board, 2008.

6. Prophet, "Prophet's View on the World of Marketing Effectiveness," New York, April 18, 2007.

7. Lenskold Group, "Lenskold Group/Kneebone 2008 Marketing OI and Measurement Study," Manasquan, New Jersey, 2008.

8. Karen Beaman, Gregory R. Guy, and Donald E. Sexton, "Managing and Measuring Return on Marketing Investment," Research Report 1435-08-RR, New York: The Conference Board, 2008.

9. Mark Clemente, "Business Gain from How You Retain: A CMO Council Study on Making the Most of Your Existing Customers," Chicago: American Marketing Association, July 9, 2008.

10. Pat La Pointe, "Building Blocks," *Marketing Management* (May-June, 2007): pp. 1–25.

11. APQC, "The State of Brand Building and Communications," Houston: 1998.

12. Joe Millich, "10 Commandments of Total Accountability," *The Advertiser* (June, 2007): pp. 19–22.

INDEX

purchase cycle measures
(marketing accountability
scorecard), 286-287

Q–R

quality, value of, 24

range of possible prices,
defined, 36
Rapid Growth stage (competitive
life cycle), 68
communications during, 256
CVA® management in, 196-198
Taster's Choice versus Maxim
example, 198-199
Reicheld, Frederick, 23
Reilly, Edward T., 255
Reiss, Al, 23
relative ability (Segment
Selection Analysis), defined, 171
relative delivered costs,
defined, 21
replacement cost method
(estimating brand equity), 87
repositioning brands, 235-236
results, steps to achieving,
295-296
capability, 301-306
effort, 299
environment, 307-309
rewards, 300-301
task clarity, 297-298
usage of marketing ROI
information, 309
return on communications
spending, 257-259
revenue
defined, 41-42, 138
market segmentation and, 221
micro-targeting and, 216-217

revenue and contribution
example, 44-45
Sexton's Revenue Law, 48-49
shifting the demand curve, 45-47
reward
defined, 295
explained, 300-301
Ries, Al, 106
ROI. *See* marketing ROI

S

Saeger, Becky, 121
sales
breakeven sales level, 139
shutdown sales level, 146
sales life cycles
during competitive life cycle
stages, 69
levels of, 66-67
Sawyer, Cheryl, 294
Segment Identification Analysis,
156-159
Segment Selection Analysis,
170-173
segmentation analysis,
defined, 155
segmenting markets. *See* market
segmentation
selecting target markets, 170-172
Sen, Kamal, 39
Sexton's Contribution Law, 50-56
Sexton's Law of Micro-Targeting,
215-219
Sexton's Revenue Law, 48-49
shakeout, defined, 74
shareholder value
contribution and, 58
defined, 77
effect of marketing on (Unum
example), 4